I0464356

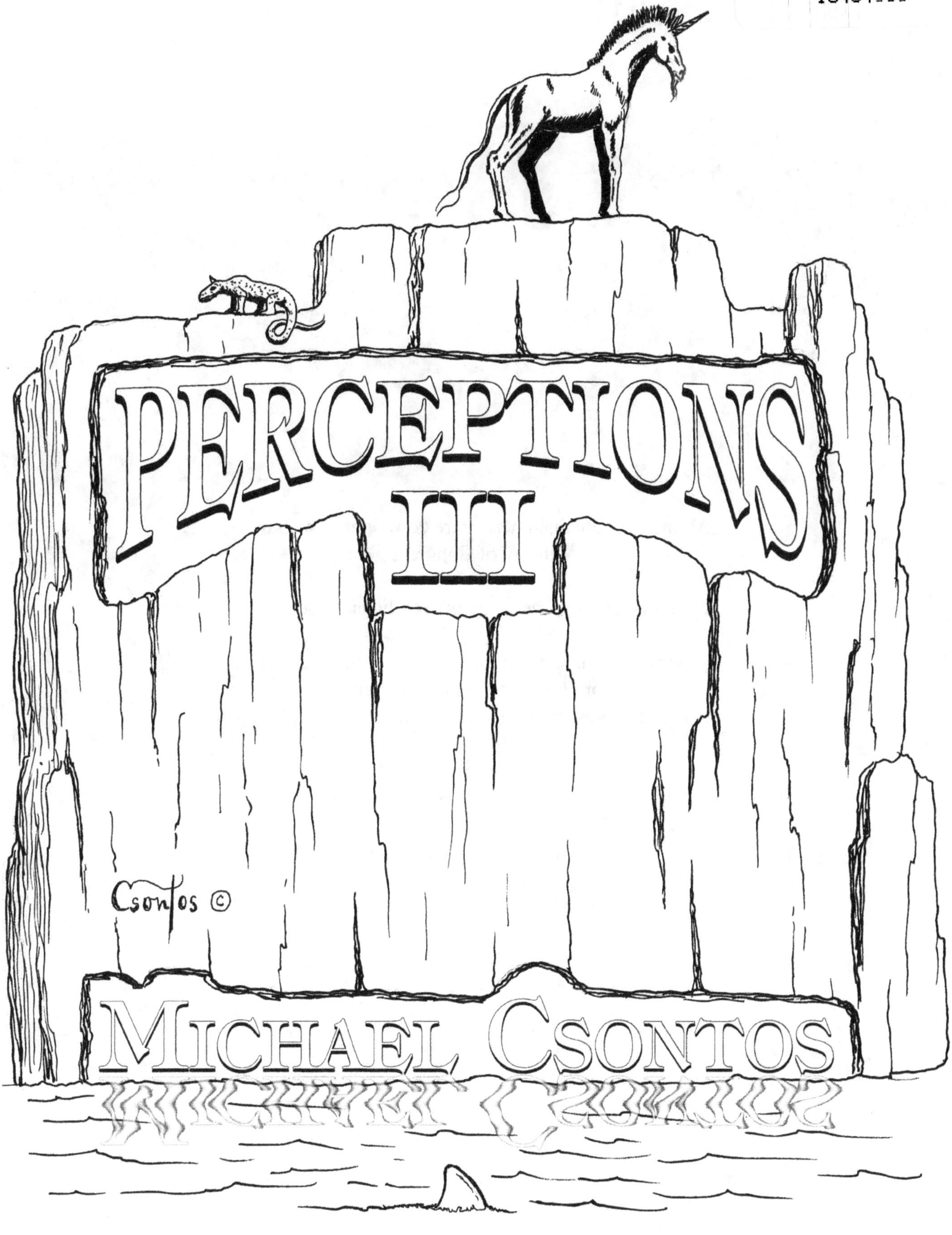

PERCEPTIONS III

Csontos ©

MICHAEL CSONTOS

All images contained herein are copyright © with the
Library of Congress

All images have been created by Michael Csontos

No portion of this book may be reproduced in any form
or duplicated in any manner
without express written permission from the author.

All rights reserved by
Michael Csontos

www.michaelcsontos.com

© 2015 First Edition

Michael Csontos resides outside of Prescott, Arizona.

DEDICATION
Even though they are gone I would like to mention their names; Salvadore Dali, Frank Frazetta and Burne Hogarth. I have learned more from these three masters than any other input since I first picked up a pencil. I had a chance to meet with you all but being a natural procrastinator I regretfully, will never have those memories. My loss. If your essence is out there somewhere, thank you all.

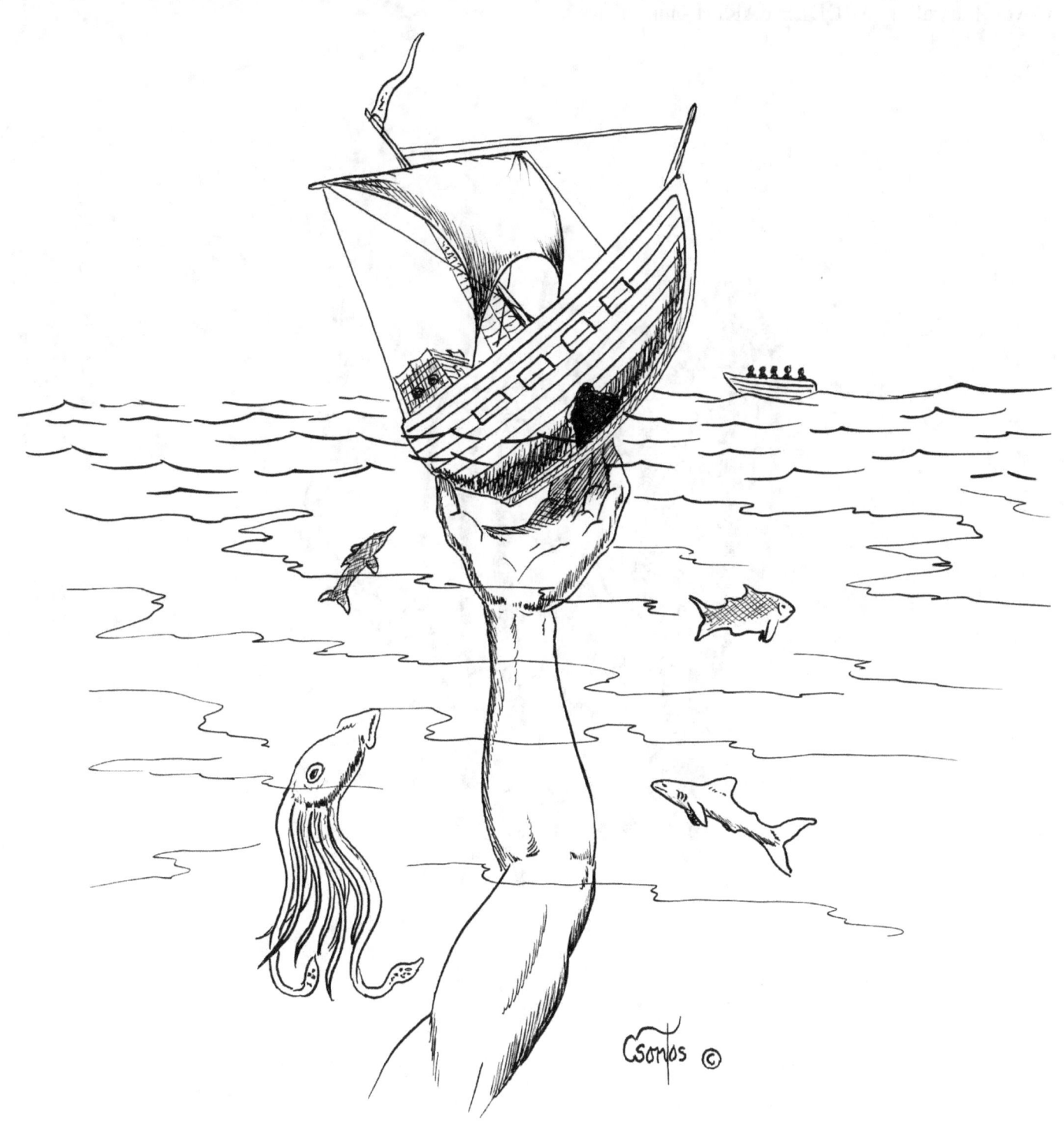

POSEIDON'S HELP - ink - pen

PREFACE

Sometimes I approach a goal with great expectations only to feel that maybe the objective might have eluded me. Was it because I lost the focus by becoming over-involved in minor intents or because I was deluding myself from the very beginning. Sometimes not even having a goal or even an expectation seems to bring about a result that is equivalent to an eureka moment. What I'm trying to get at in my usual round-a-bout way is that I occasionally over think myself. Were my first books adequate in what I was trying to portray? If not then maybe this forth one will get my sometimes aimless point across about visualizing (mostly from an abstract beginning). It was also inspired by the book 'The Arcane Eye of Hogarth'. Please enjoy.

Cover illustration: MIDDLE EARTH - ink - pen

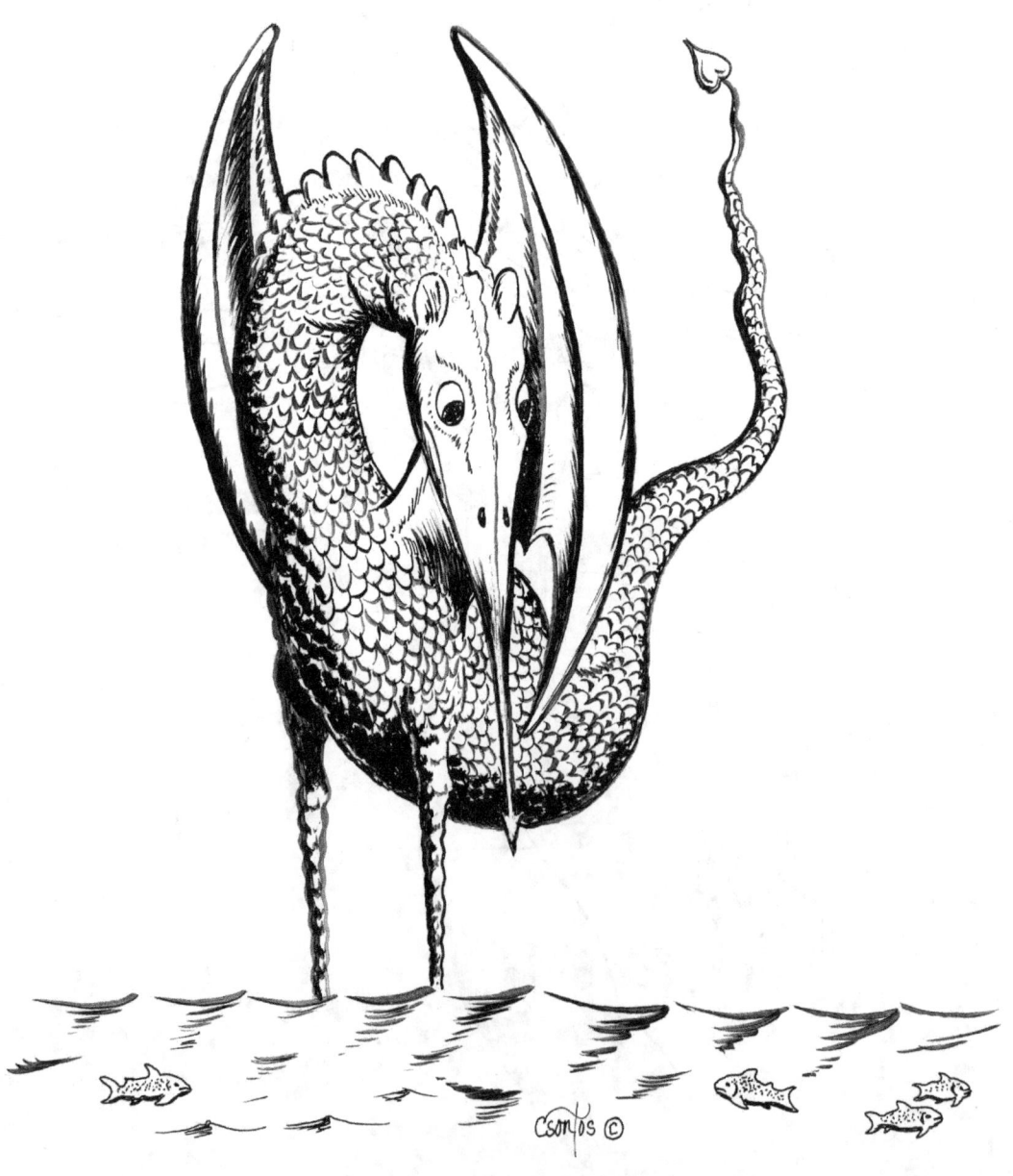

WAITING FOR A FISH - ink - pen & brush

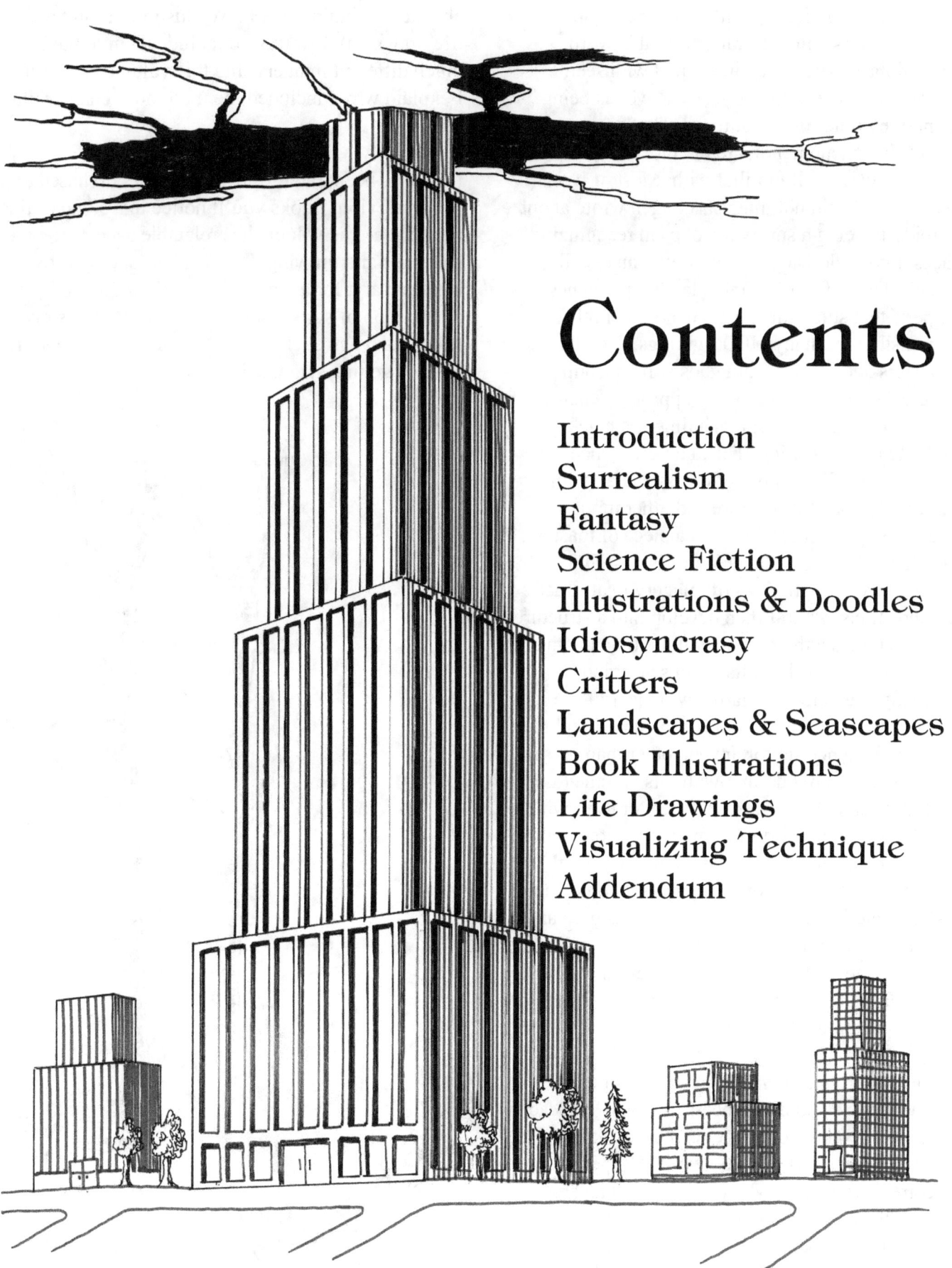

Contents

TOO TALL FOR THE SKY - ink - pen & brush

INTRODUCTION

While I was coming up with different sections of text for this volume I ran across this word: 'pareidolia'. It was used in context with seeing images from the Mars Curiosity Rover as being something other than just rocks. The most common use of this phenomenon are ink blot tests, which I believe we are all familiar with. Most of us can see something in nothing. Carl Sagen wrote about pareidolia being a survival tool as in recognizing faces. Leonardo Da Vinci felt it was an excellent artist's device for developing landscape scenes. Experts that study this phenomenon feel it is responsible for many UFO sightings, deep lake monsters and sounds from ghosts. It's meaning is actually quite similar to my approach when developing imagery for a painting or a black and white composition. The main difference is that pareidolia is more often associated with misconceptions from nature and other input. For example; I do not see Jesus on a piece of toast nor do I believe the planet Venus is a UFO. I do, however see all kinds of imagery in abstract compositions which I then develop into a structure that resembles a theme. Most of the time the theme is surreal but it still has its origins abstractly. Recently I tend to disregard any imagery I see in the abstract beginnings of an art piece if I feel they are too idiosyncratic for anyone other than myself. However, I did not do that with this volume (as I included many haphazard sketches) or even with everything I've ever done. On another note, unless everything an artist creates is a commission, then it would seem that a bit of idiosyncrasy would show itself sooner or later. A lot of the images give an indication of simulacrums. But if you can tell what I'm trying to portray then that is okay as well. After all, fantasy and surrealism only deal with reality on a representational basis.

Switching from a standard number 2 pencil to initialize the sketching process to a wide 6B lead has proven to be more beneficial to invoking an internal response (thought/action). The pencil becomes even wider when laid down at an angle. This helped in establishing a shadow effect, which in turn gave visualizing another aspect as opposed to just seeing outlines of objects. Using the wider, softer 6B pencil allowed me to come up with almost five times as much imagery in a given time.

As for the two sections that do not deal with an abstract beginning (the book illustrations and the life drawings), I wanted to include them to have as much different imagery into this volume as I could. I explain why I included them on those chapter title pages.

If you've been to the website or have purchased any of my previous books you'll notice that some of the imagery in this volume has relatable aspects to other paintings and drawings. Once an artist (any artist) has been at it for a while, there will undoubtedly be a repetition of sorts of ideas or themes. That's my excuse and I'm sticking to it. Could also be that my brain is getting stagnated.

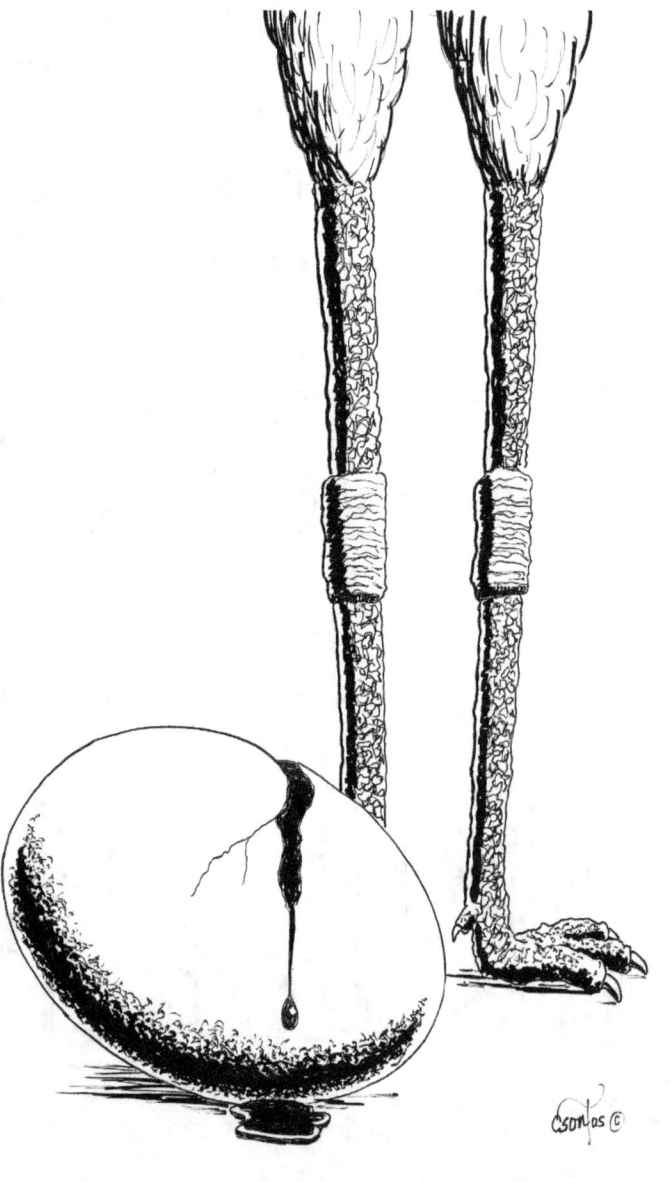

DROPPED IT TOO FAR - ink - pen

Surrealism

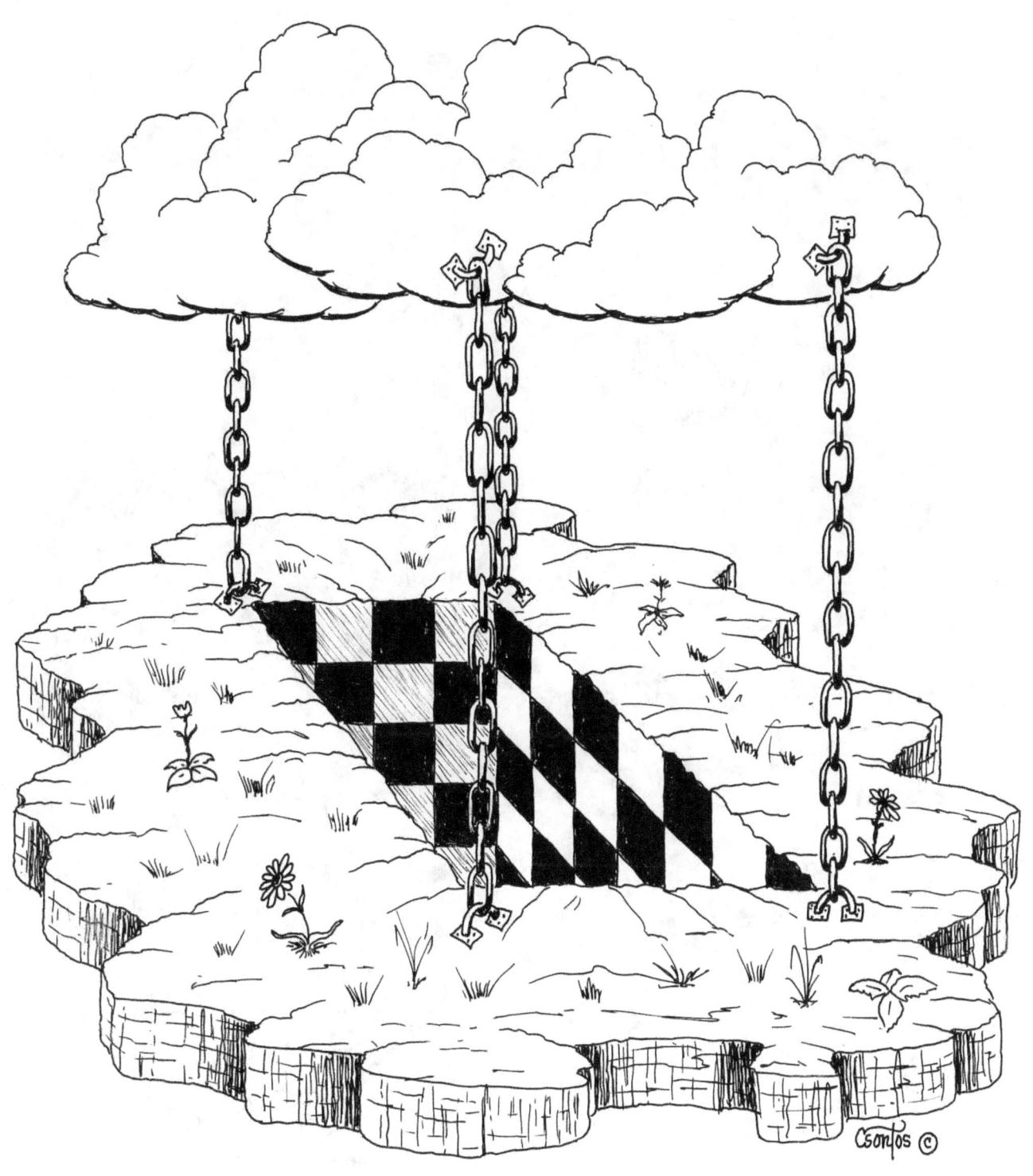

HOLDING UP A HOLE - ink - pen & brush

Surrealism has always been my favorite theme, as long as I do it right. Even after 40 years of painting in this style I'm still not sure why I prefer it over other themes. Probably just can't deal with absolute reality.

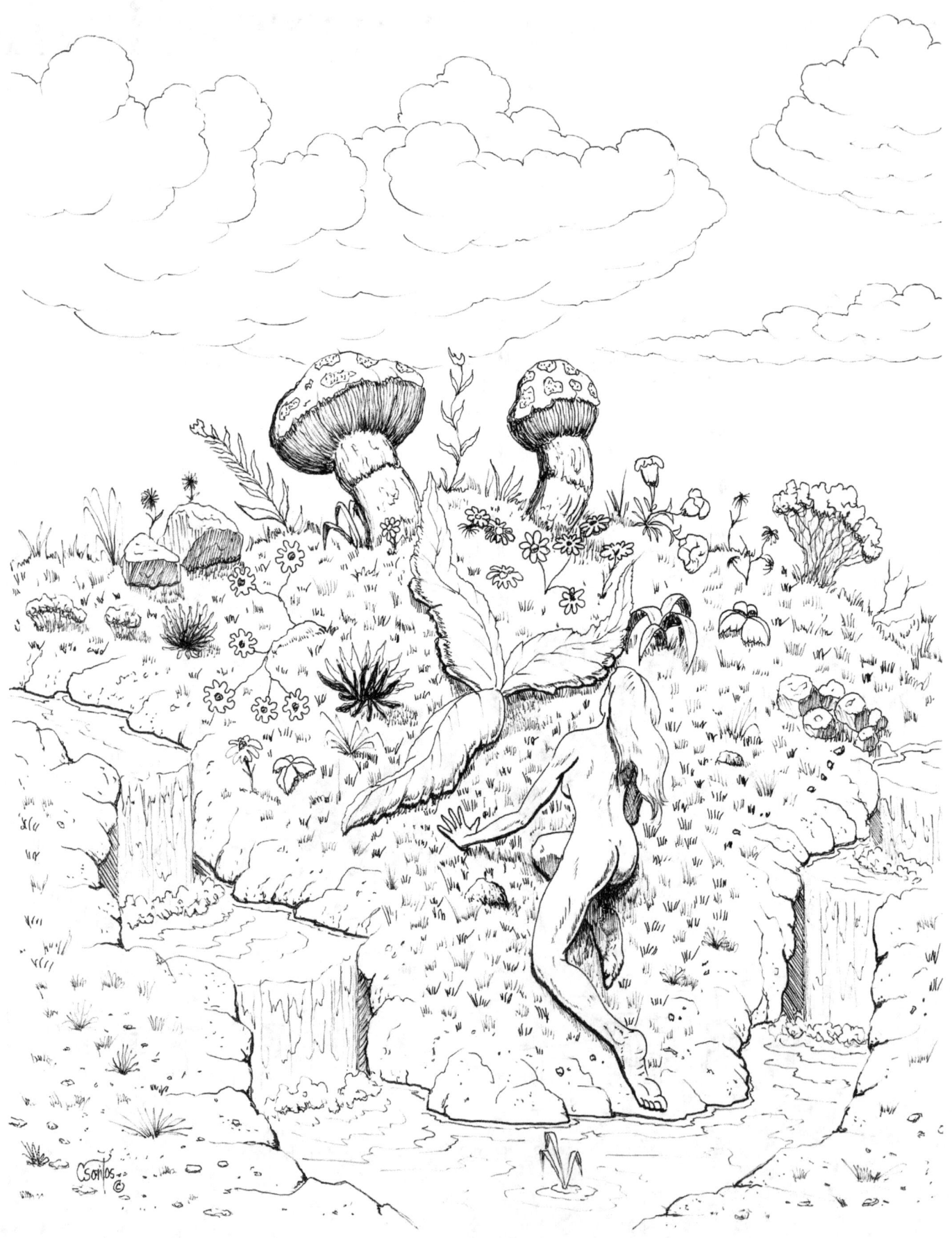

MUSHROOM HILL - ink - pen

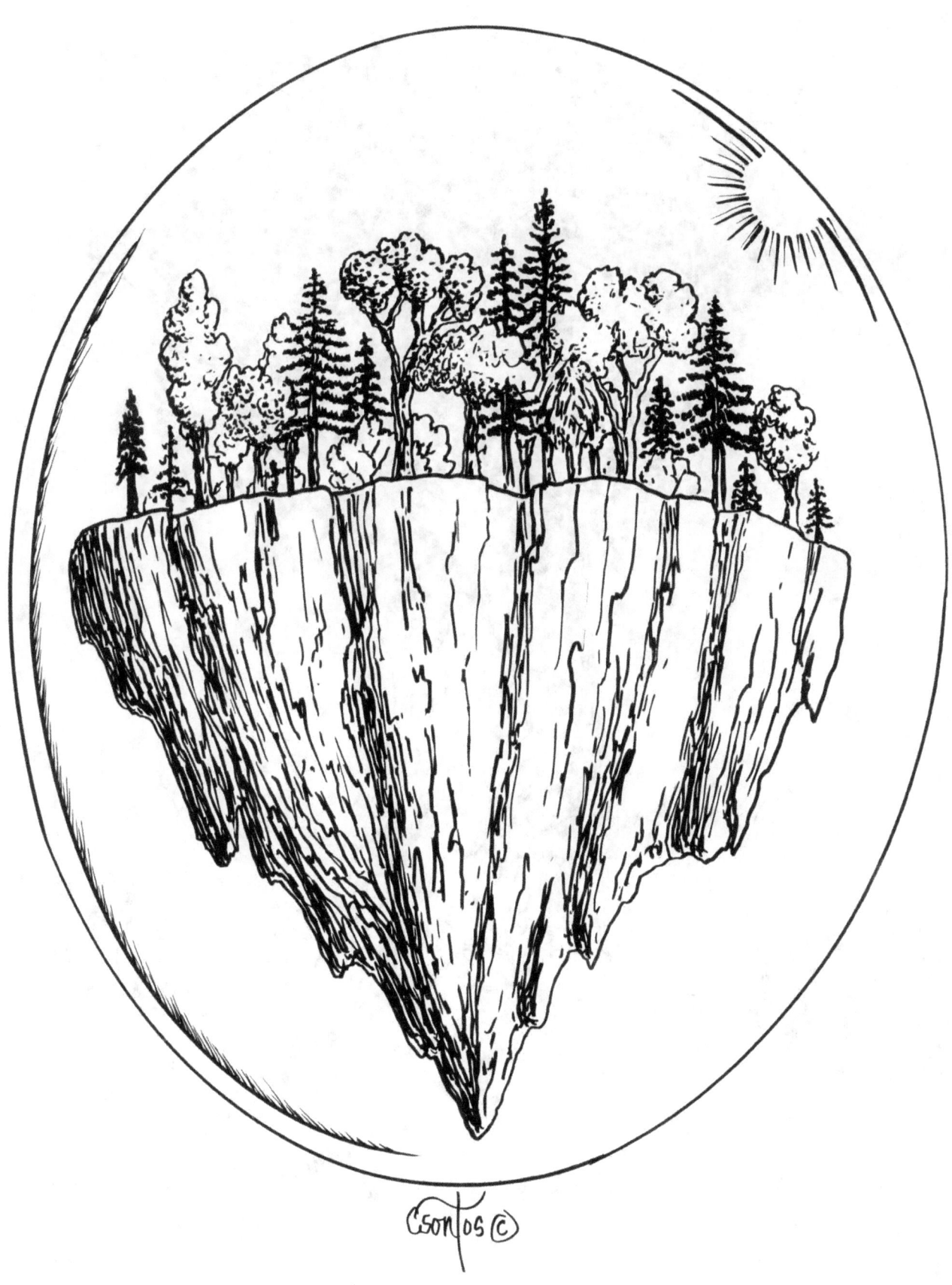

A NEW LAND - ink - fine tip marker

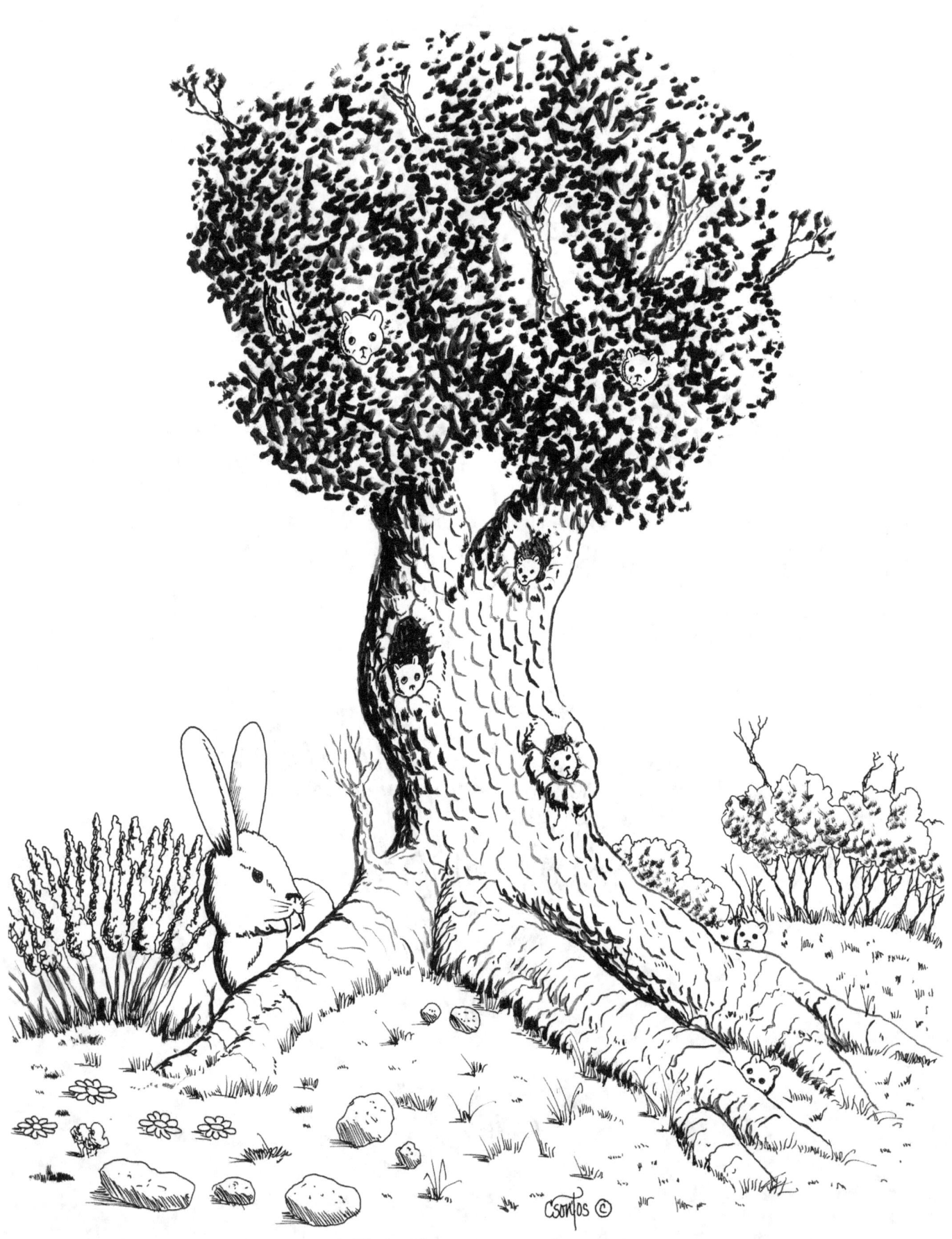

HIDING FROM THE CARNIVOROUS RABBIT - ink - pen & brush

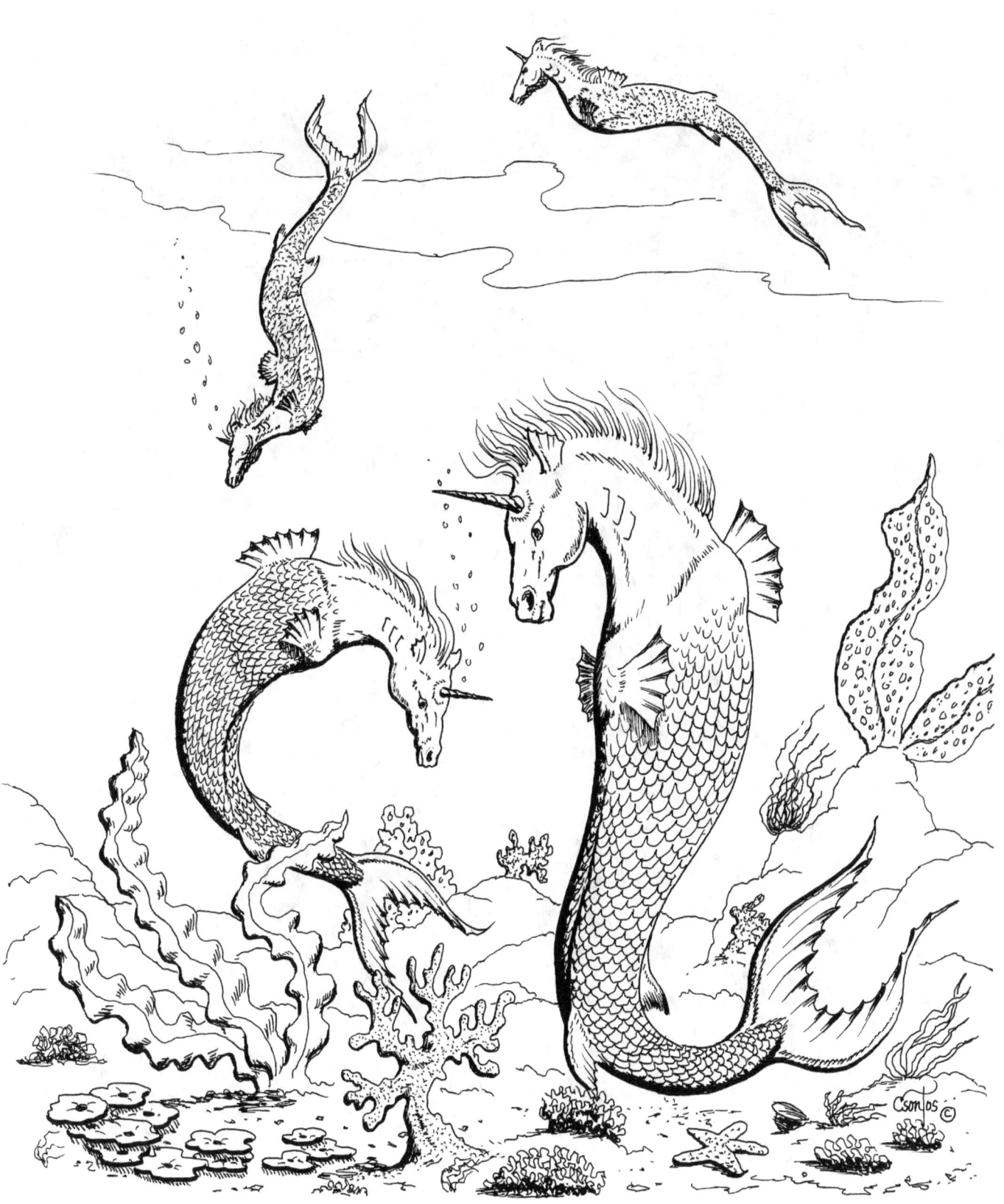

SEA HORSES - ink - pen

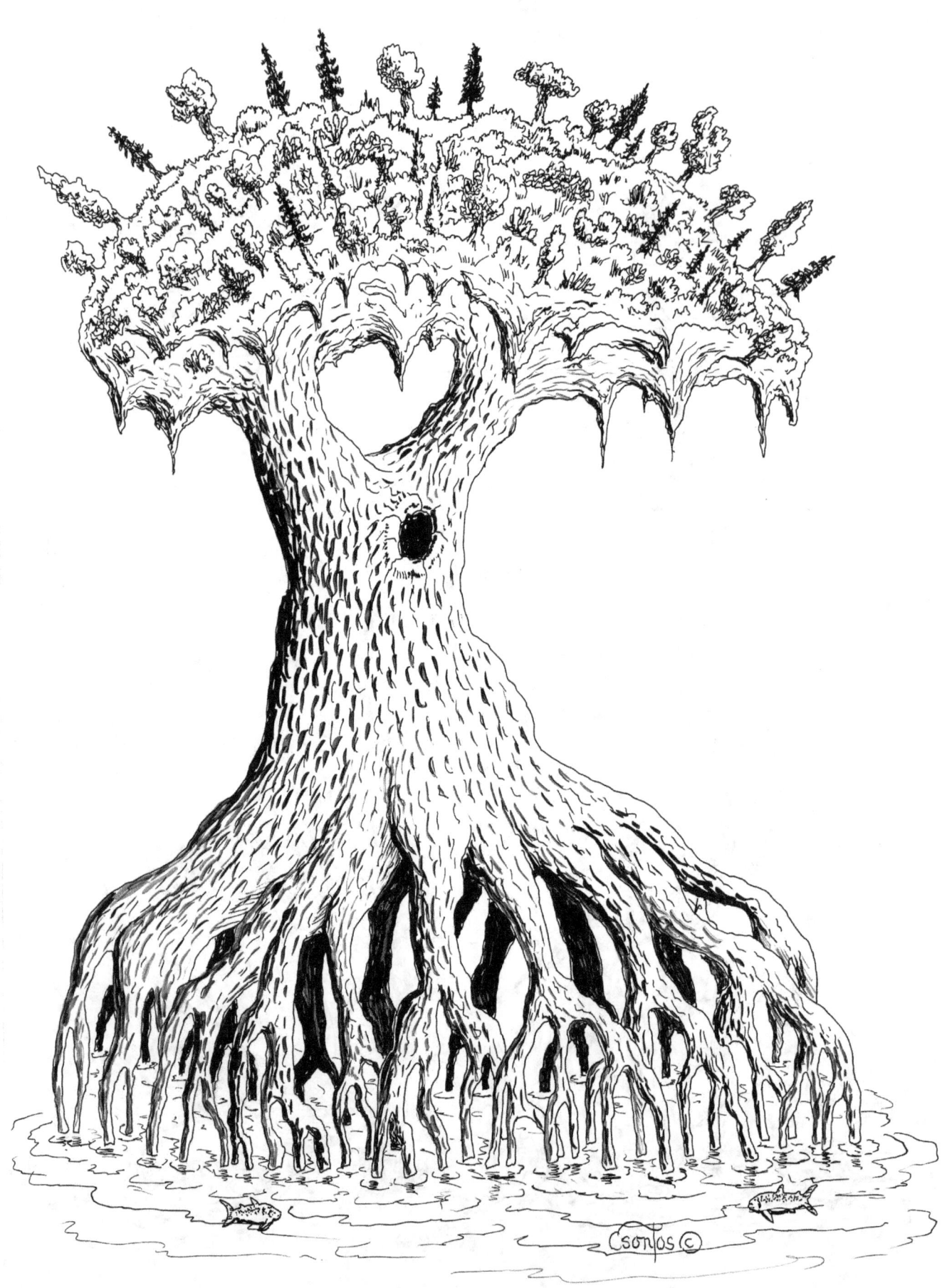

GROWING A FOREST IN THE BANDI TREE - ink - pen & brush

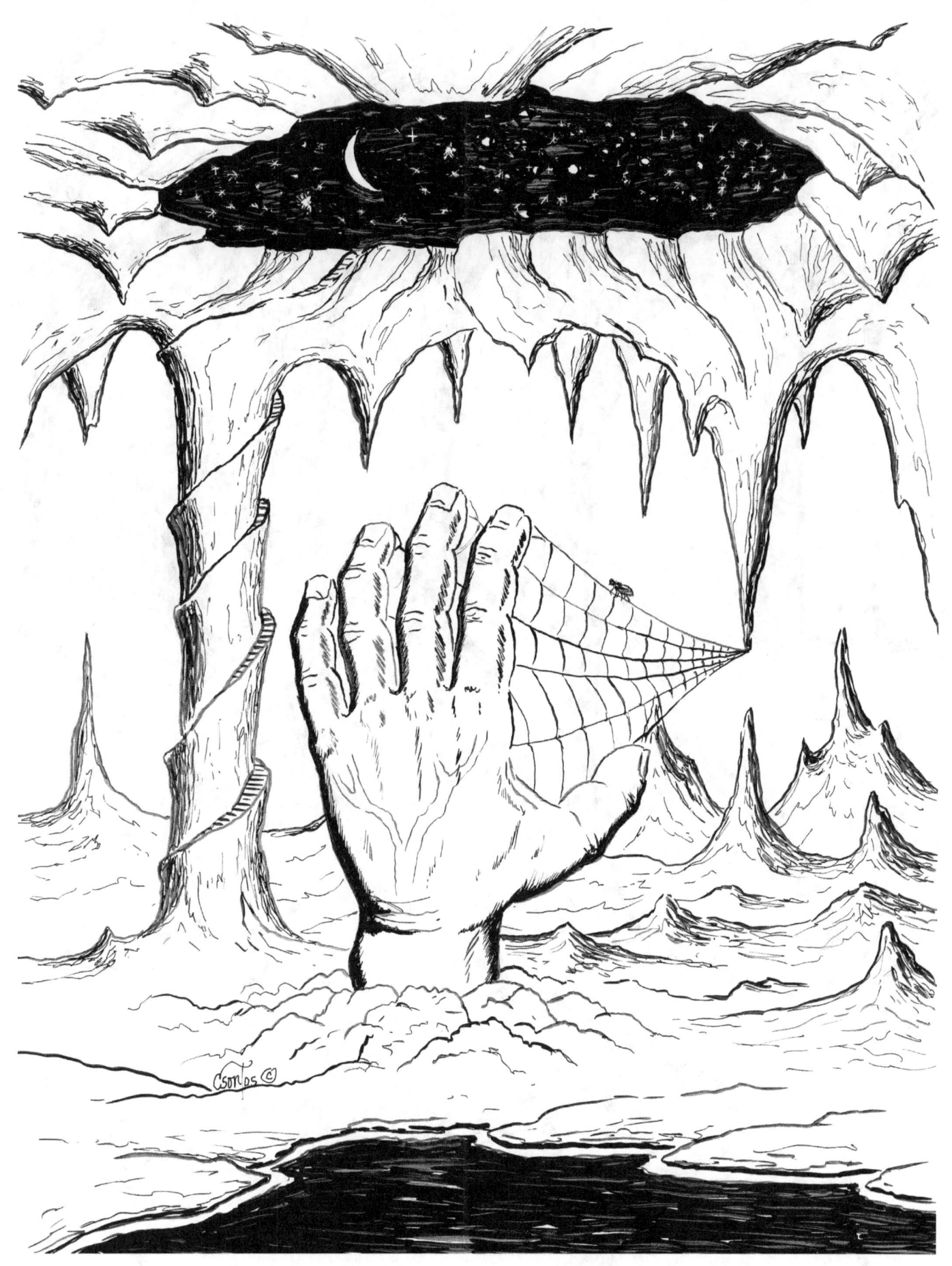

STAIRWAY TO HEAVEN - ink - pen & brush

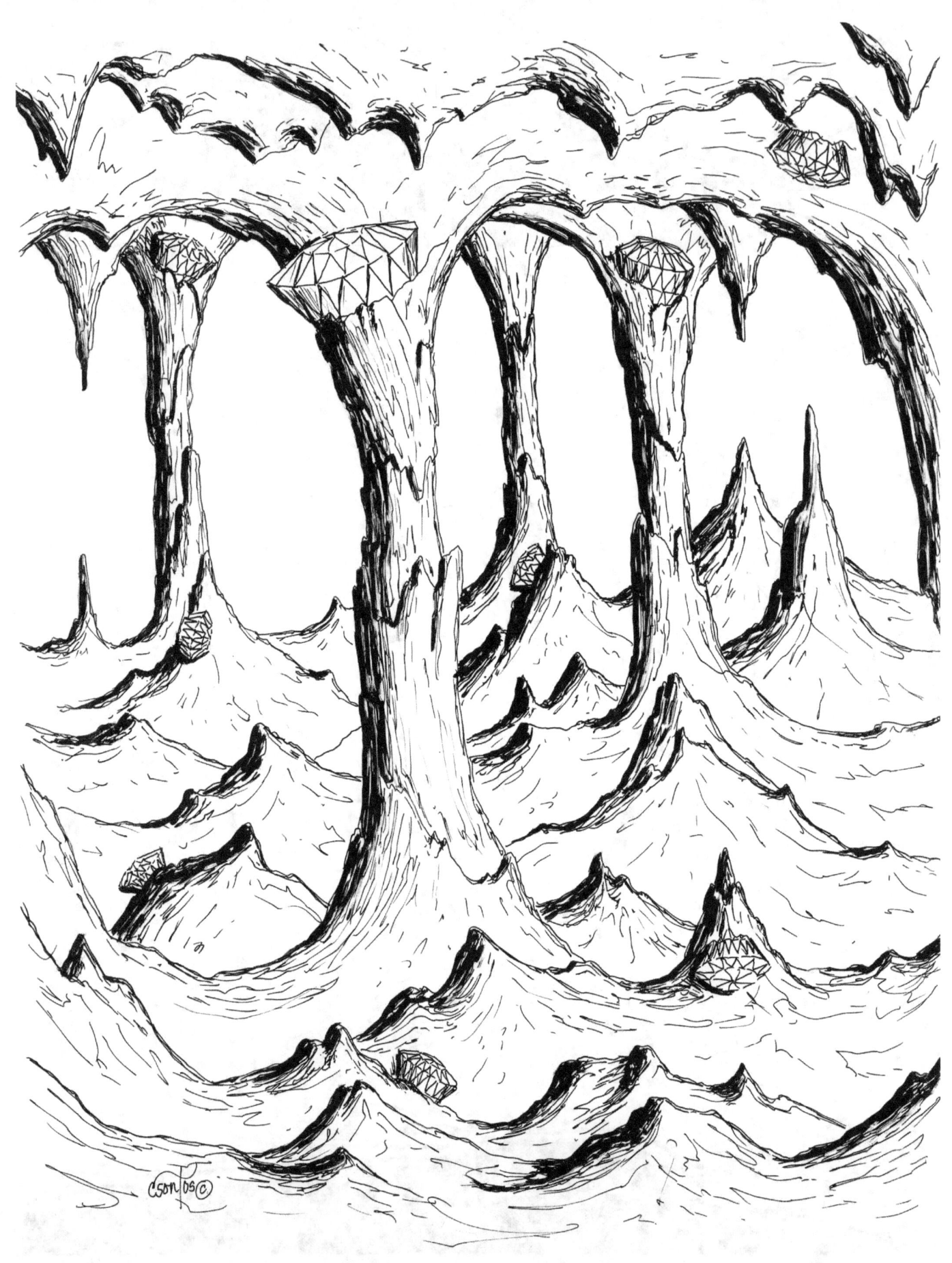

DIAMOND MINE - ink - pen & brush

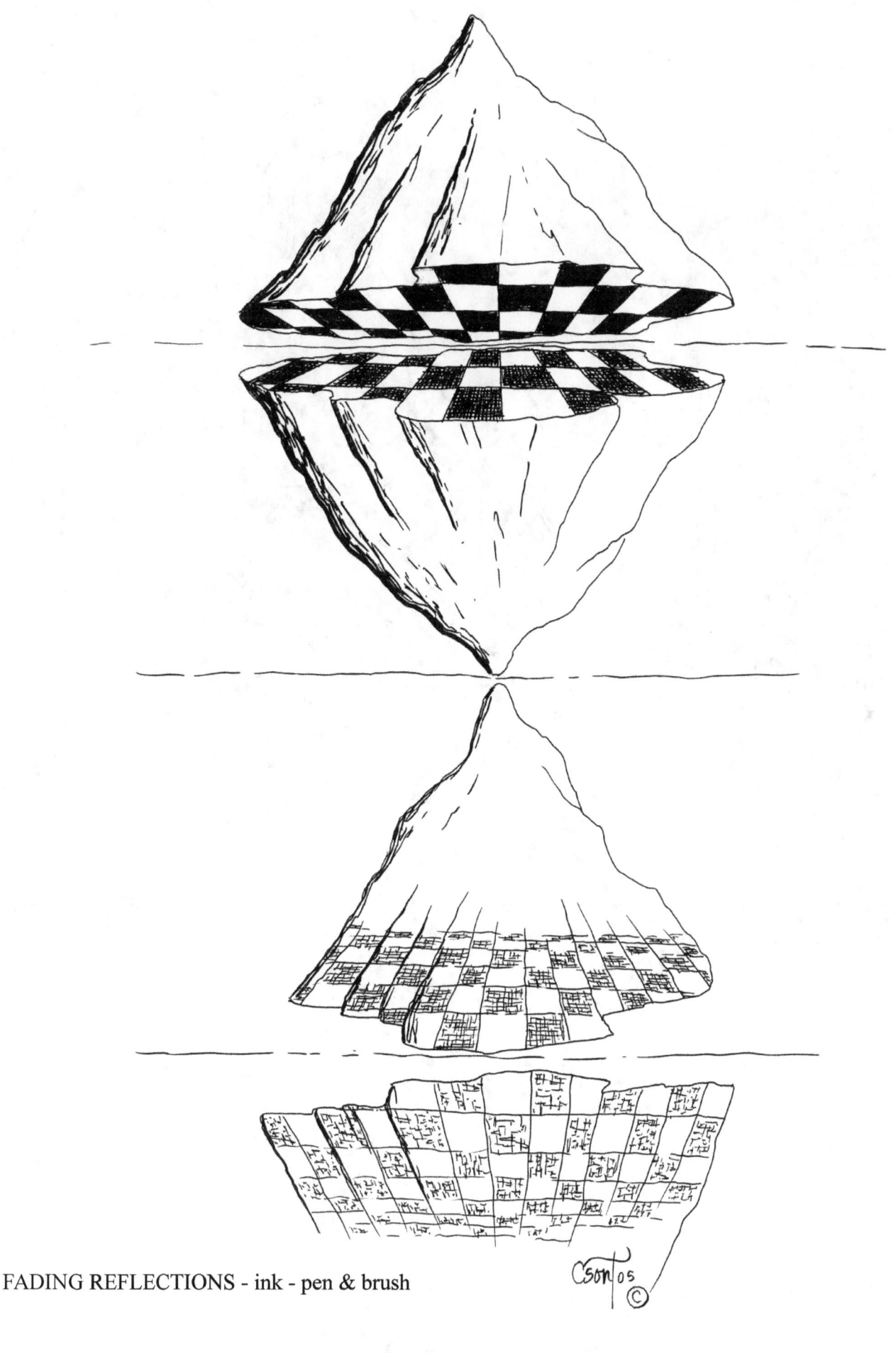

FADING REFLECTIONS - ink - pen & brush

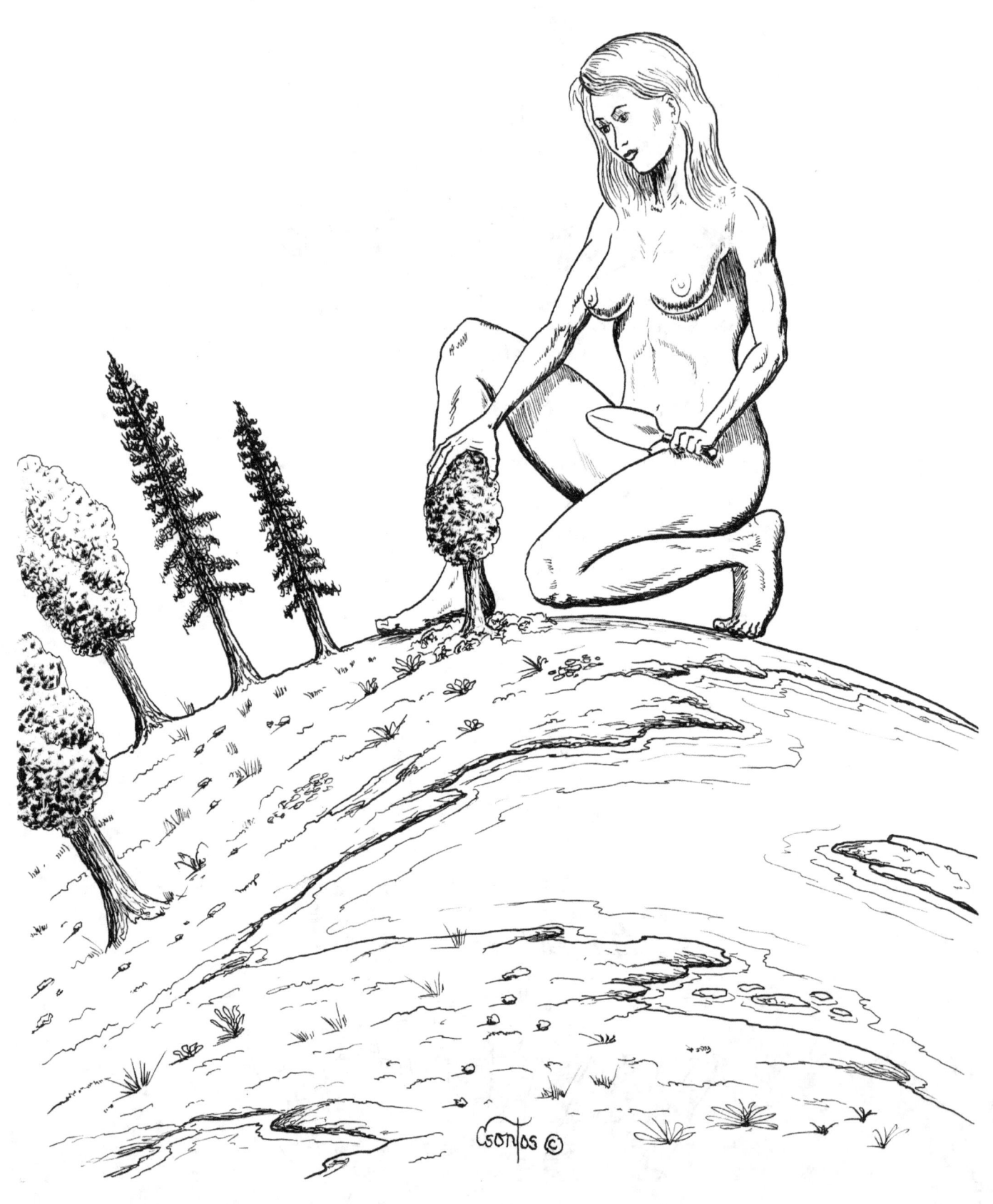

PLANTING A TREE - ink - pen & brush

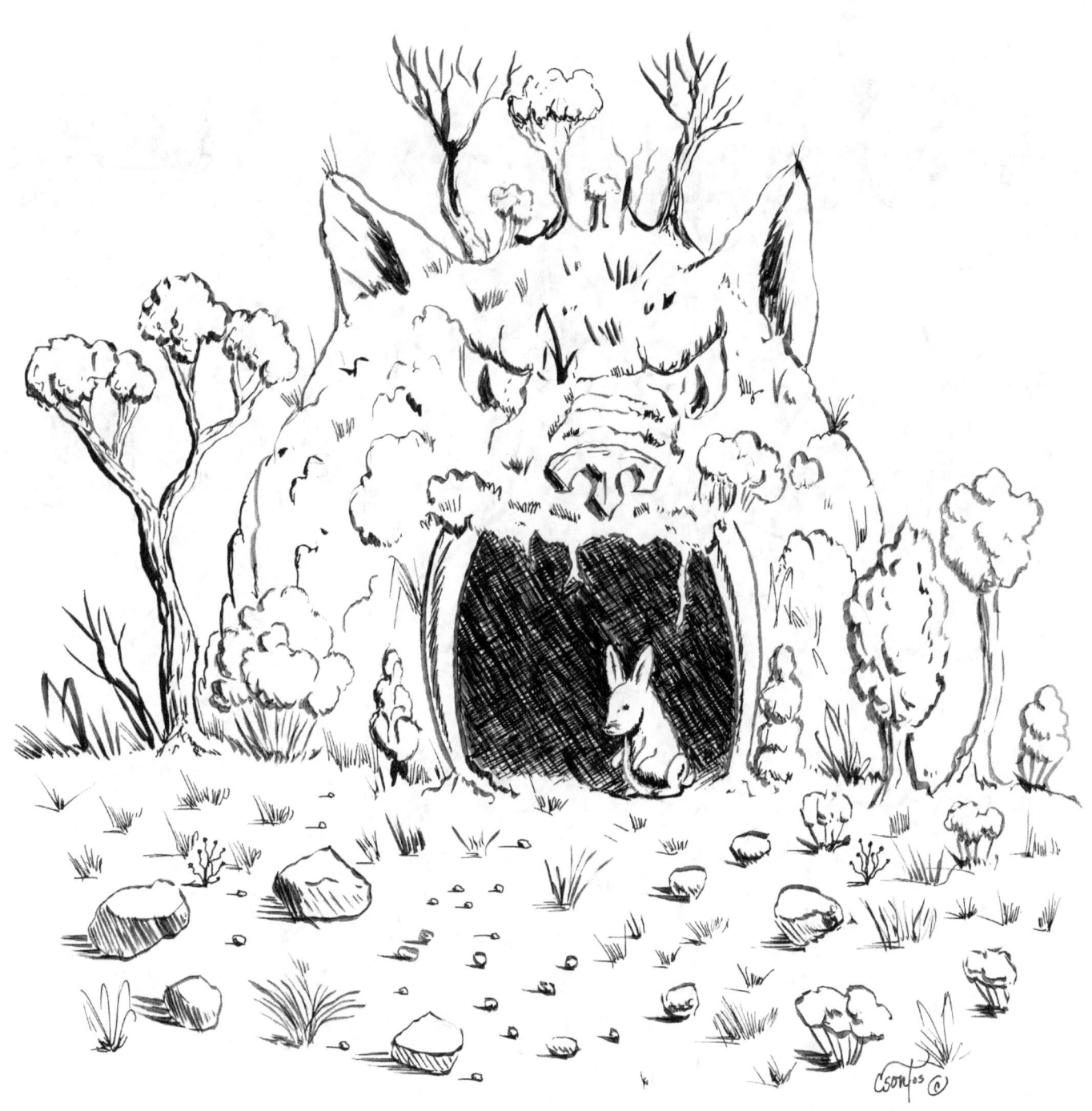

THE BURROW - ink - pen

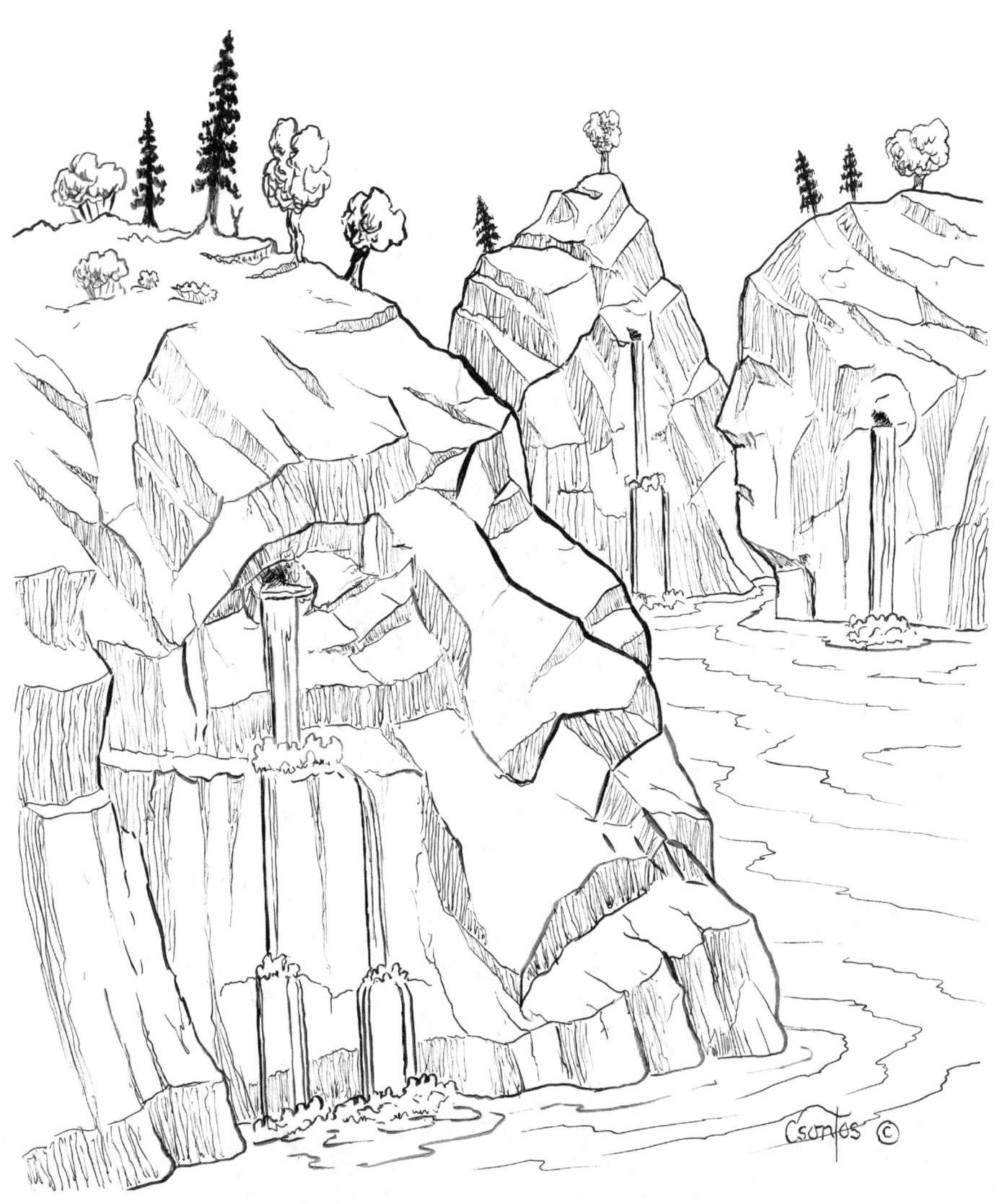

STONE FACES - ink - pen & brush

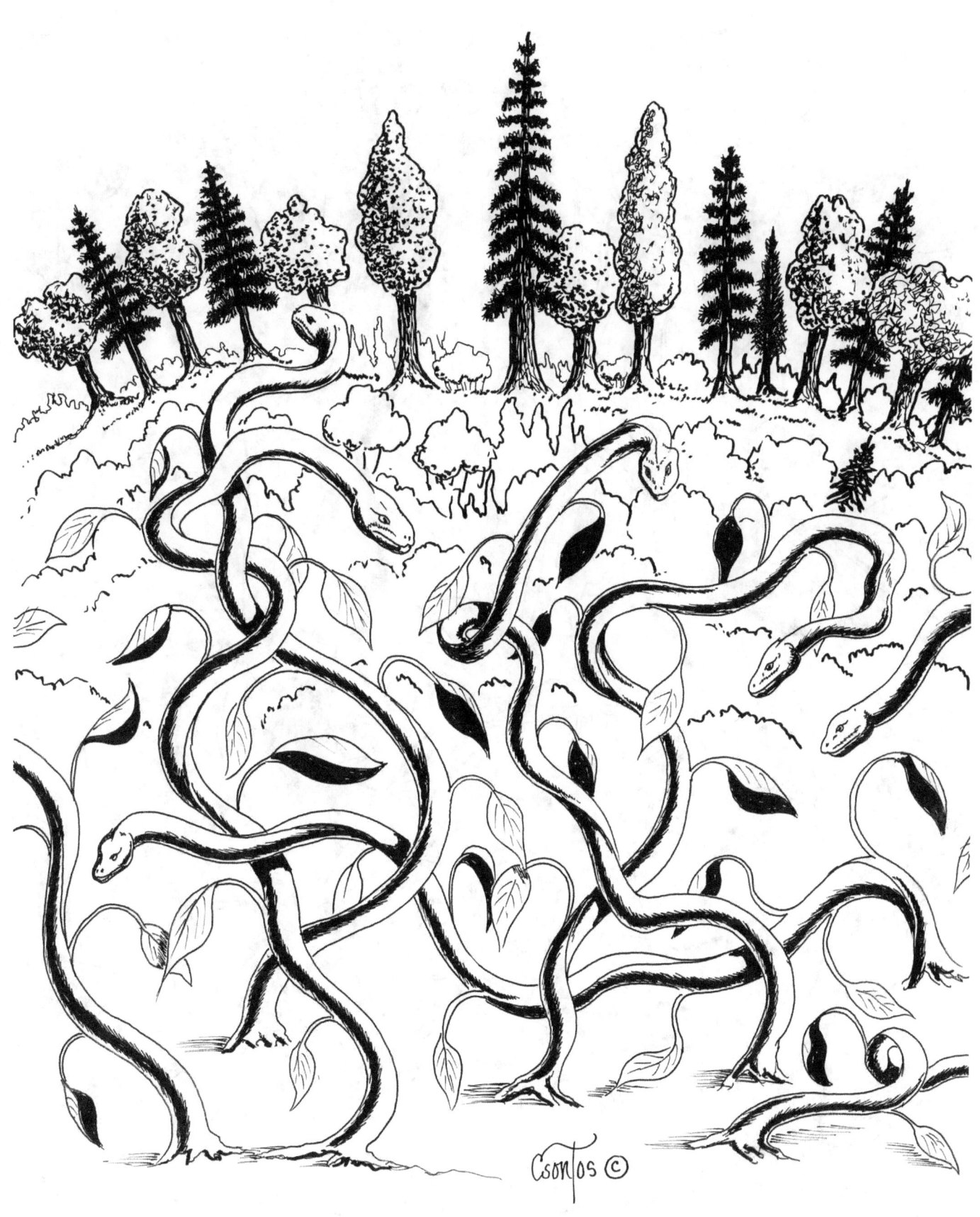

VINE LIFE - ink - pen & brush

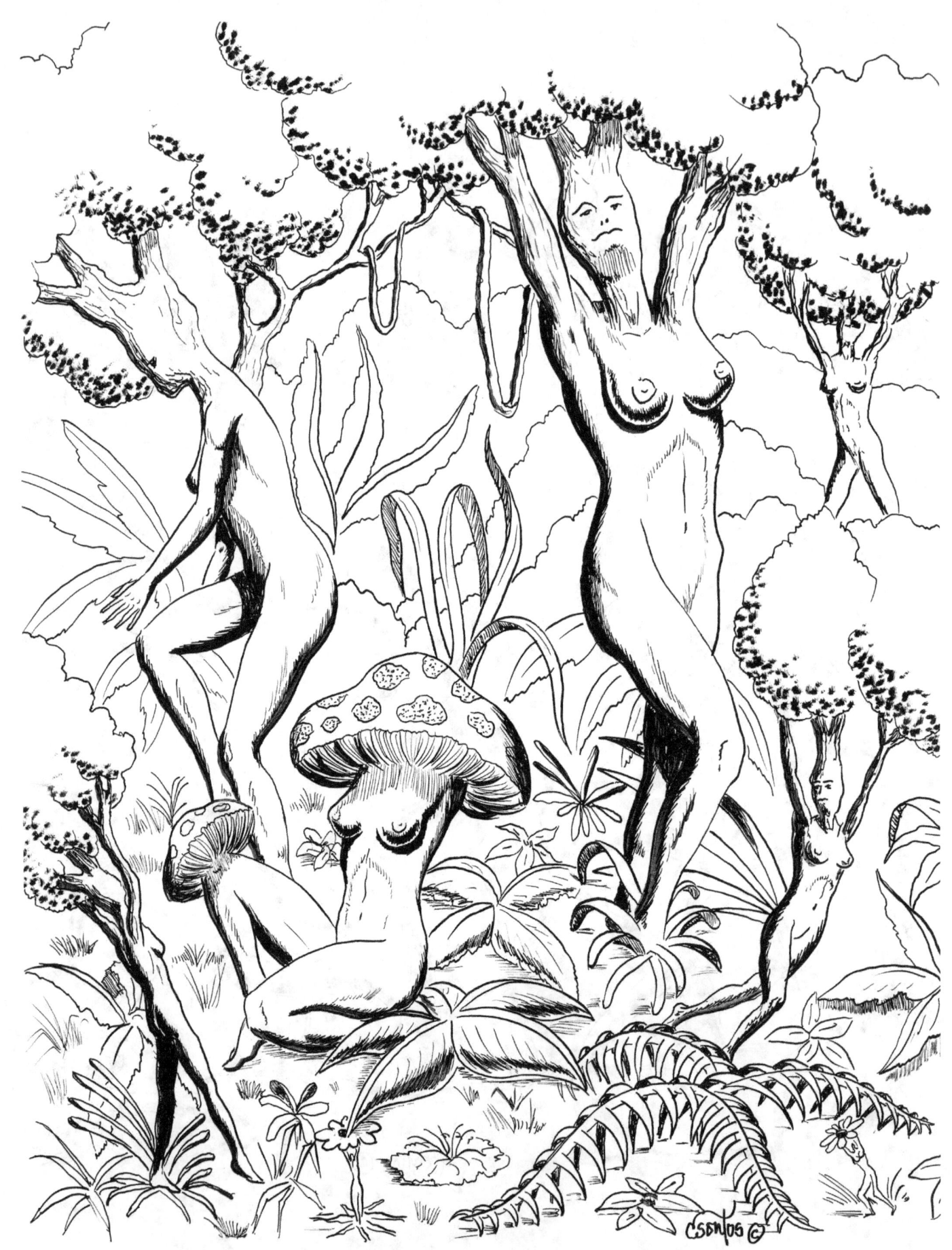

LADYSCAPE - ink - pen & brush

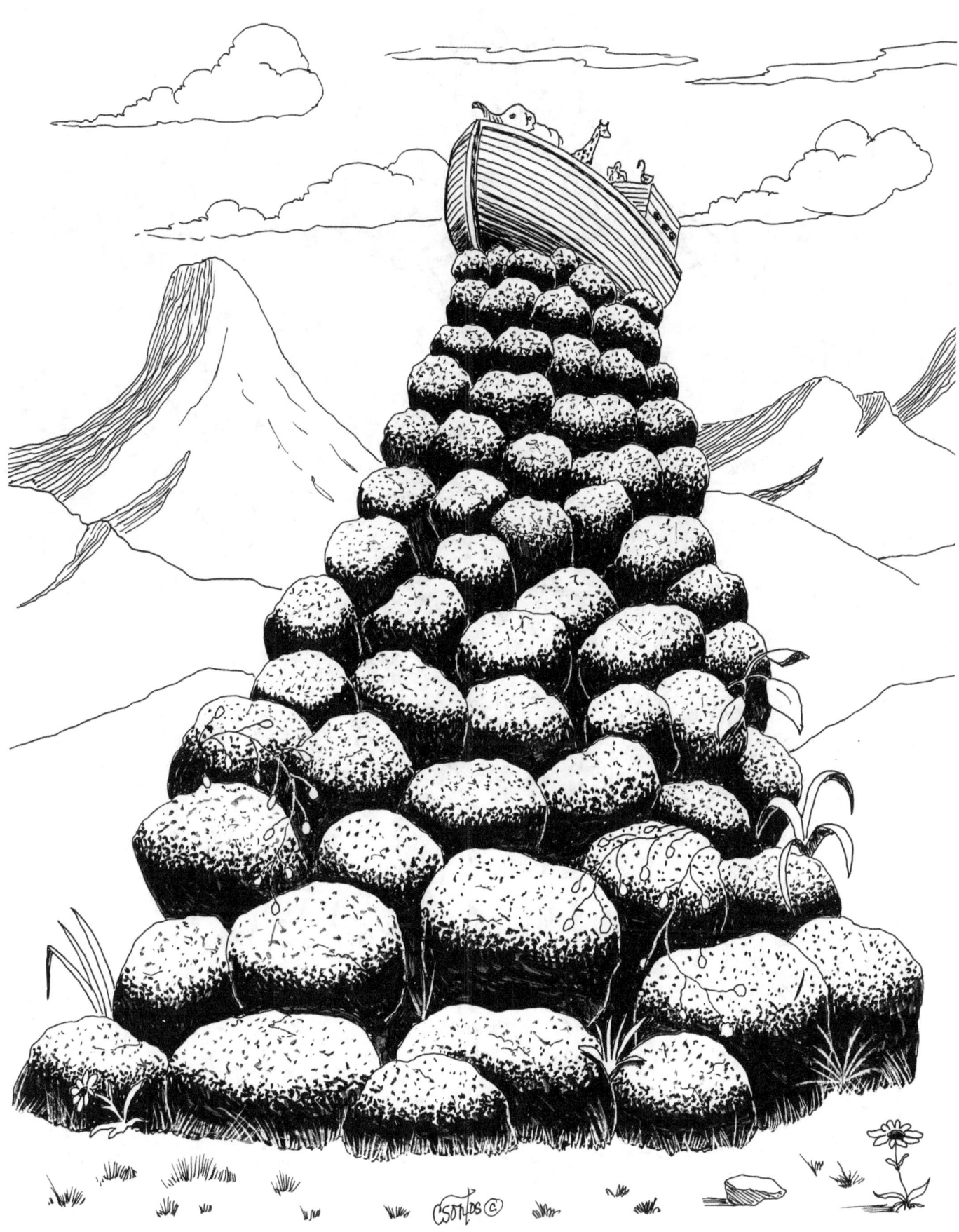

ROCK TOWER - ink - pen & brush

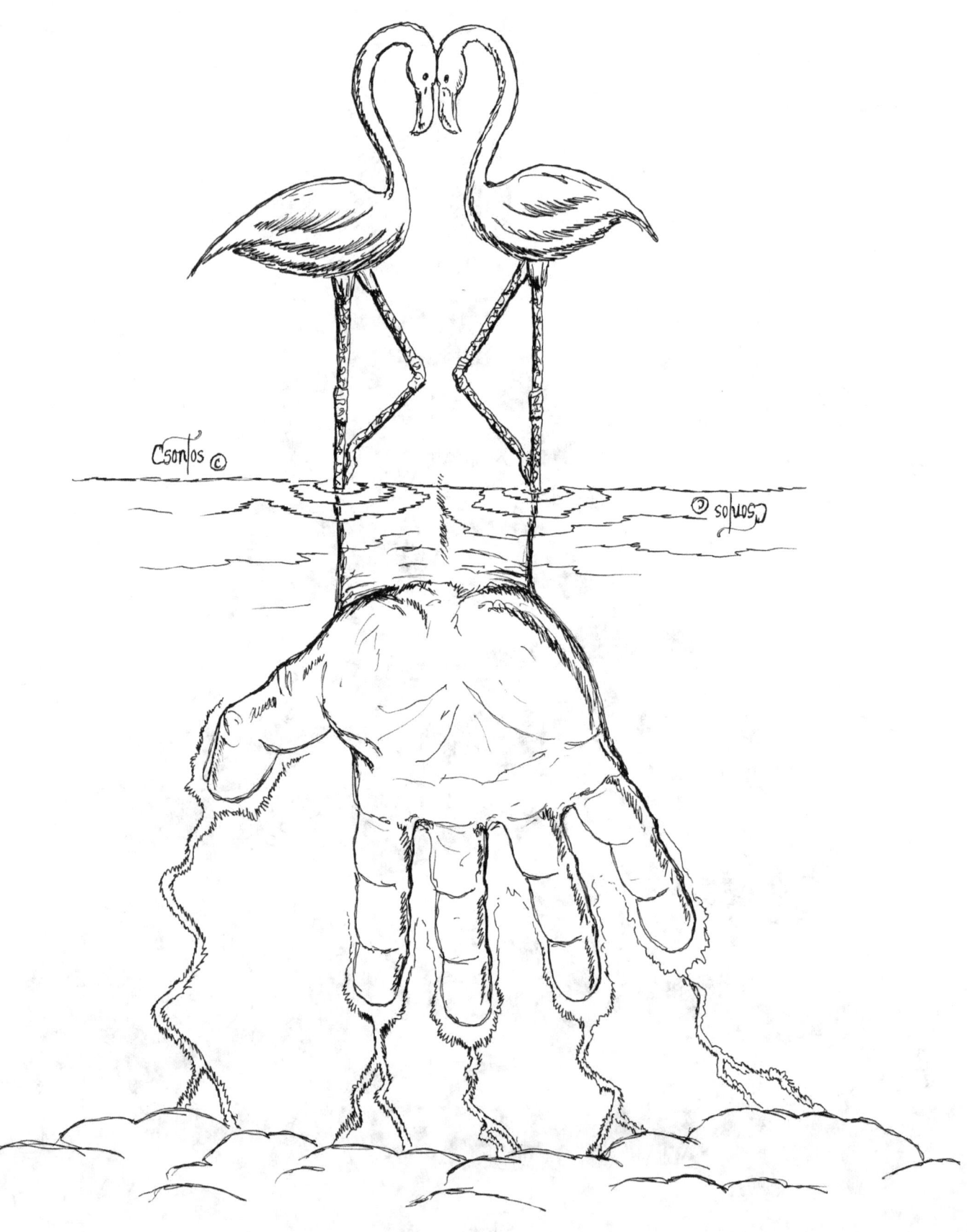

TRANSFERENCE - ink - pen

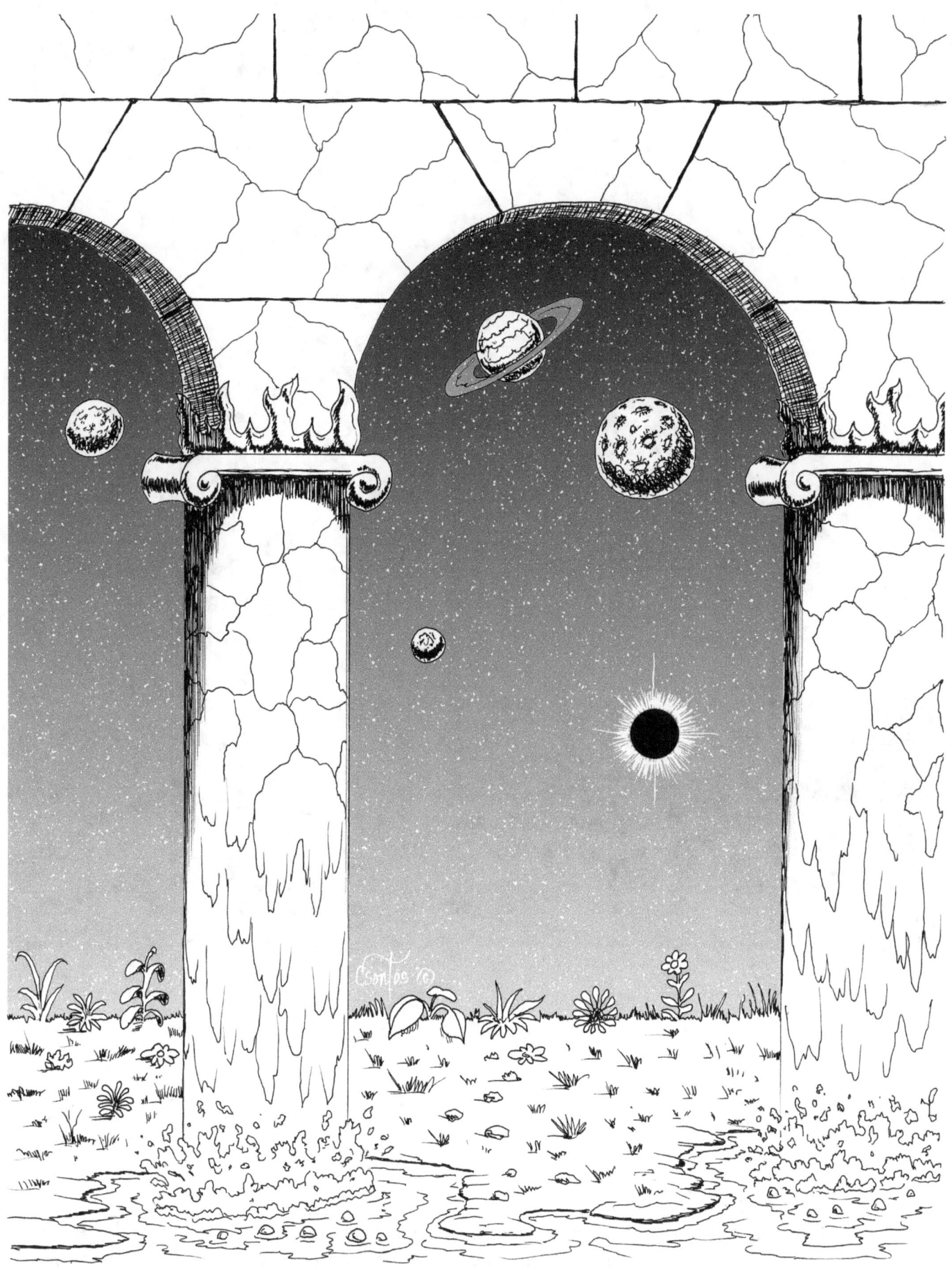

PORTAL - ink - pen & Photoshop

Fantasy

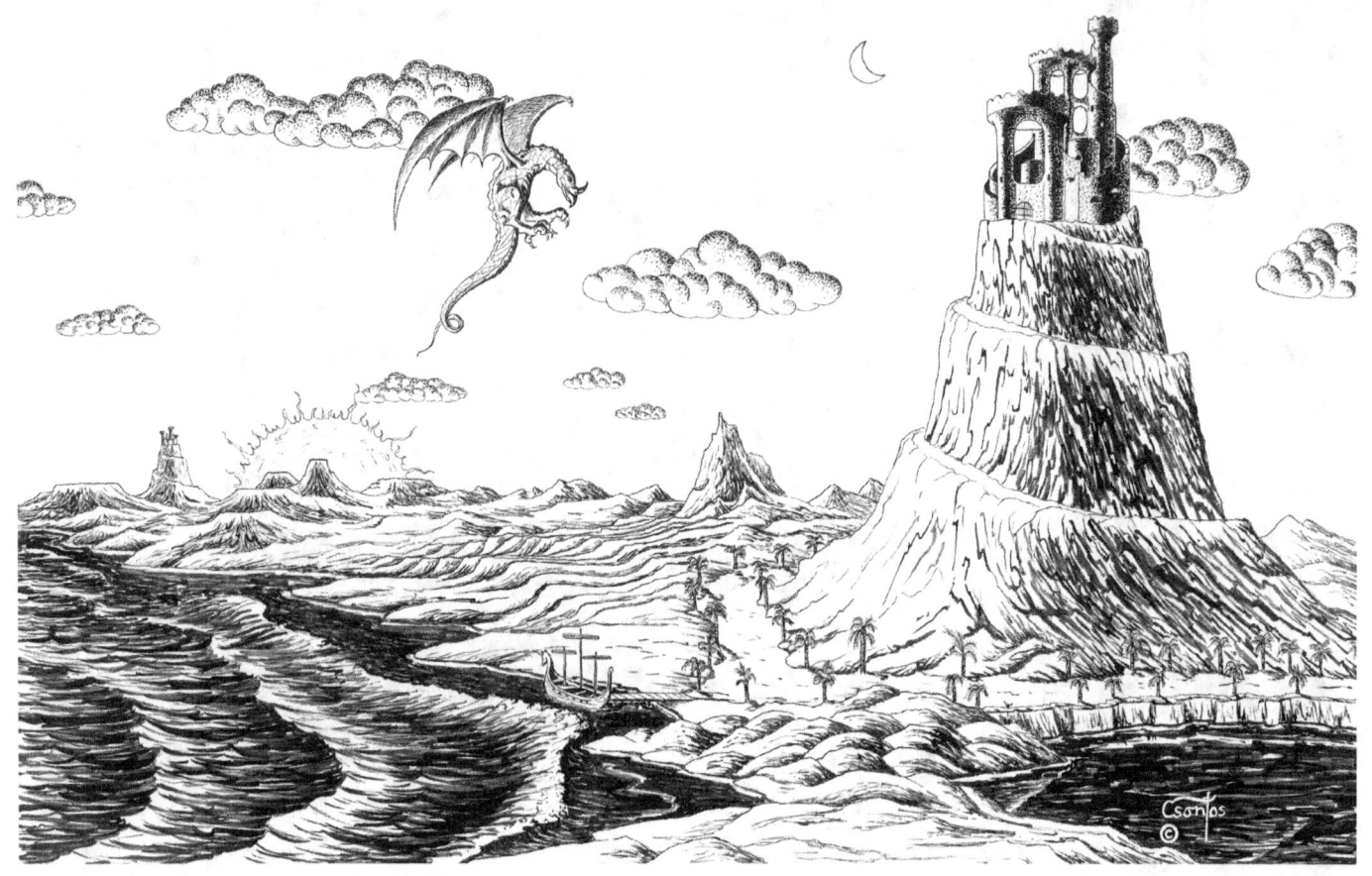

MEDIEVAL SCENE - ink - pen & brush

I was never much of a fantasy buff reader as I prefer to draw and paint. I did read "The Lord of the Rings' when I had a rather easy job many, many years ago. I do however, love the imagery. Especially the dynamic imagery of Frank Frazetta. Most of the fantasy paintings I've done are in 'Perceptions I & II'.

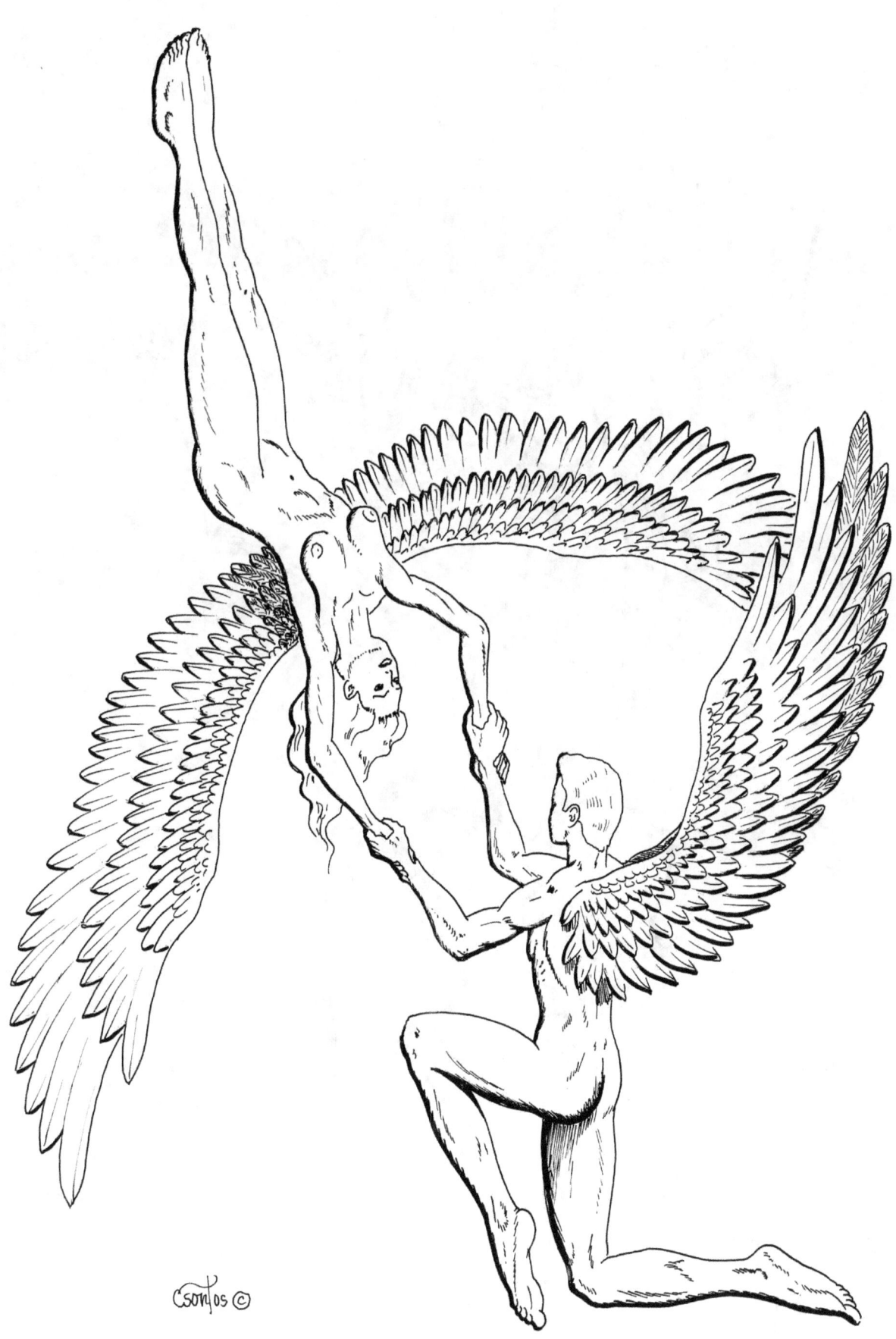

AERIAL ACROBATICS - ink - pen & brush

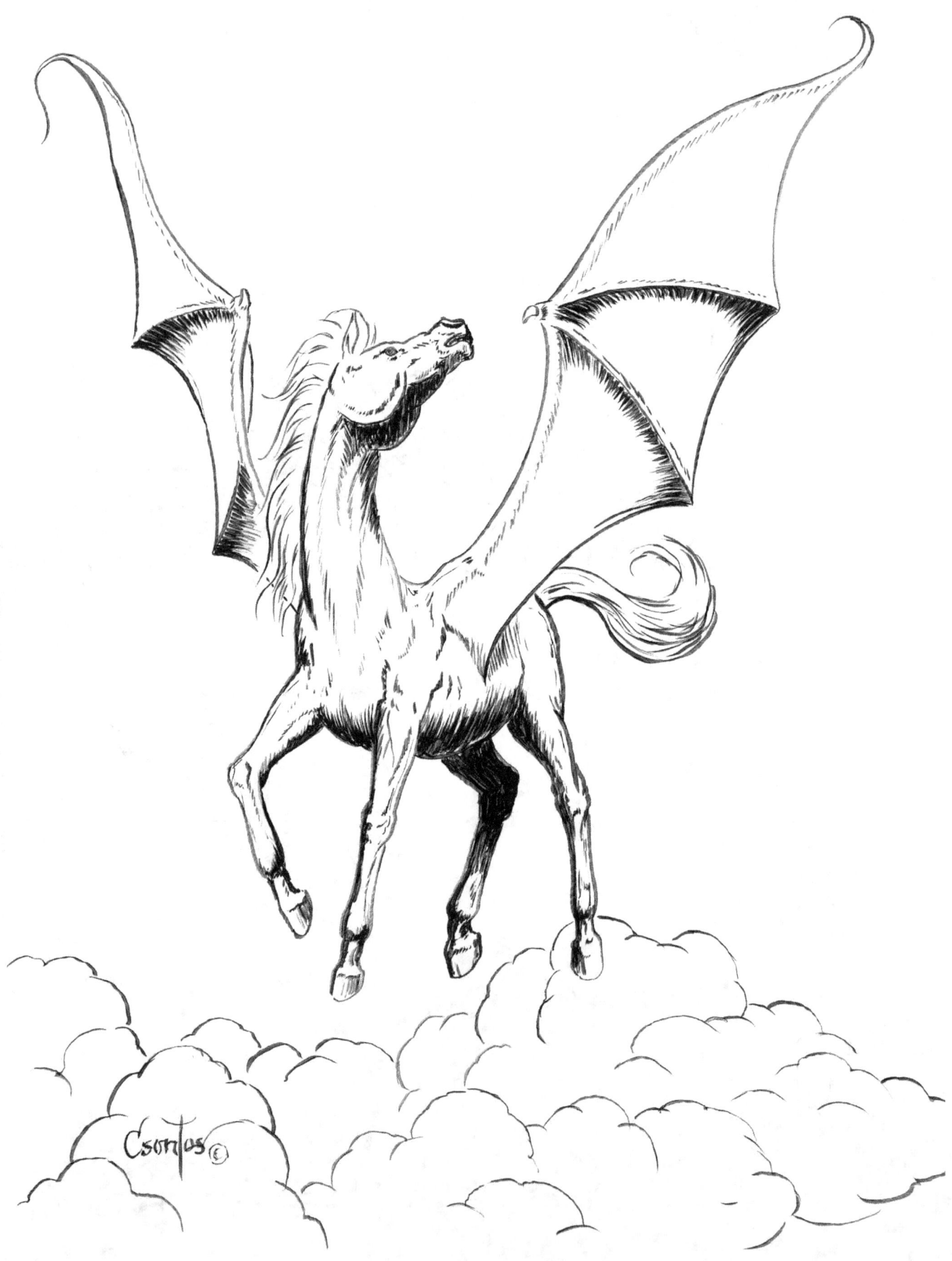

A DIFFERENT KIND OF PEGASUS - ink - pen & brush

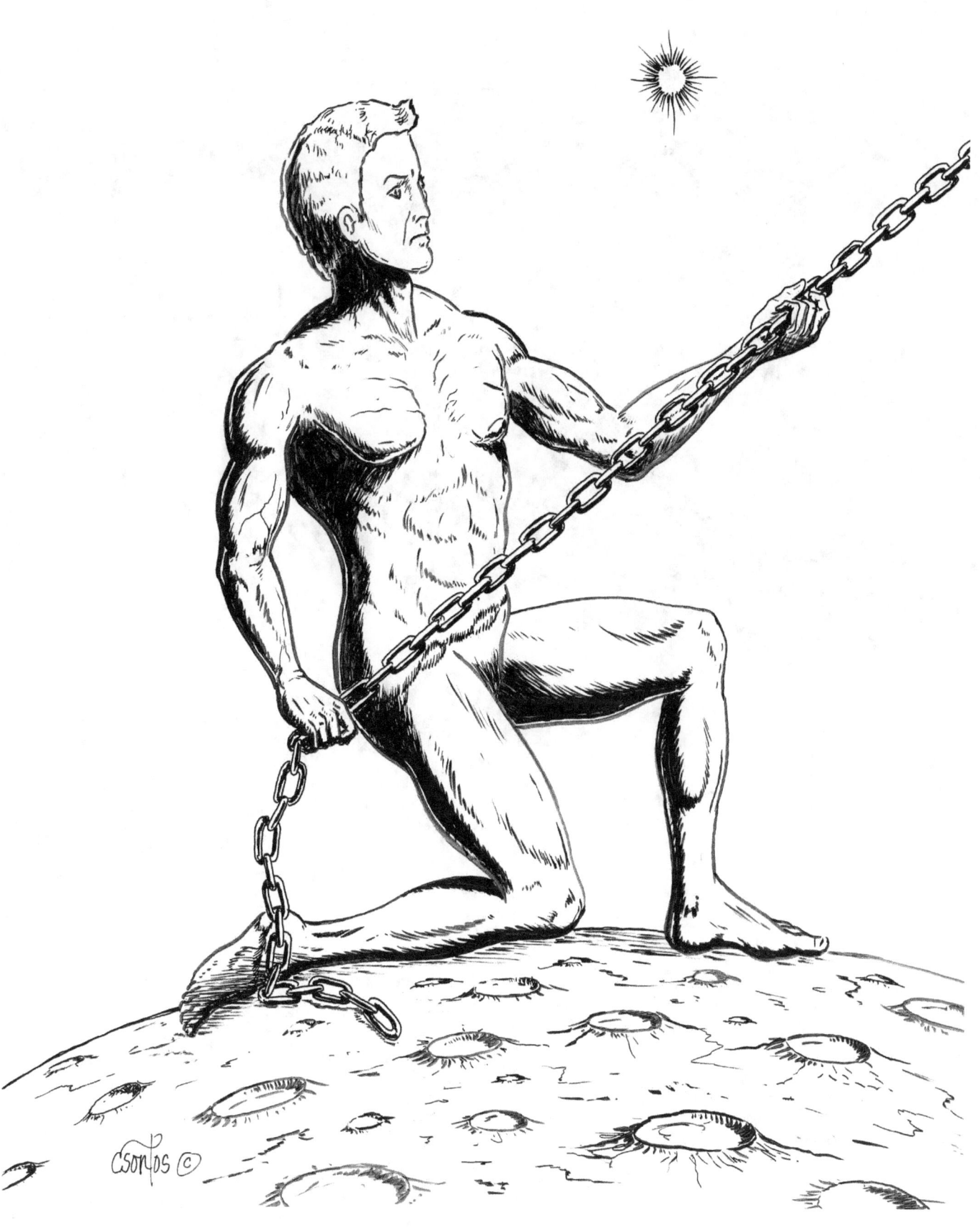

AN ATLAS - ink - pen & brush

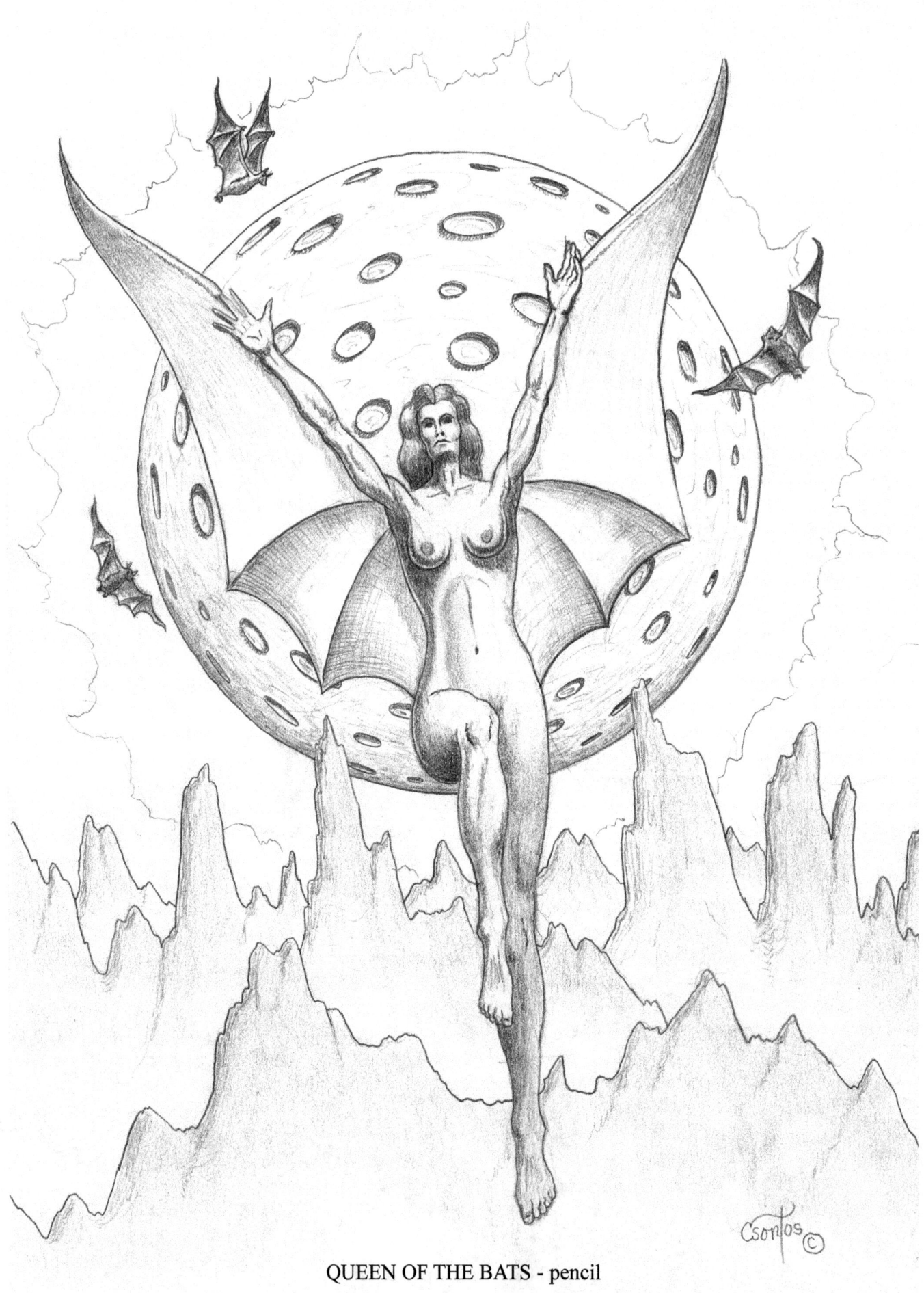

QUEEN OF THE BATS - pencil

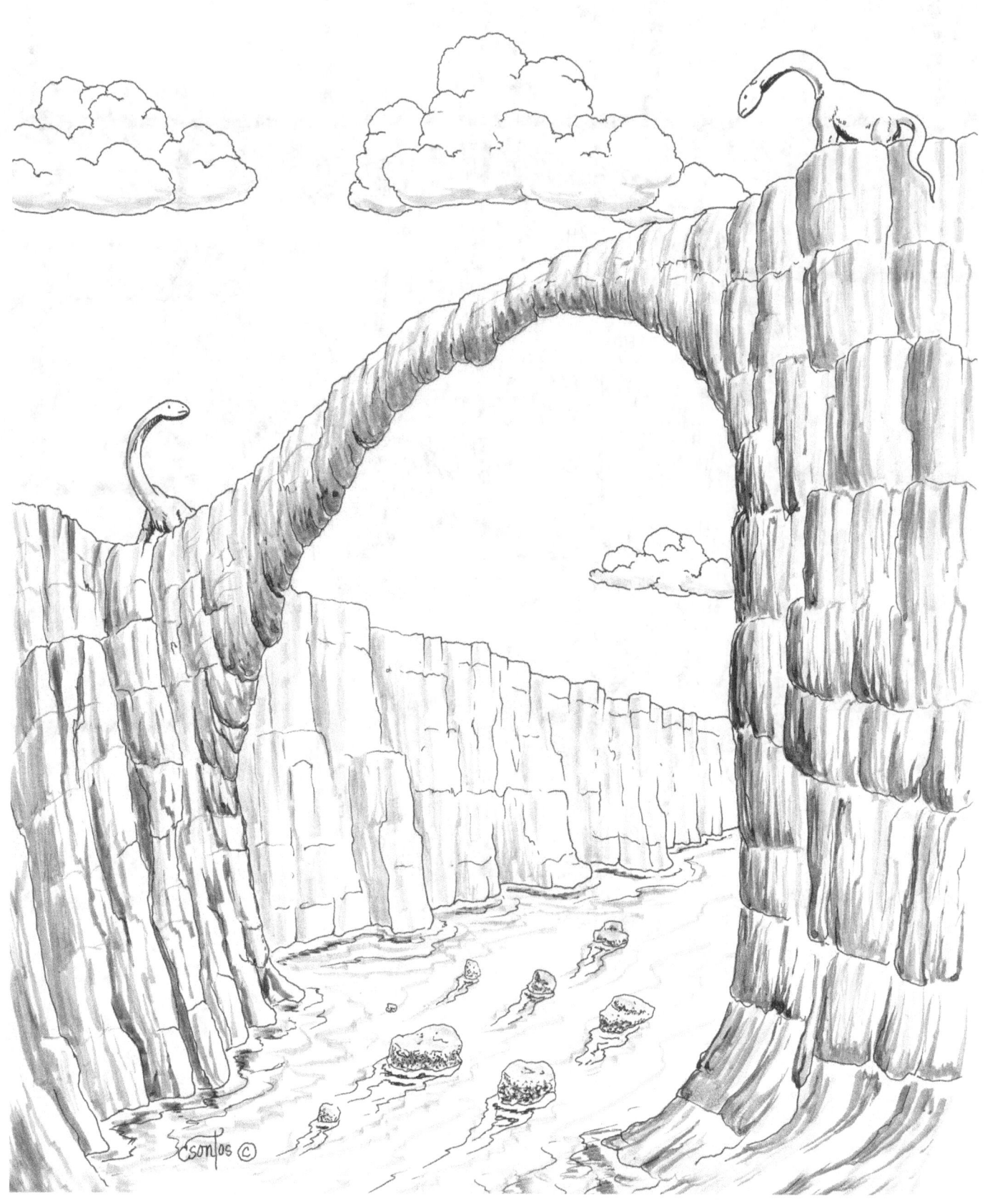

DECISIONS, DECISIONS - ink & ink wash - pen & brush

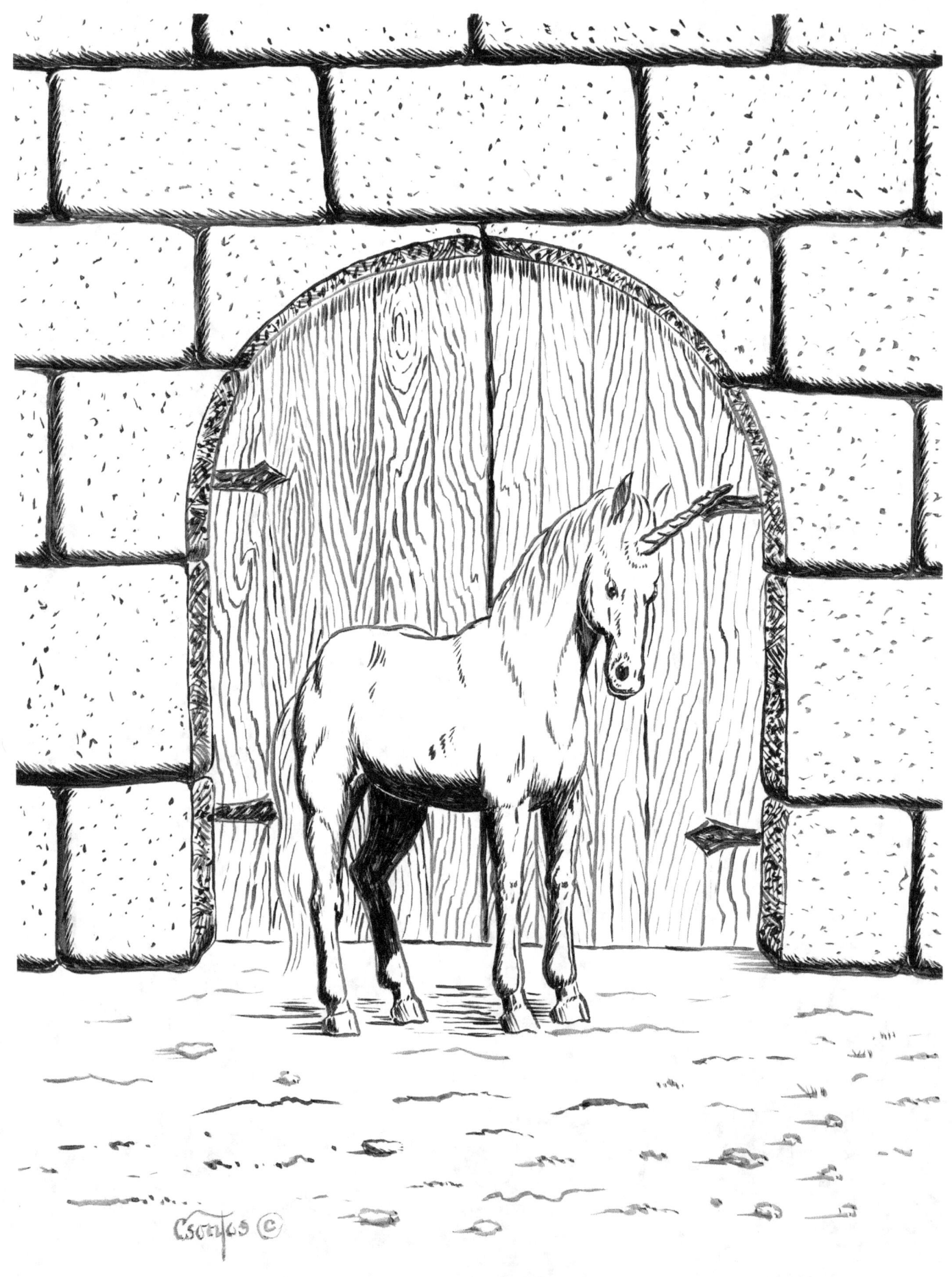

GUARDIAN OF THE GATE - ink - pen & brush

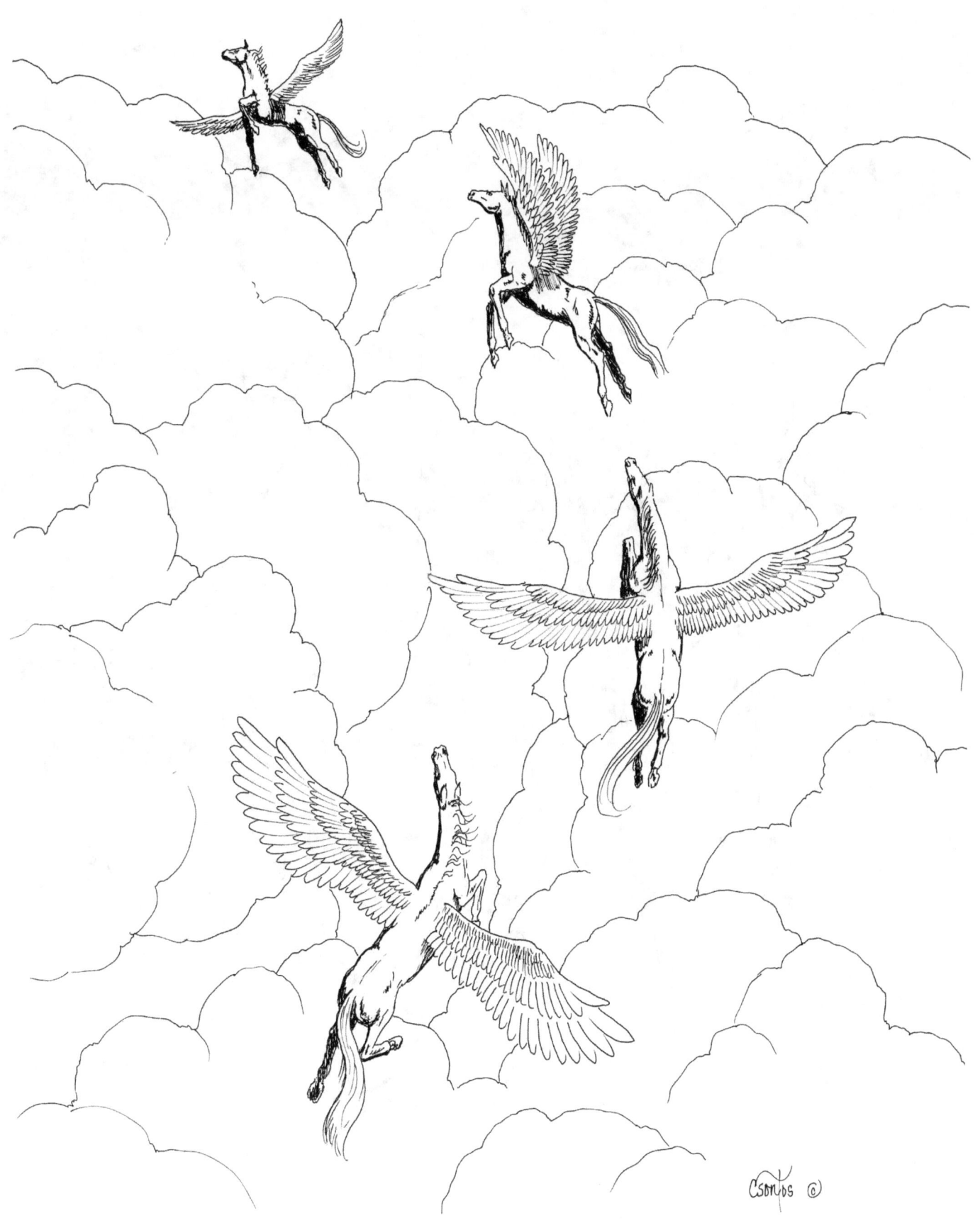

FOLLOW THE LEADER - ink - pen

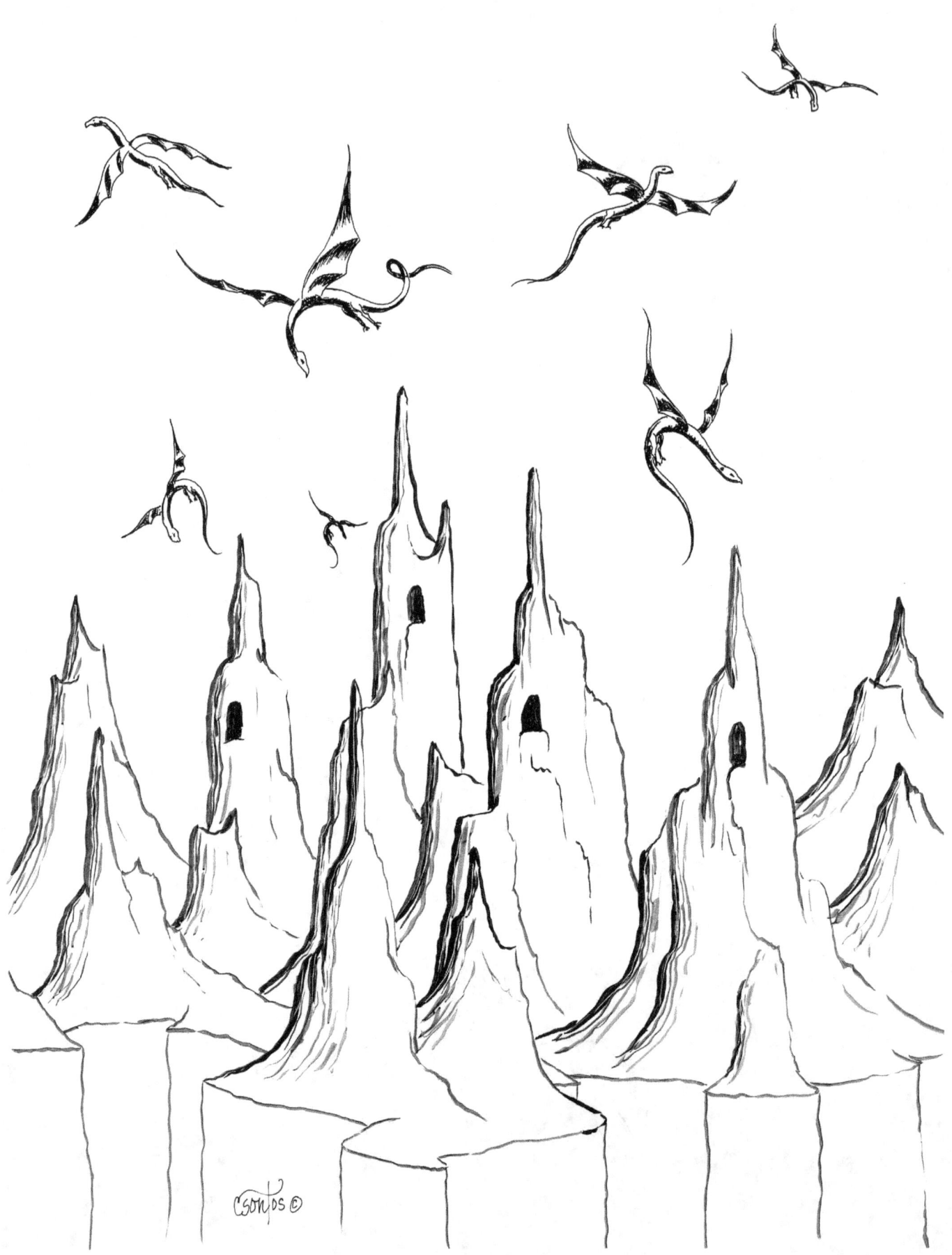

DRAGON LAND - ink - pen & brush

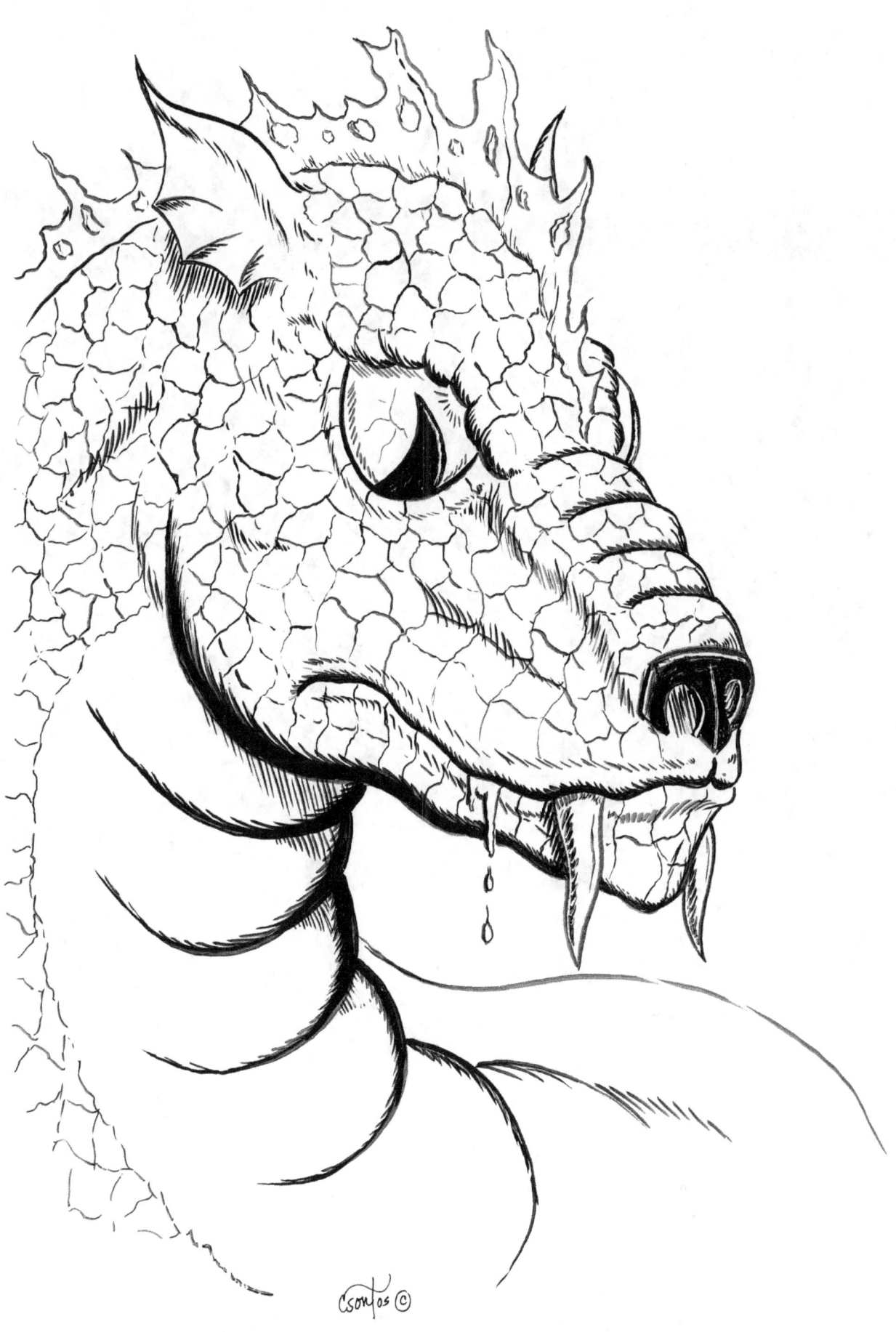

Csontos ©

REPTILIUS - ink - brush

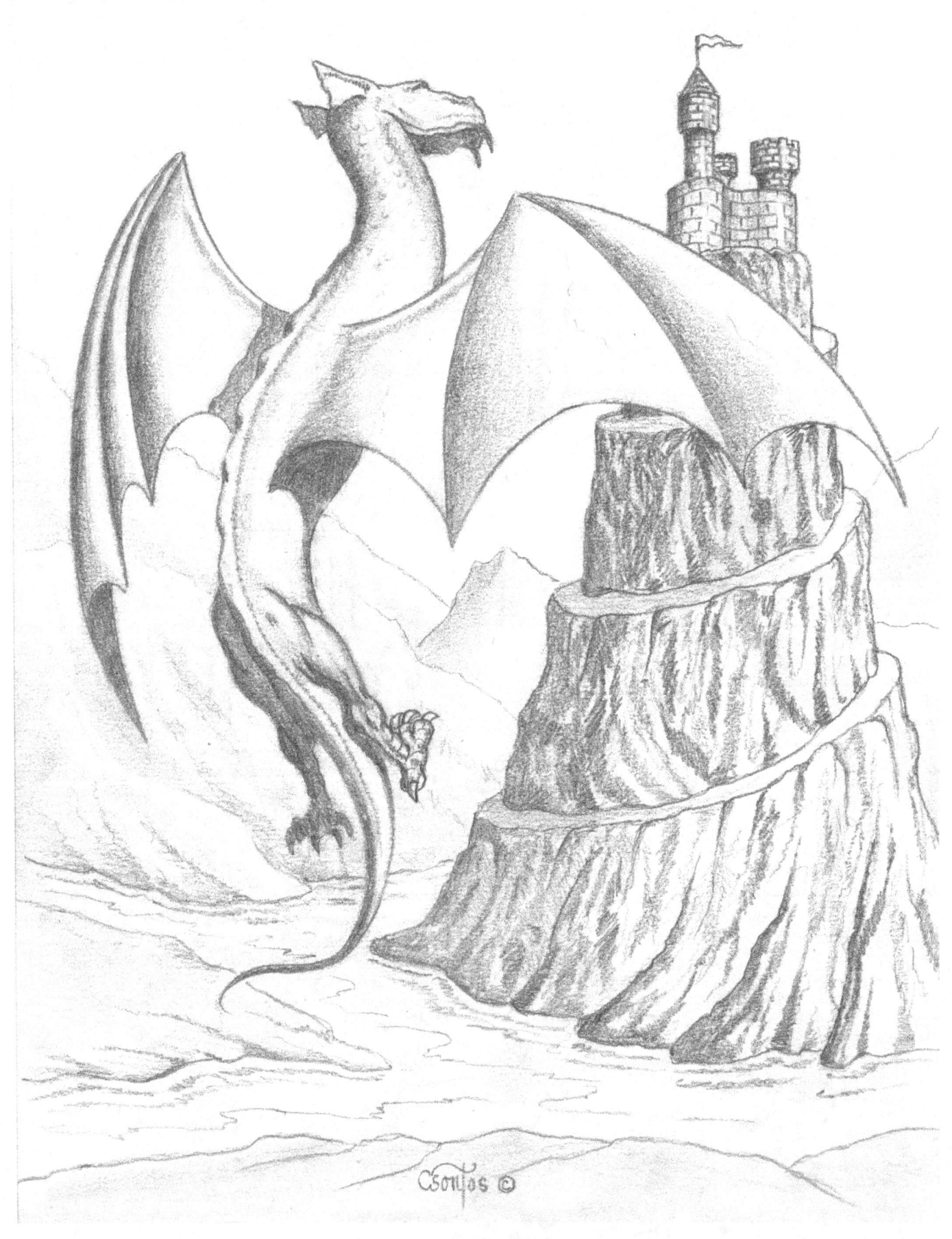

WHY TAKE THE TRAIL WHEN YOU CAN FLY - pencil

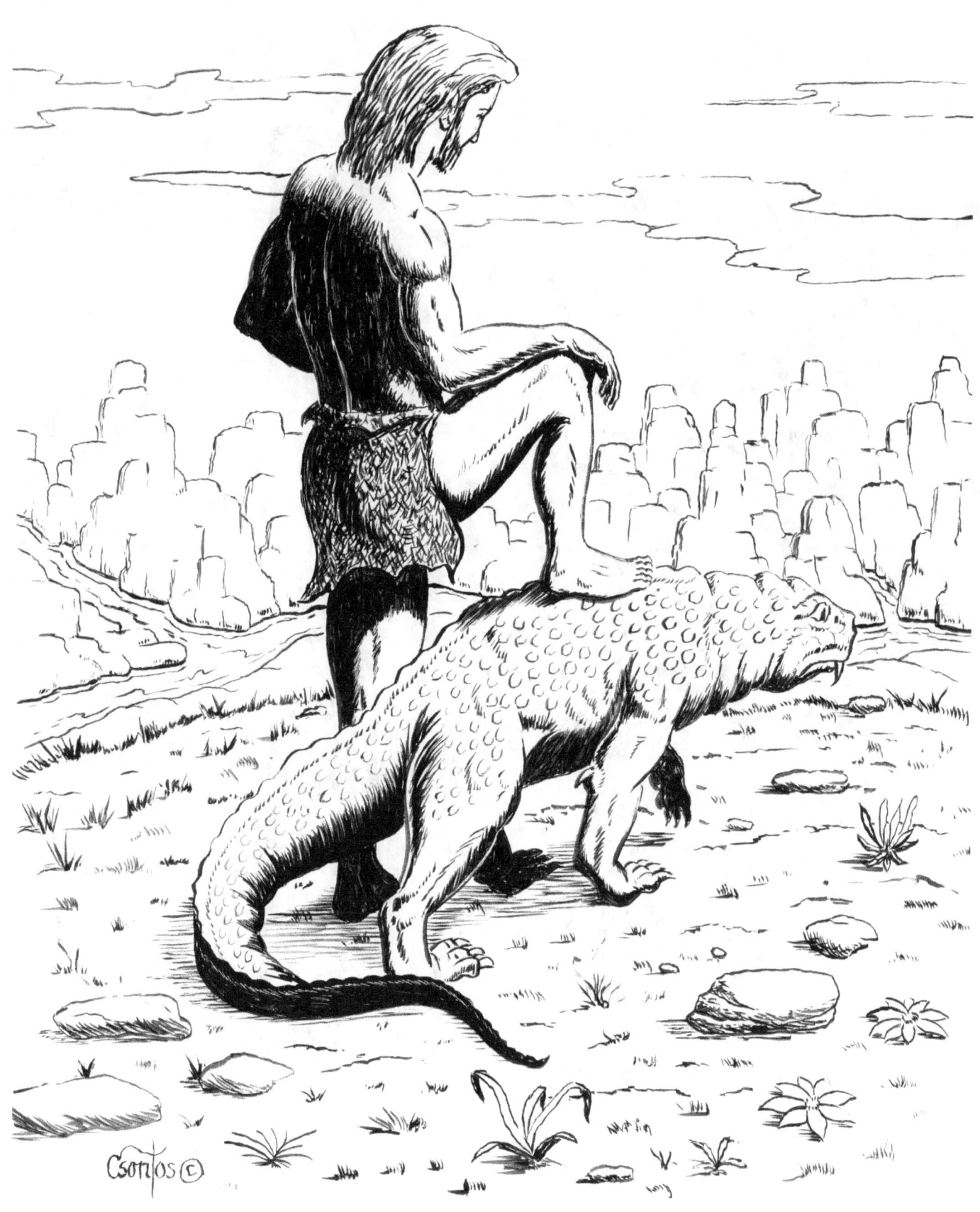

TAKING IN THE OVERLOOK - ink - brush

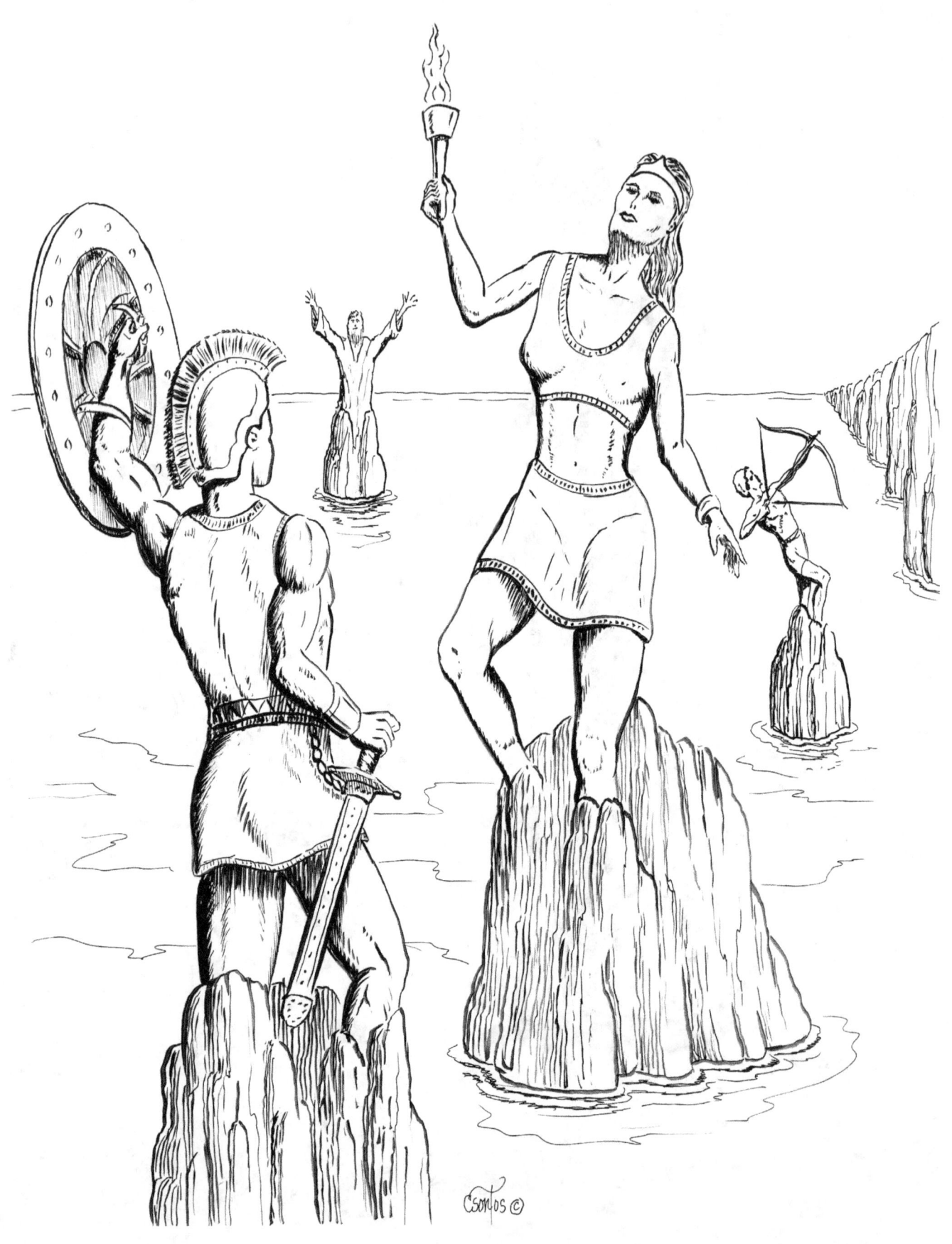

TITANS - ink - brush

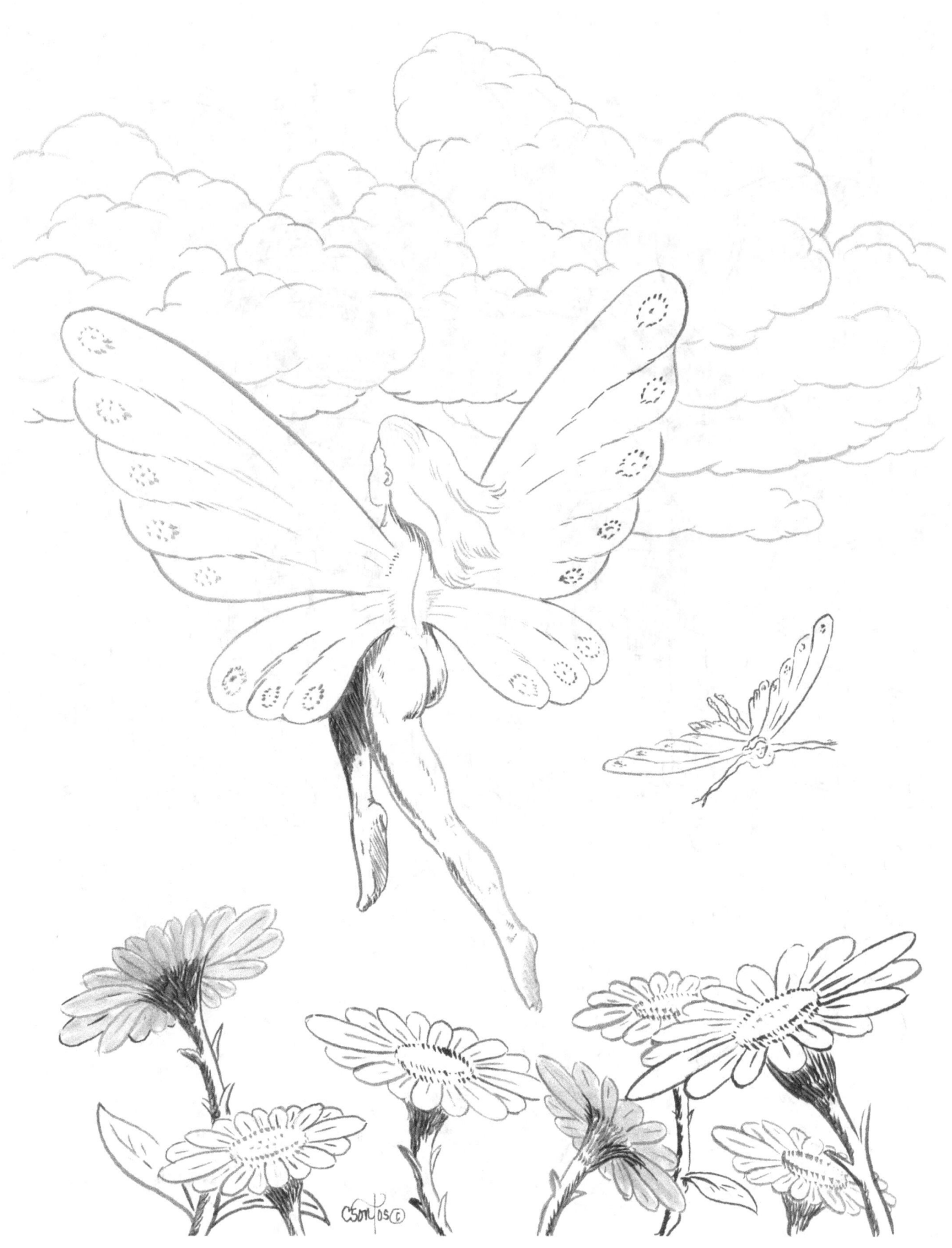

TAKING FLIGHT - ink - brush

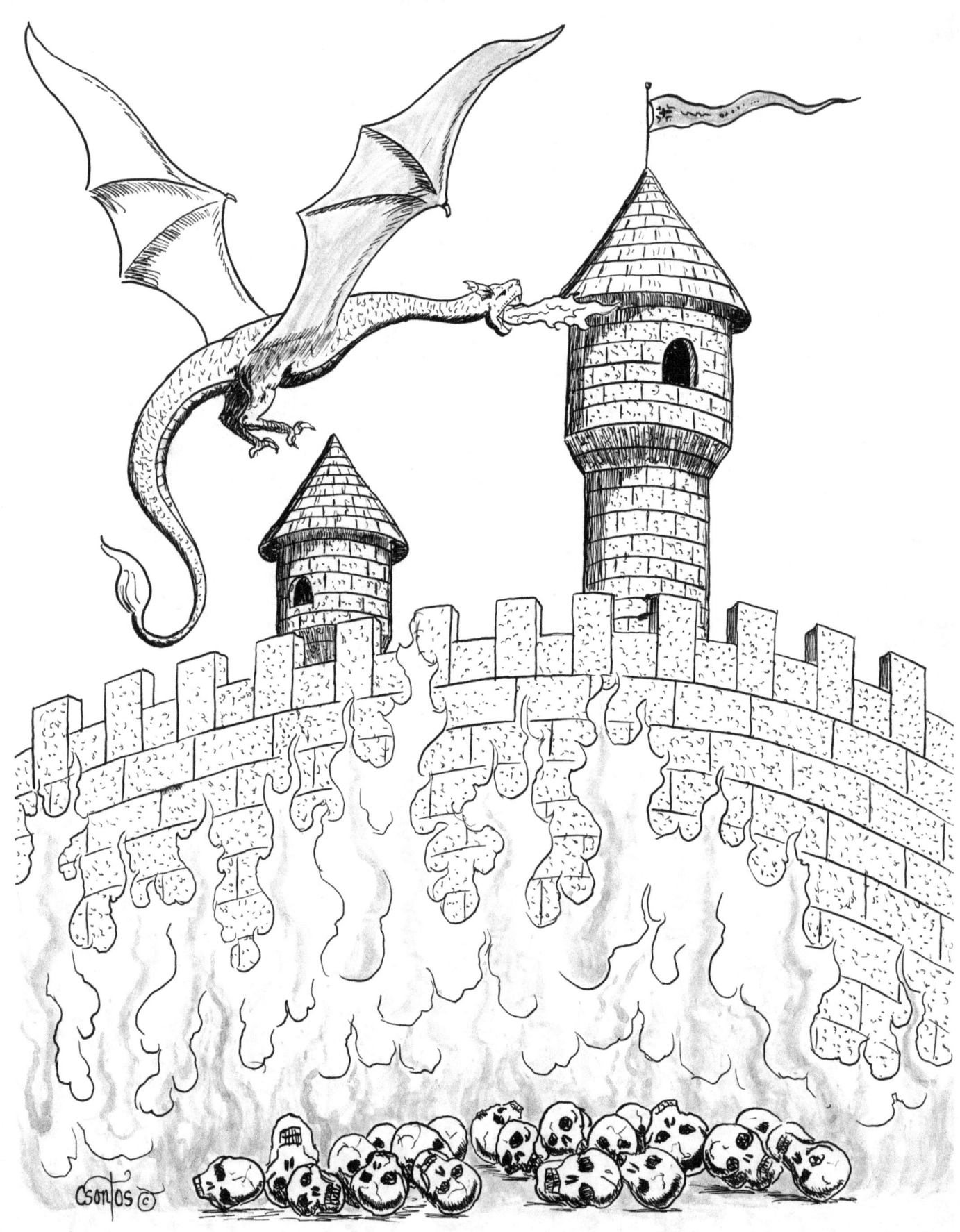

REVENGE - ink & ink wash - pen & brush

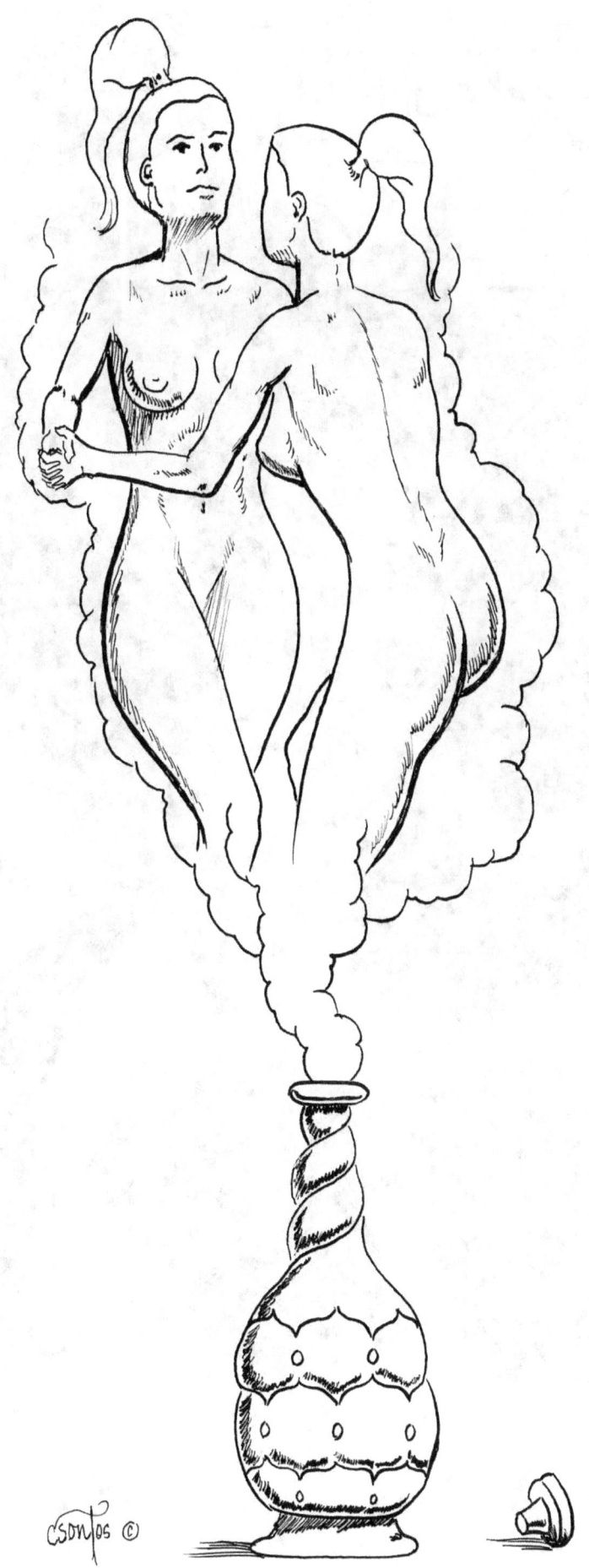

JINN SISTERS - ink - pen

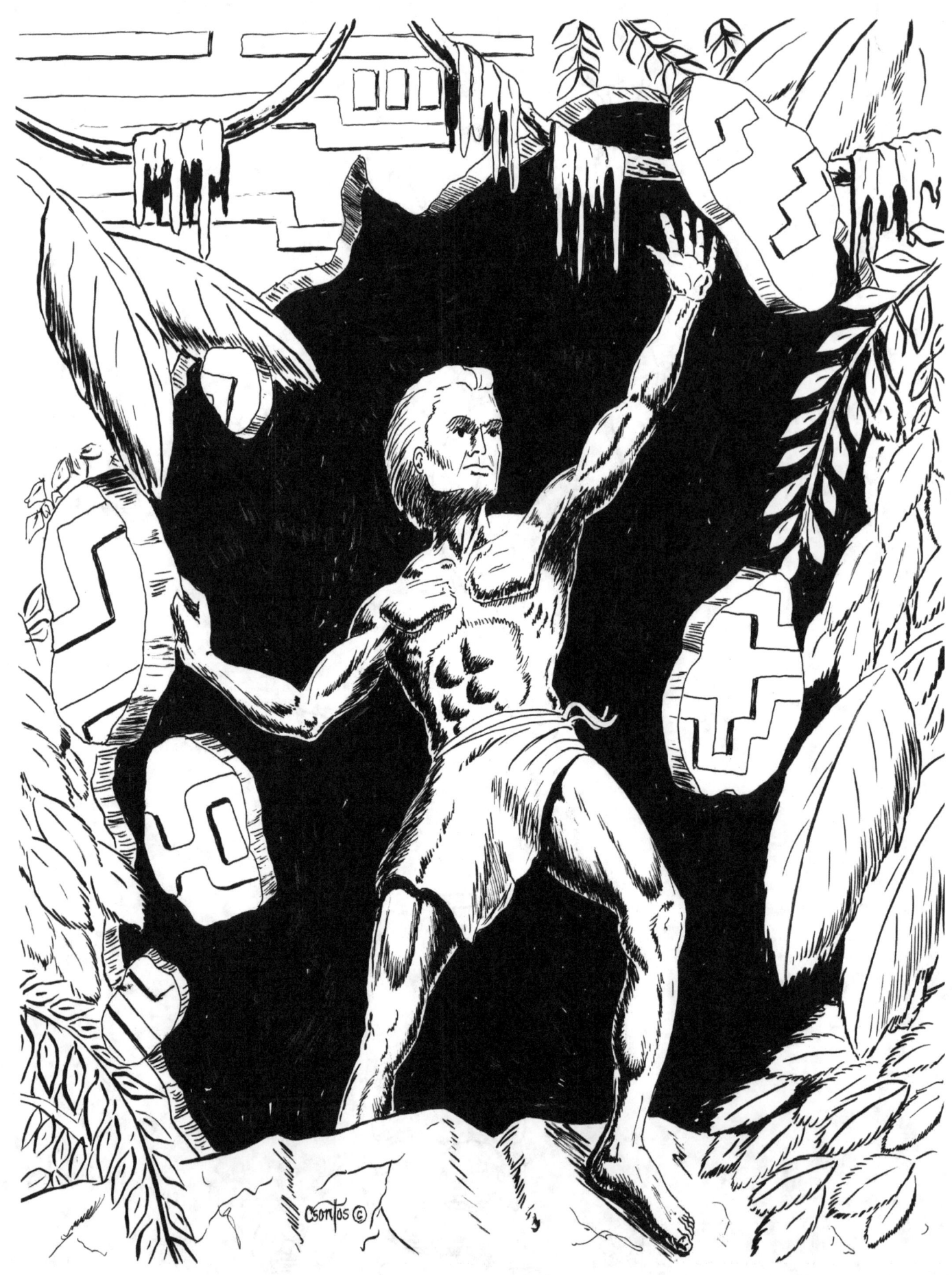

RESURRECTION - ink - pen & brush

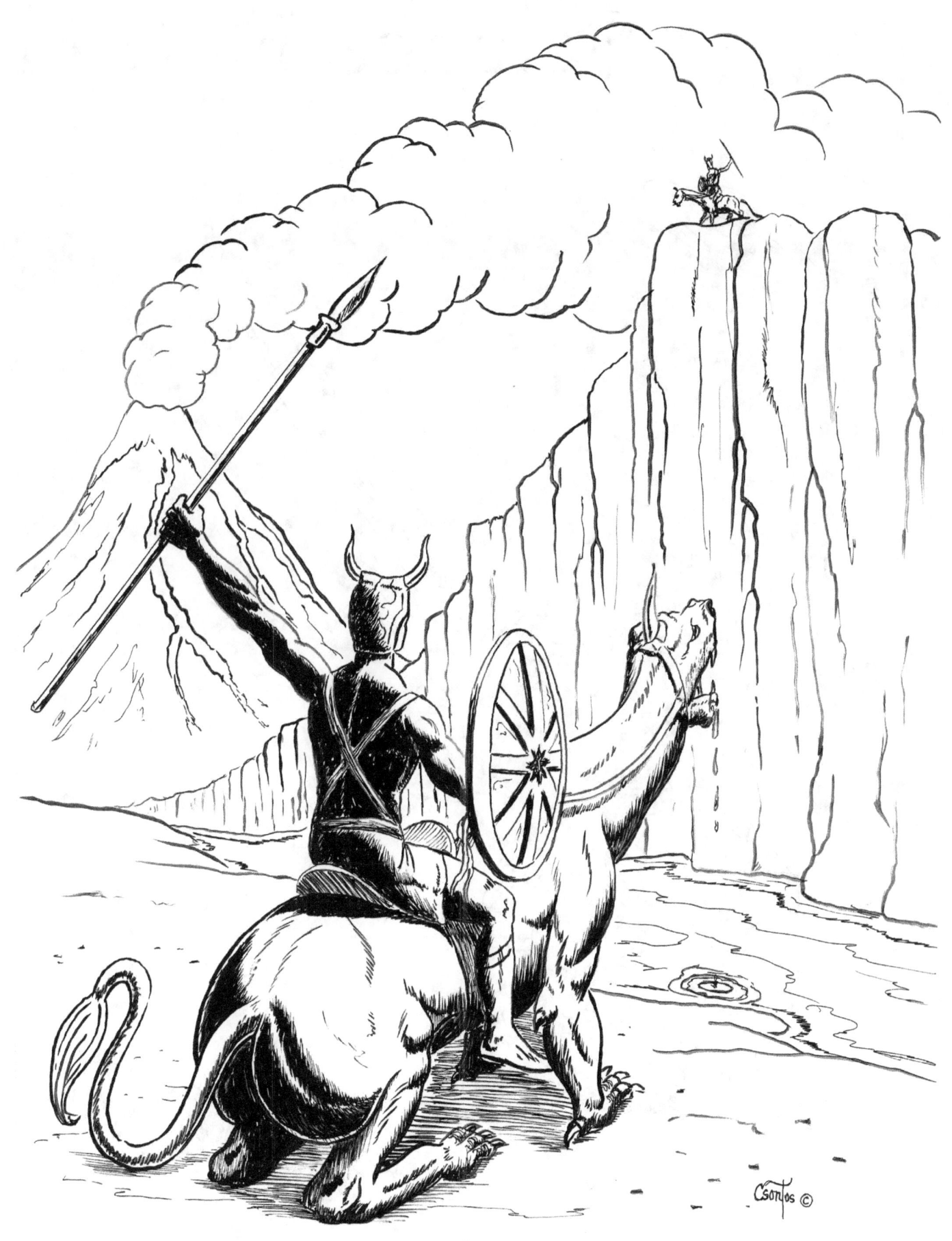

SALUTATION - ink - pen & brush

Science Fiction

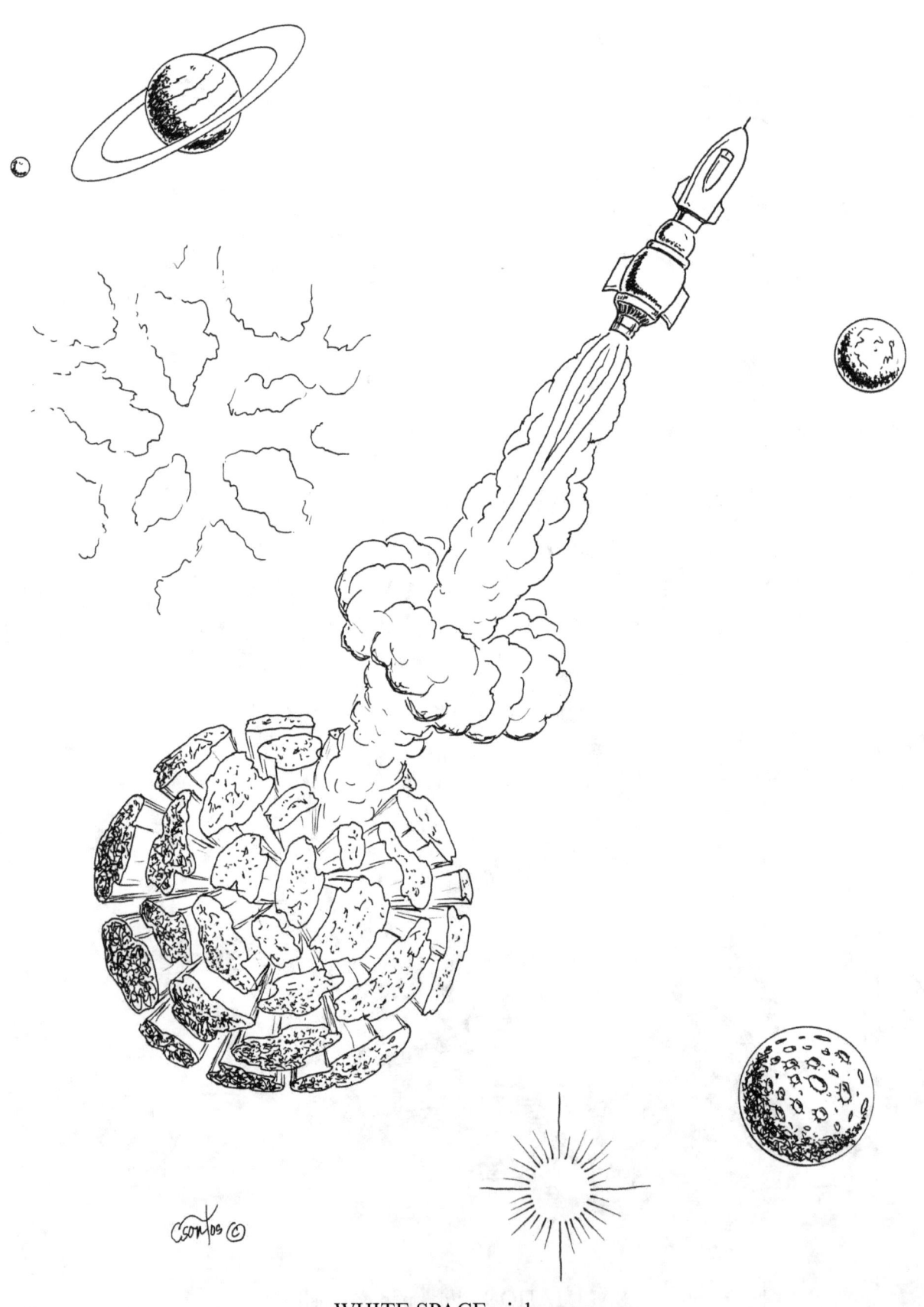

WHITE SPACE - ink - pen

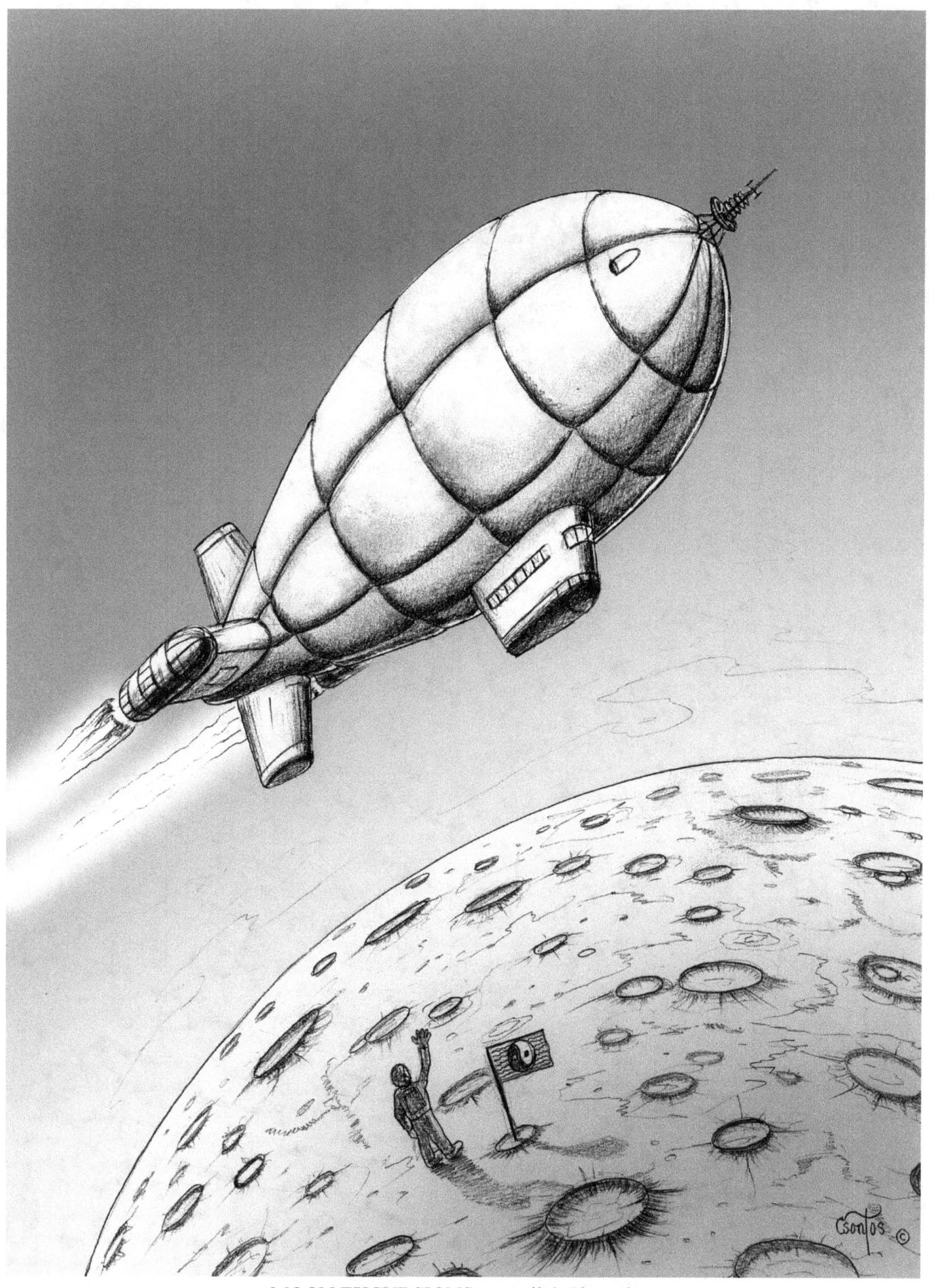

MOON EXCURSIONS - pencil & Photoshop

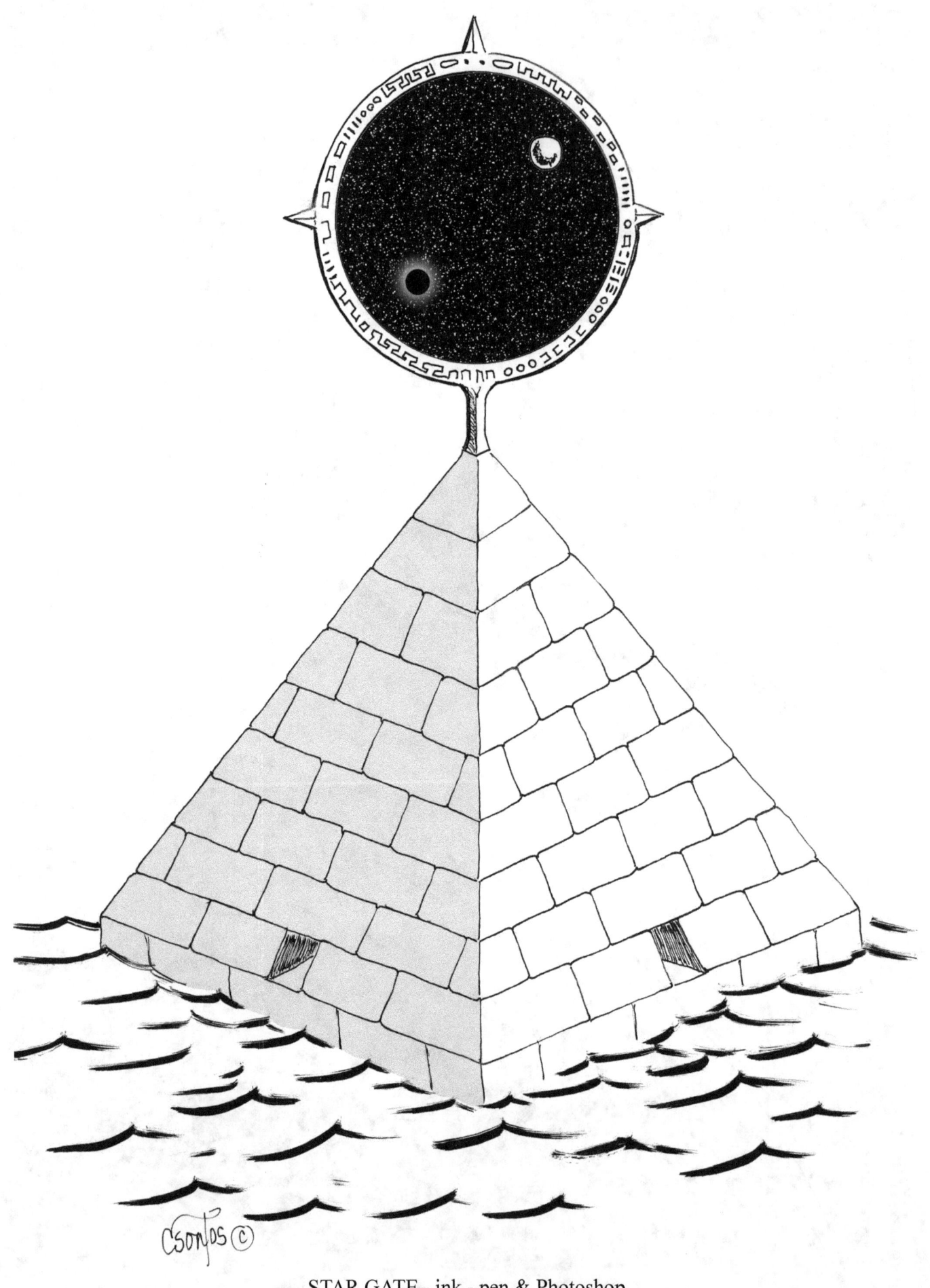

STAR GATE - ink - pen & Photoshop

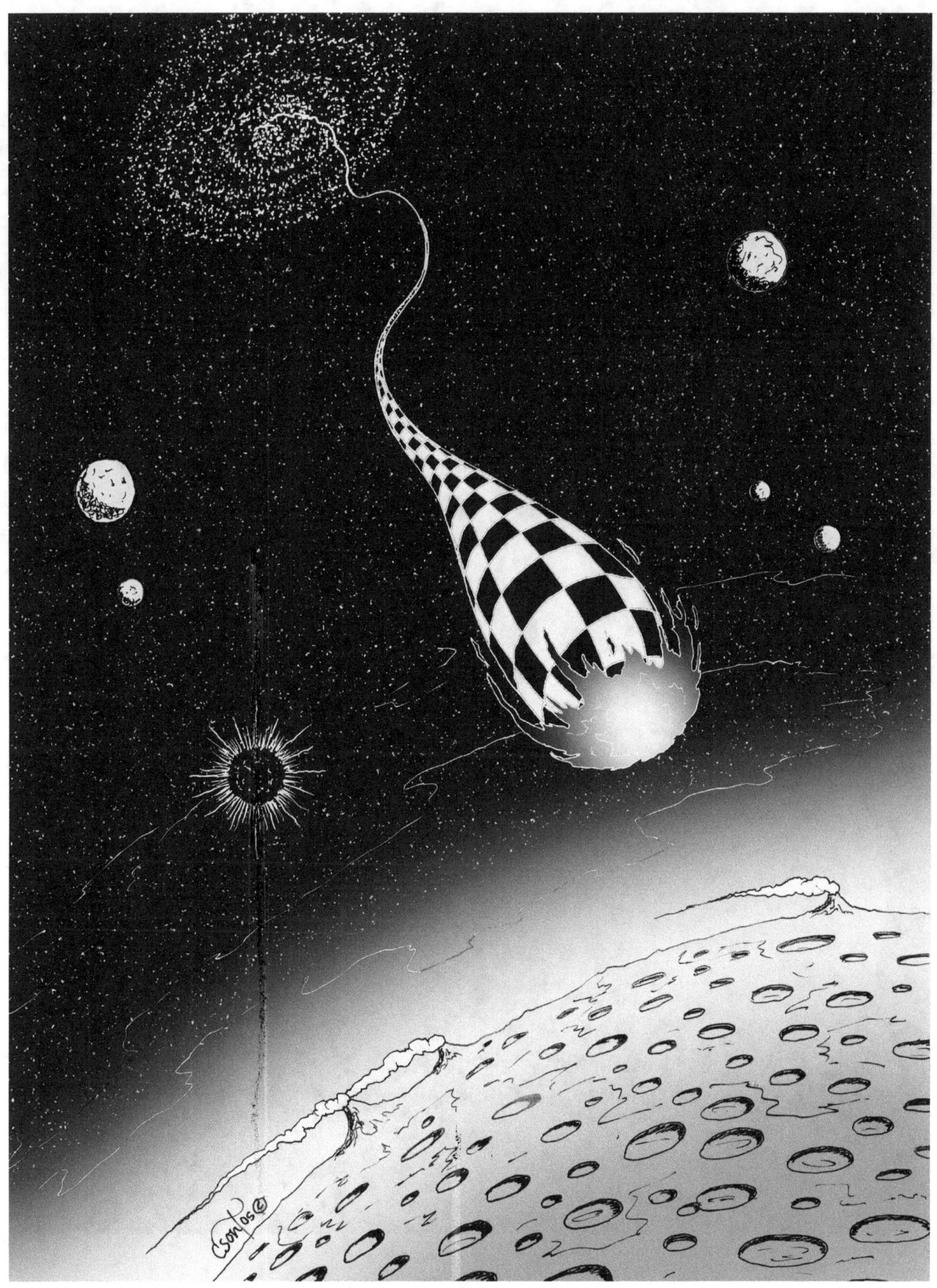

OP-ART METEORITE - ink - pen, brush & Photoshop

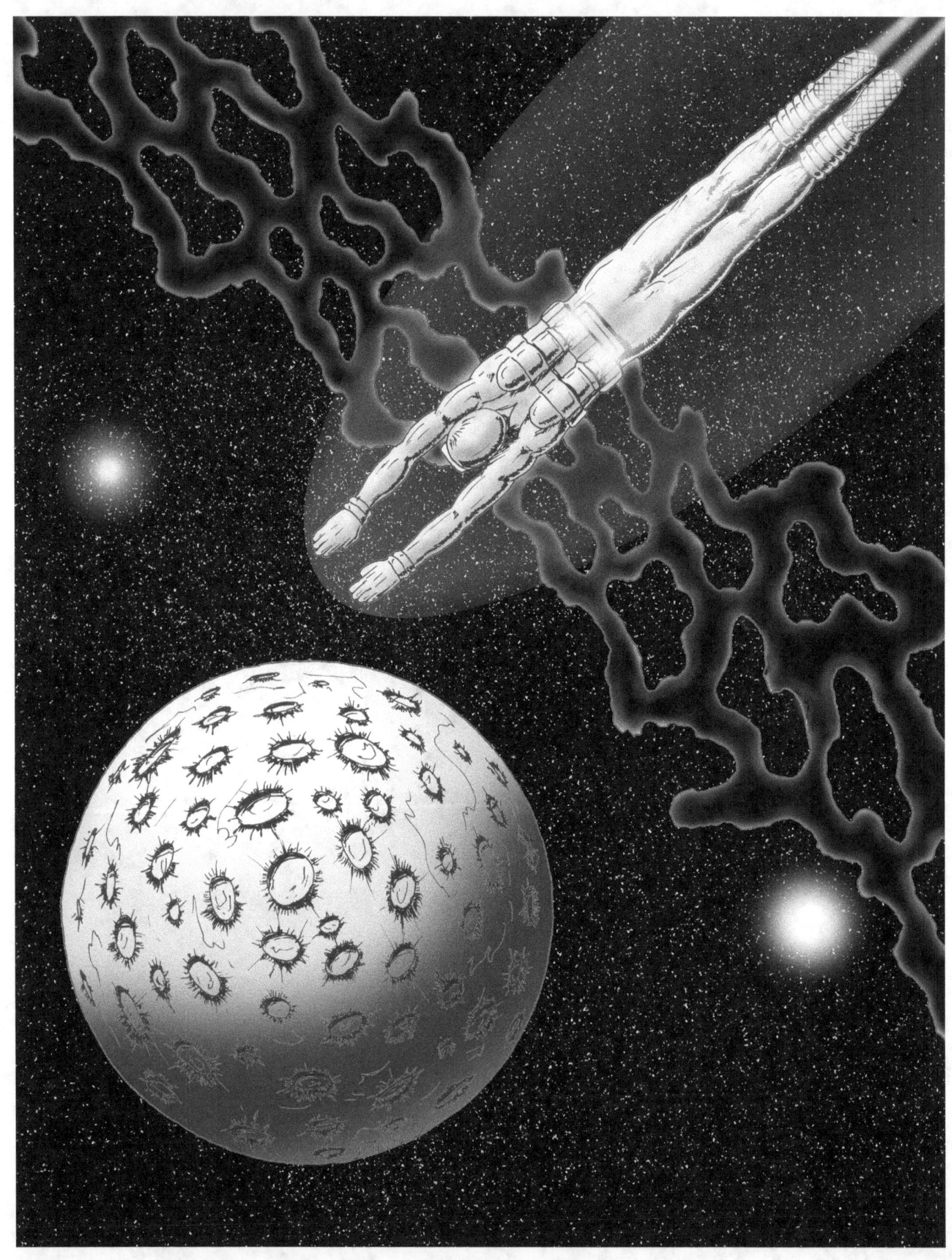

ROCKET MAN - ink - pen & Photoshop

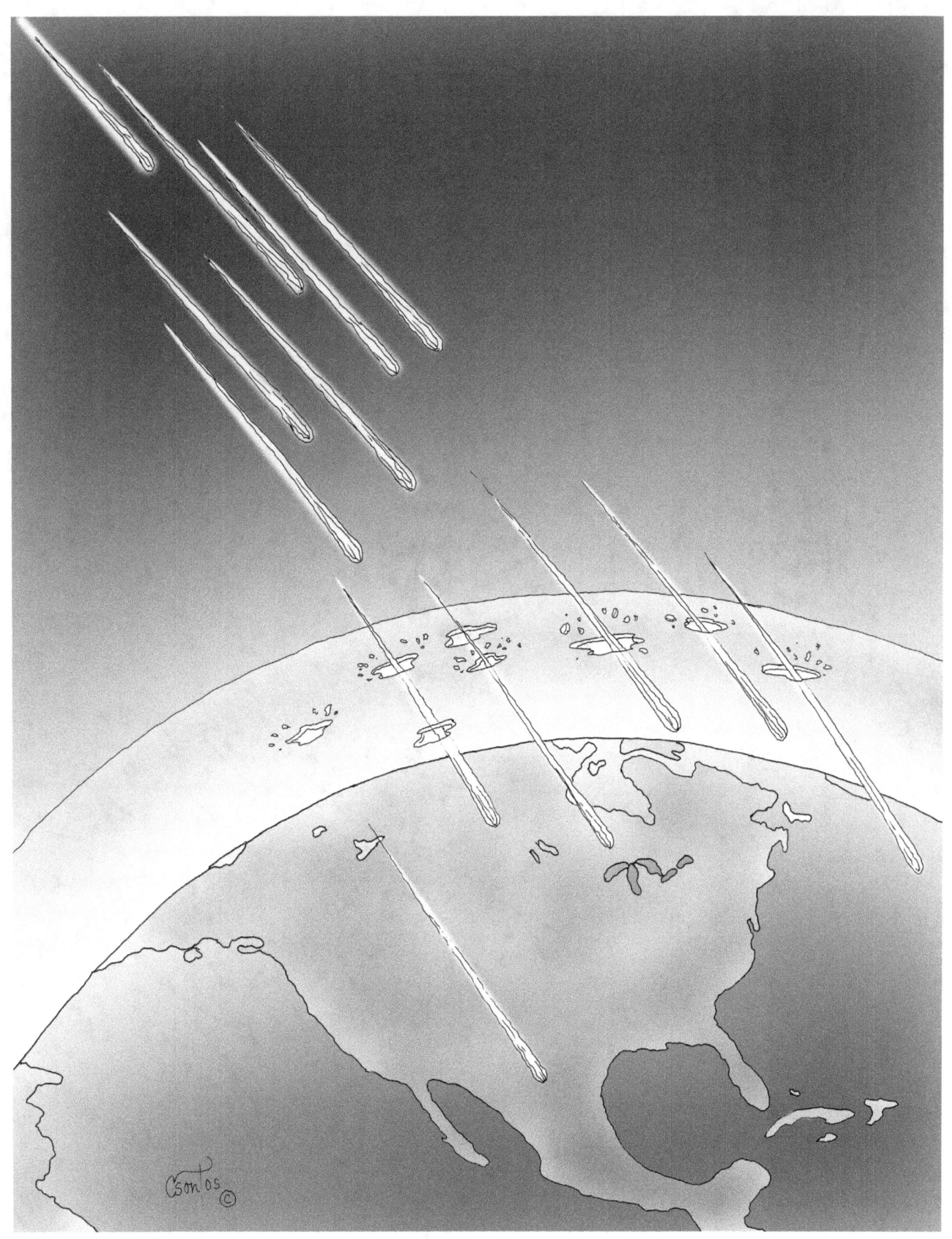

PUNCHING THROUGH THE OZONE - ink - pen & Photoshop

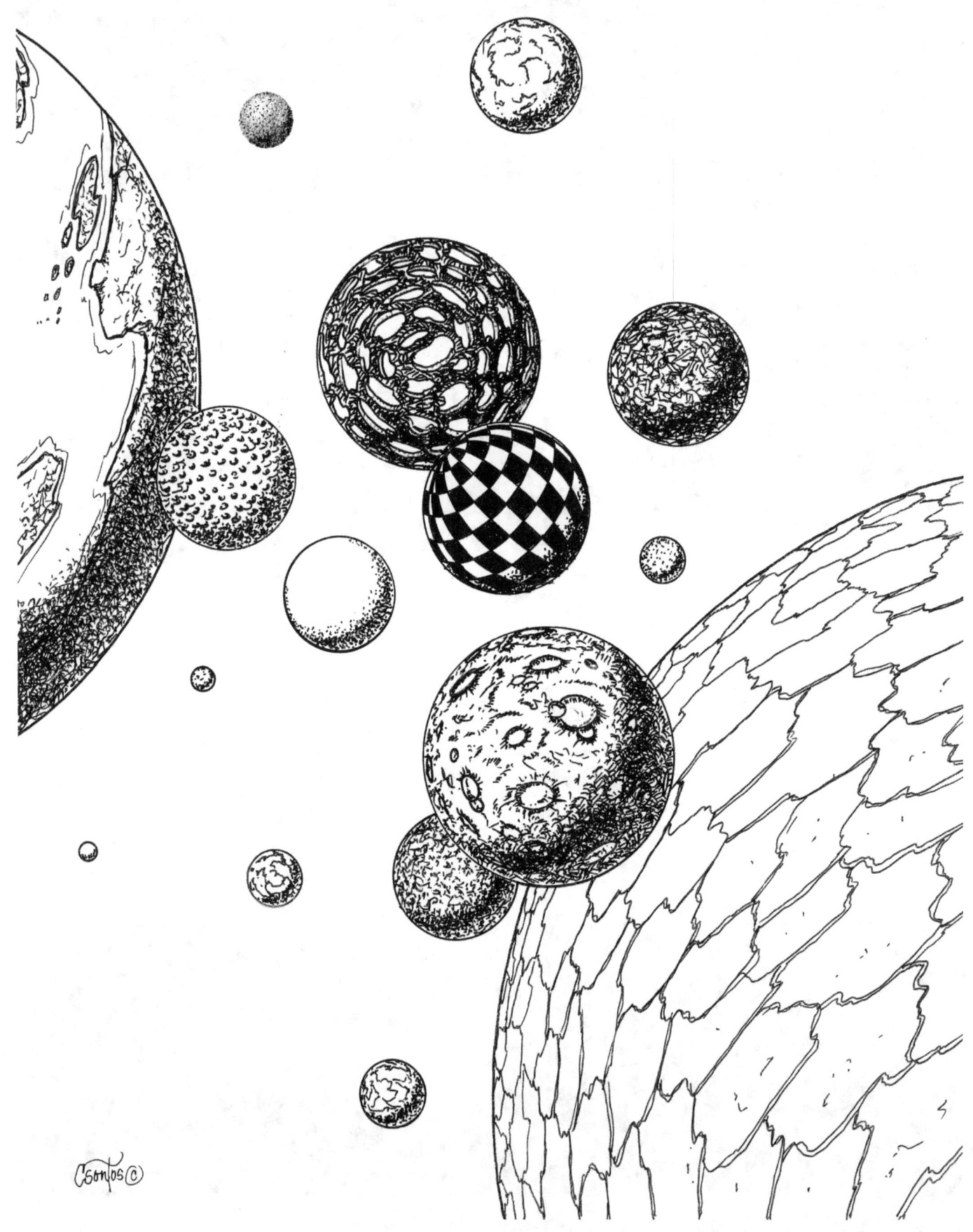

SPHERES - ink - pen & brush

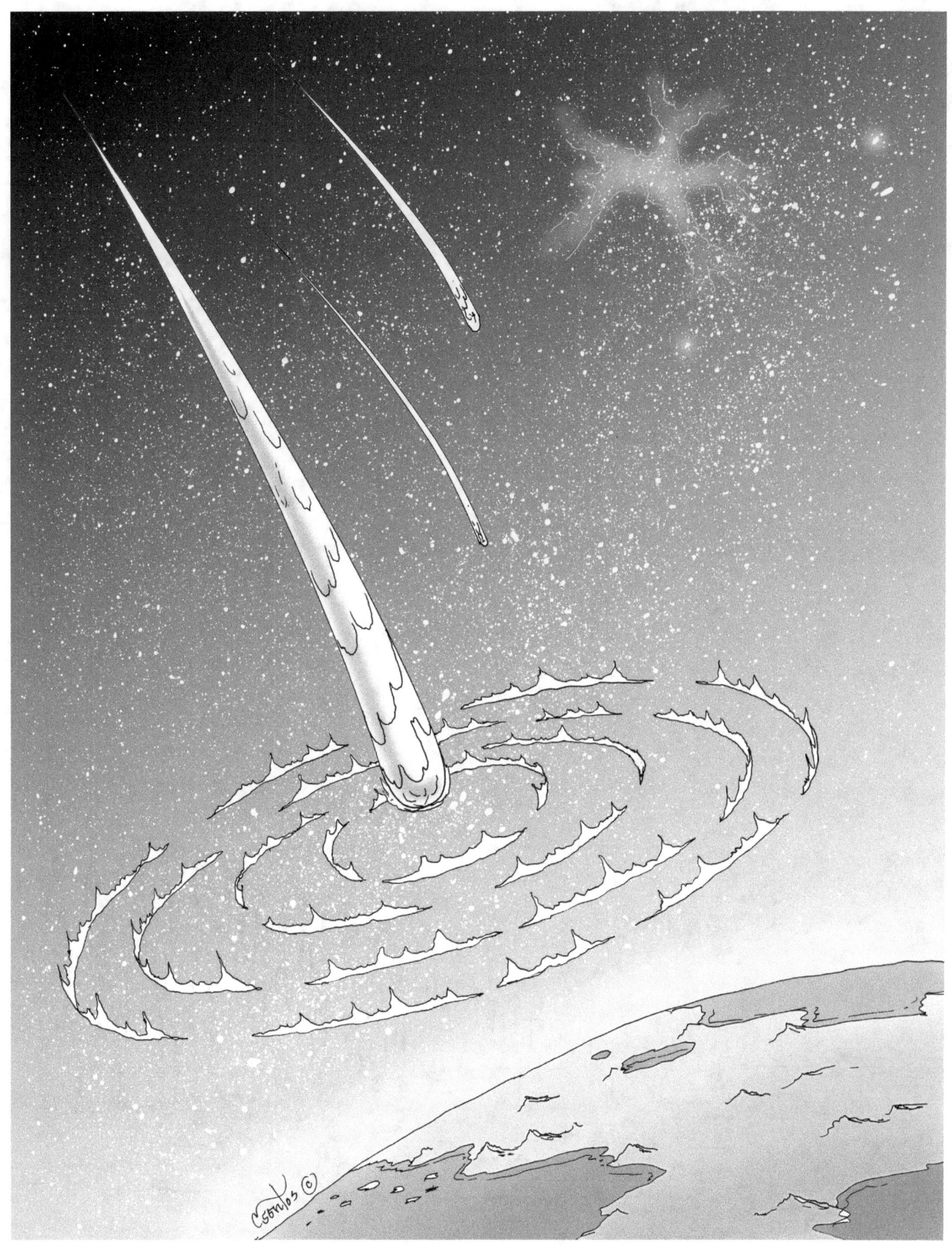

SHOCK WAVE - ink - pen & Photoshop

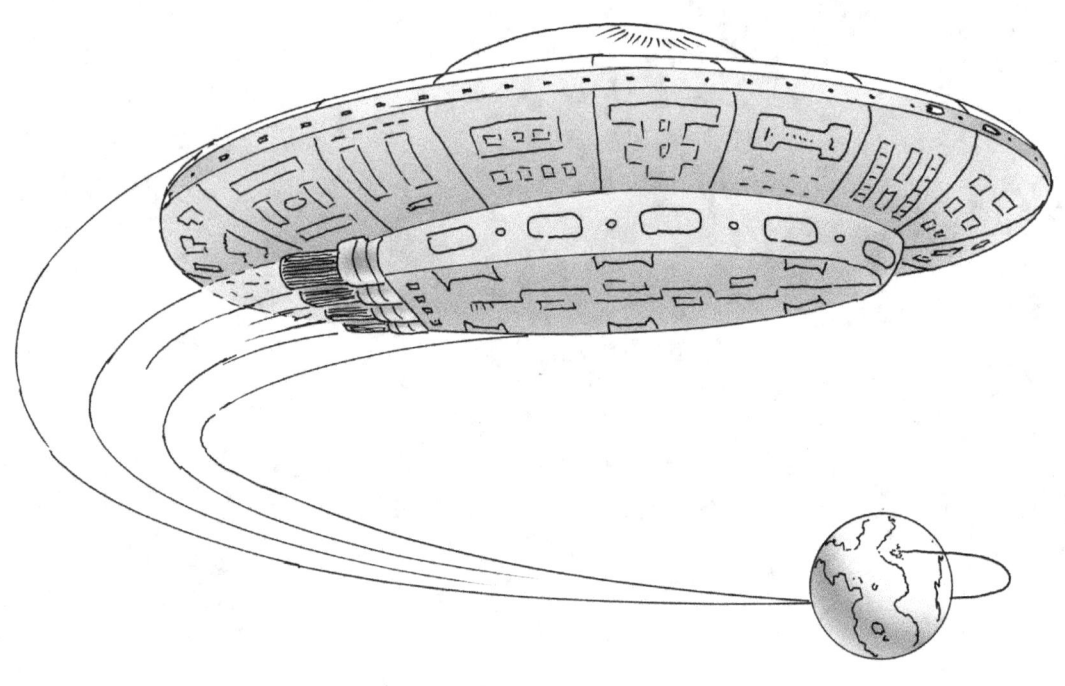

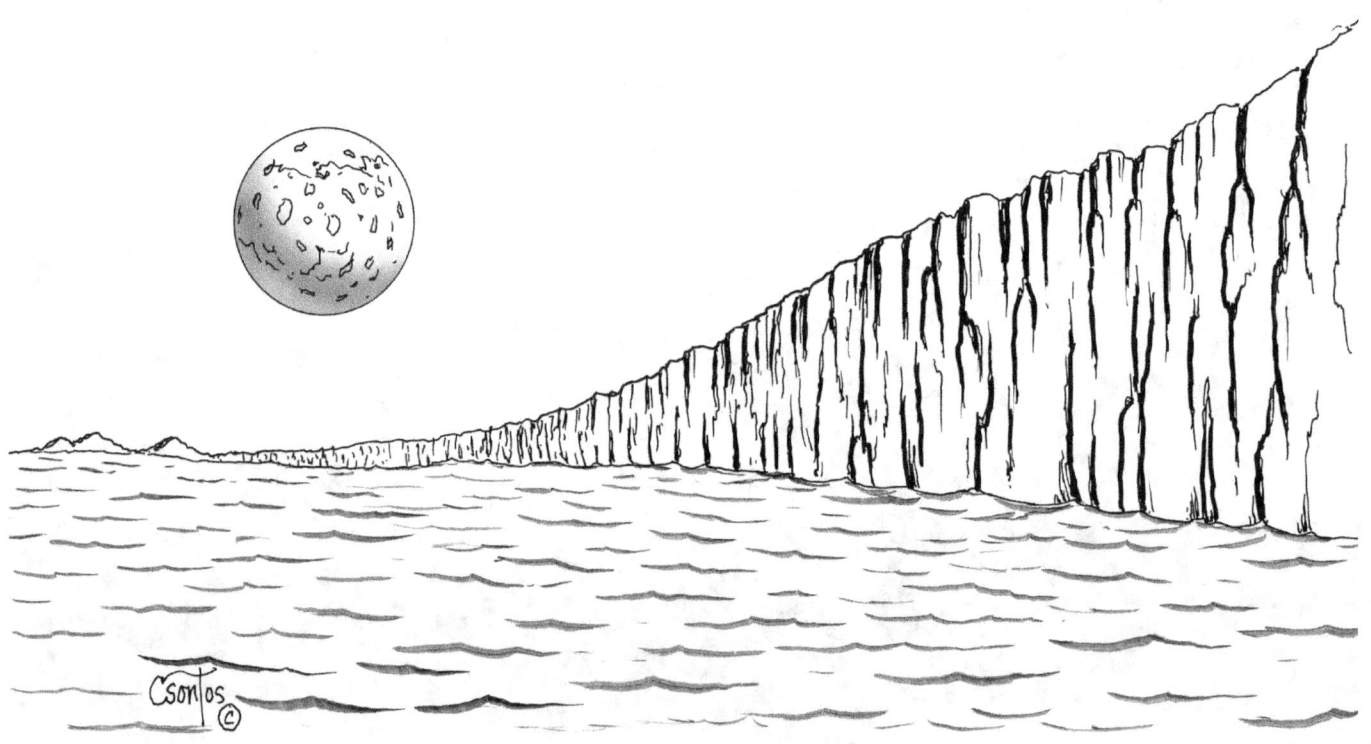

TEST FLIGHT - ink - pen & Photoshop

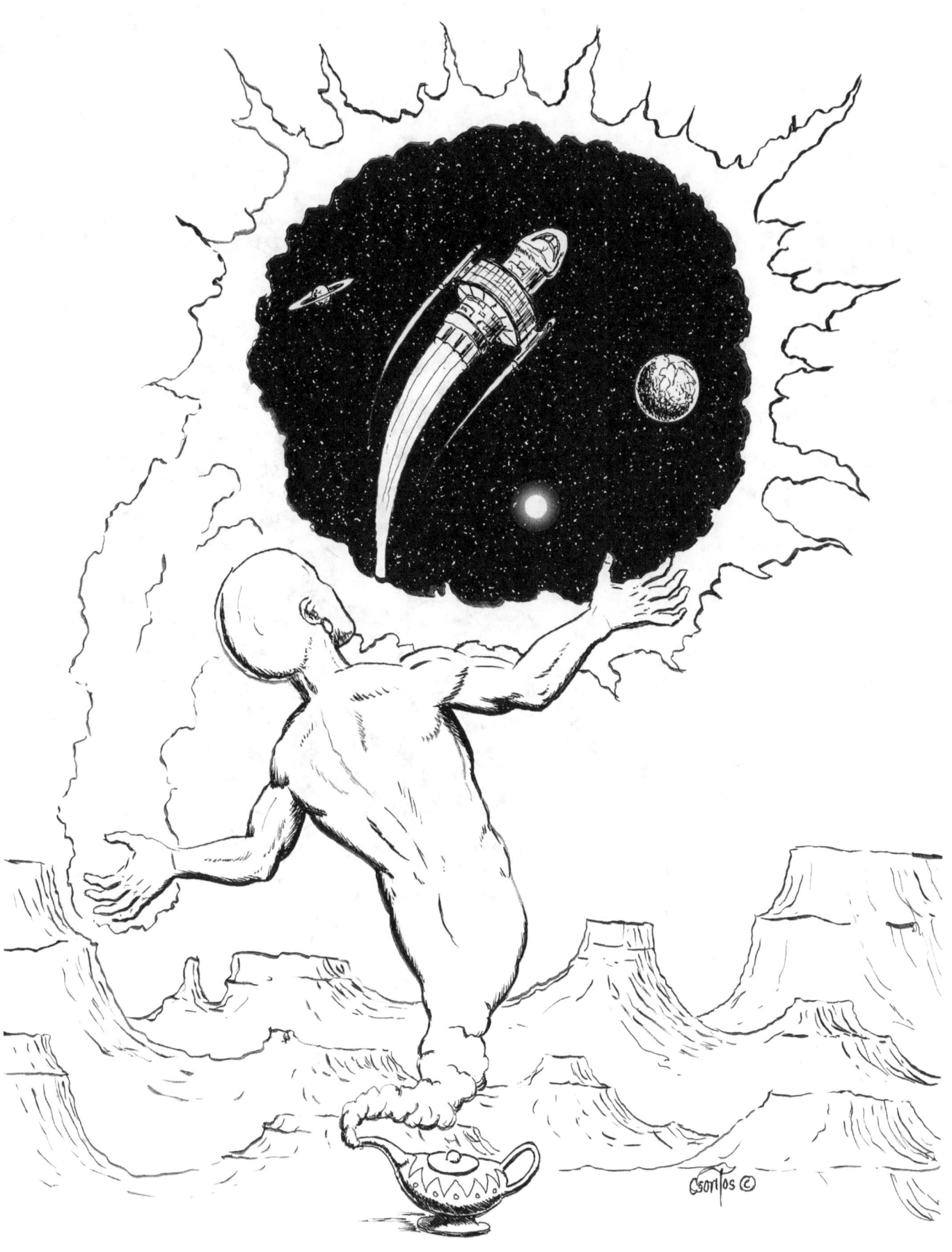

SEEING THE FUTURE - ink - pen, brush & Photoshop

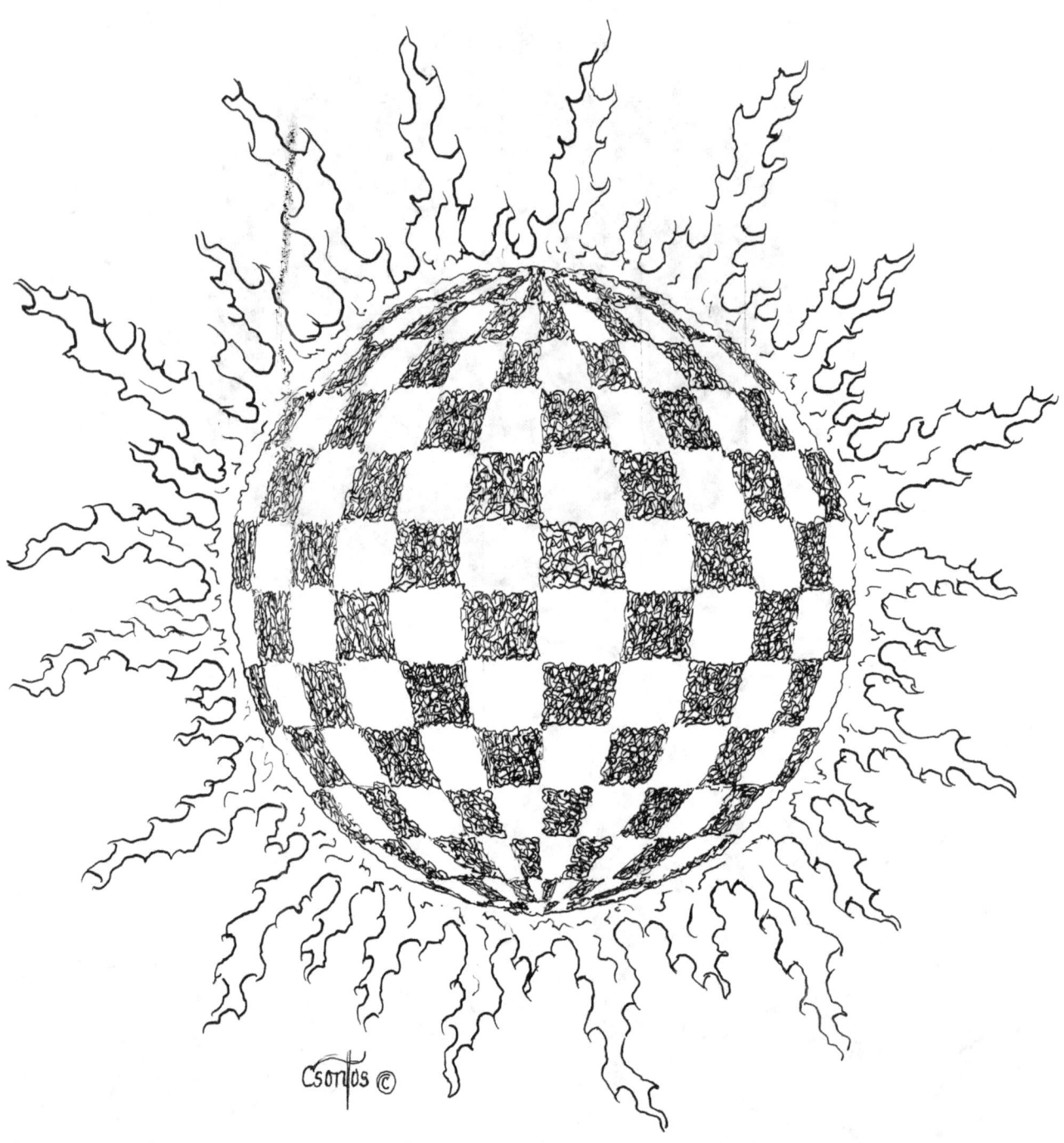

NOVA - ink - pen

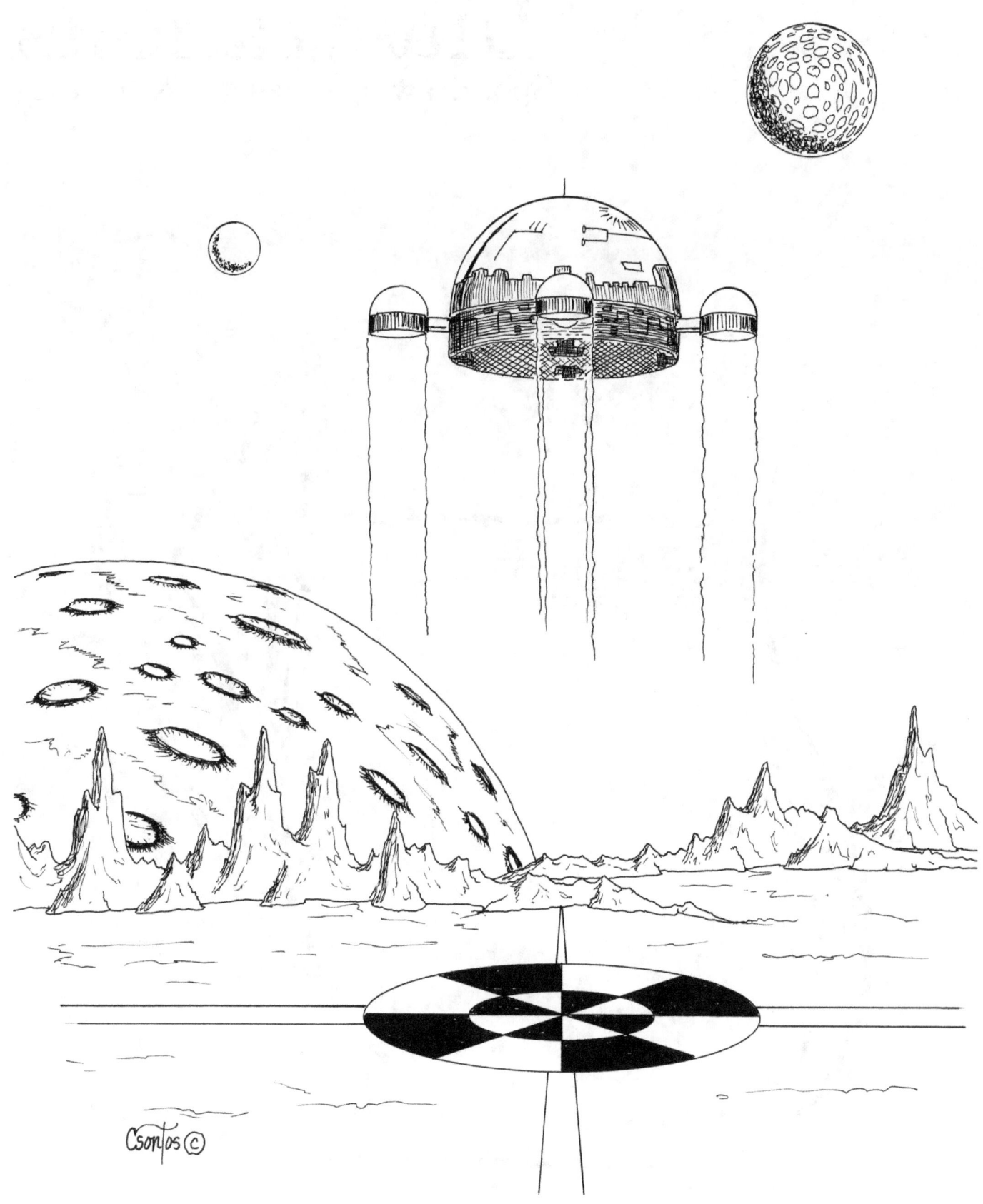

POD - ink - pen & brush

Illustrations
Spot drawings, designs & doodles

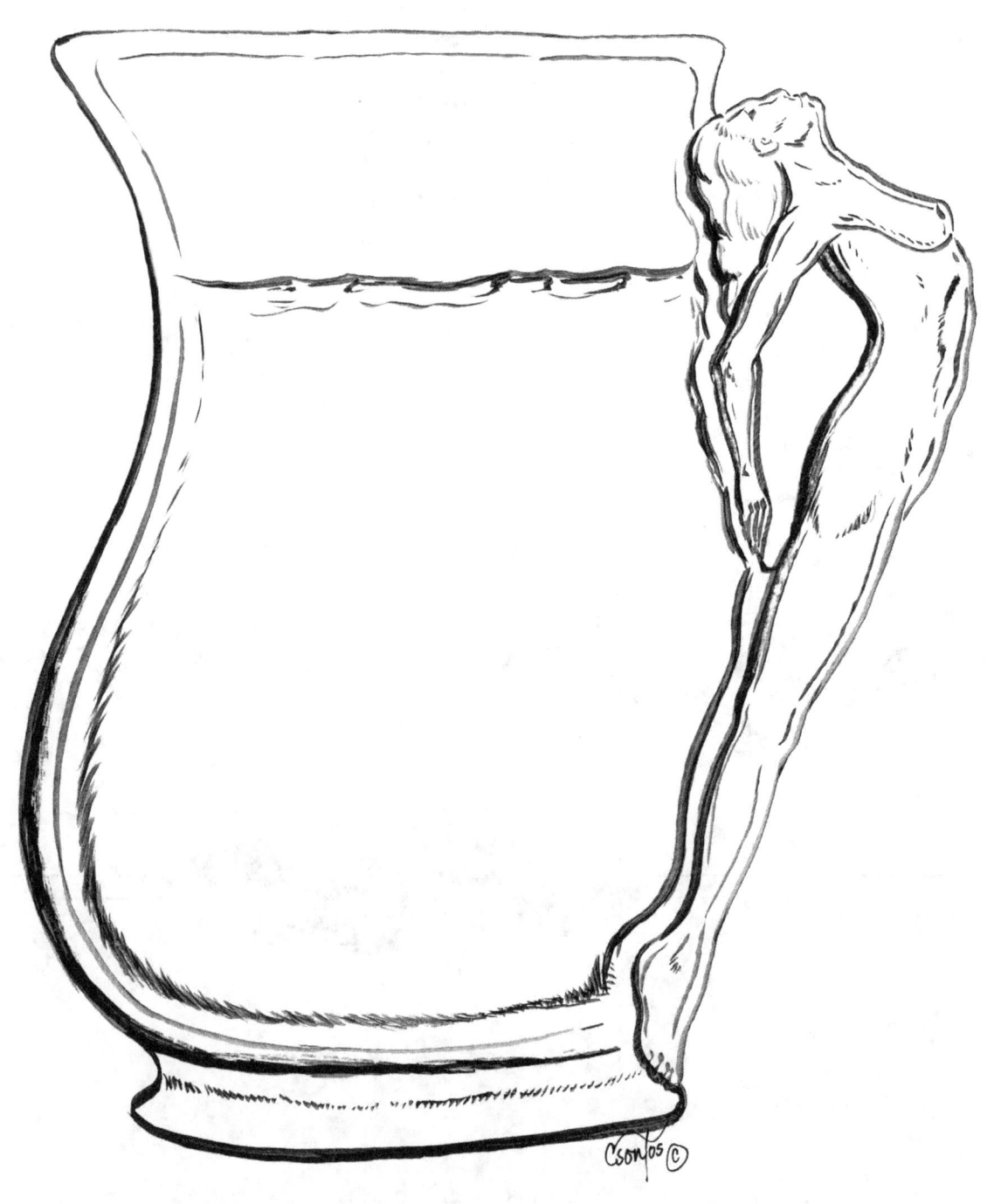

GLASS PITCHER - ink - brush

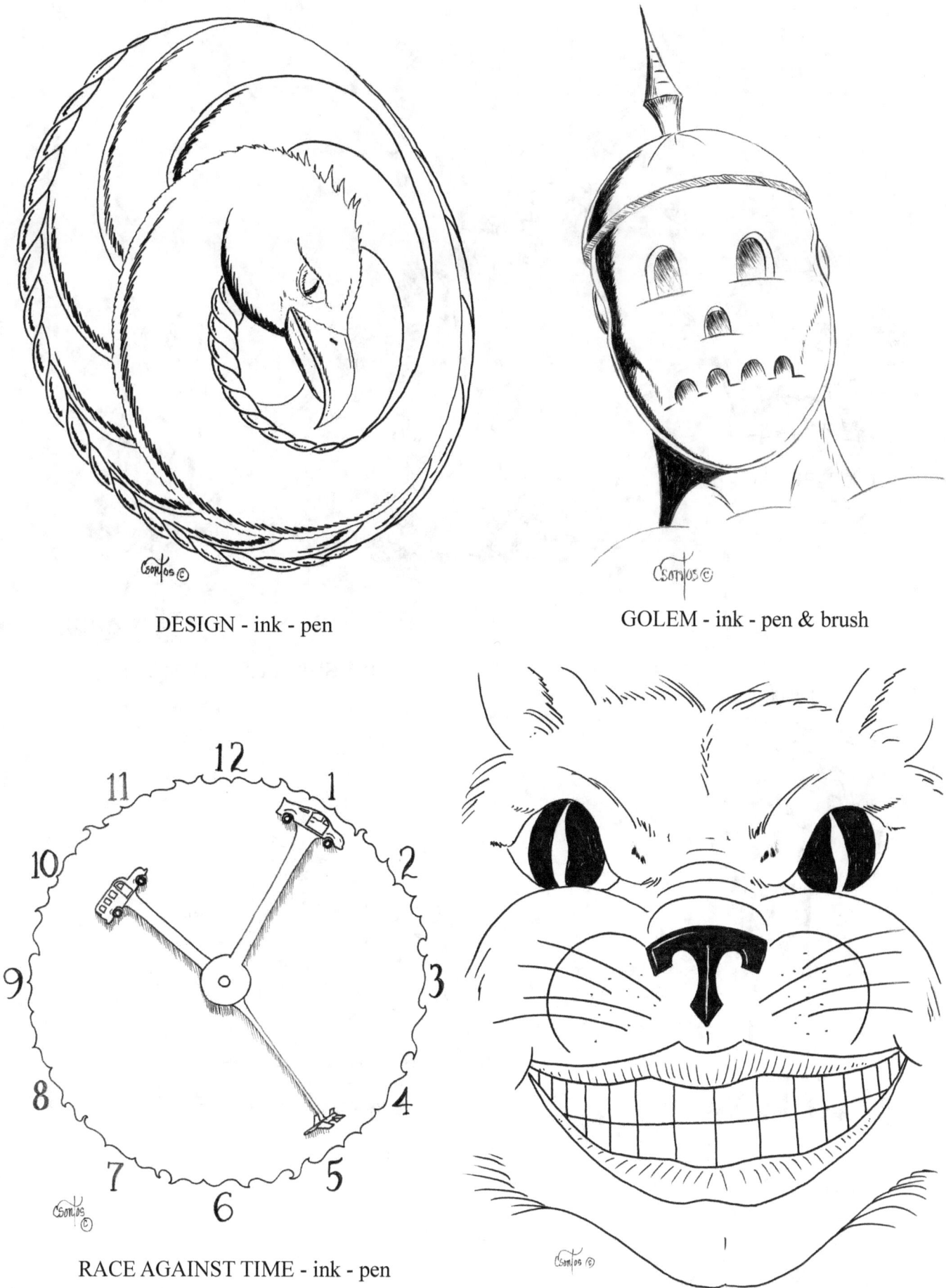

DESIGN - ink - pen

GOLEM - ink - pen & brush

RACE AGAINST TIME - ink - pen

DESIGN - CHESHIRE CAT - ink - pen & brush

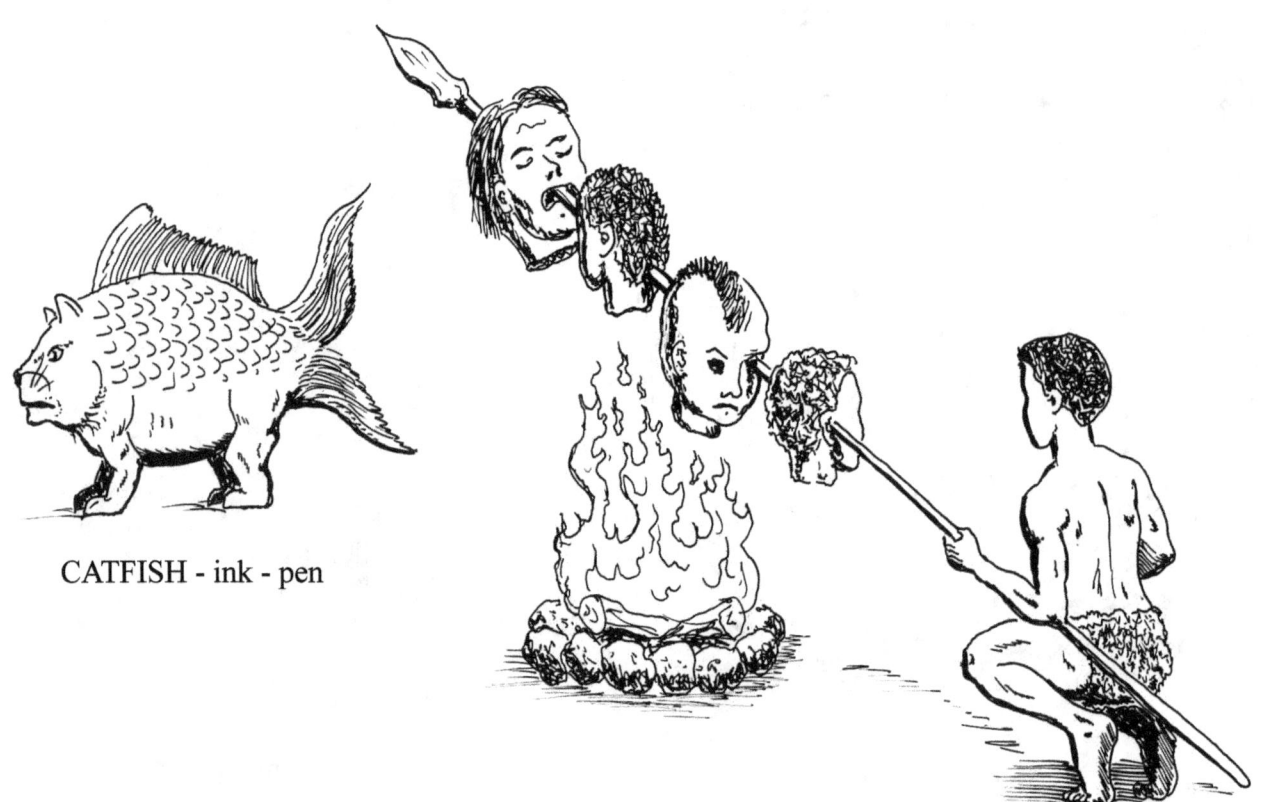

CATFISH - ink - pen

HEAD HUNTER'S SHISH KEBAB - ink - pen

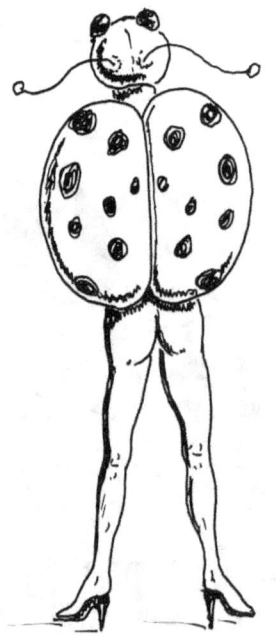

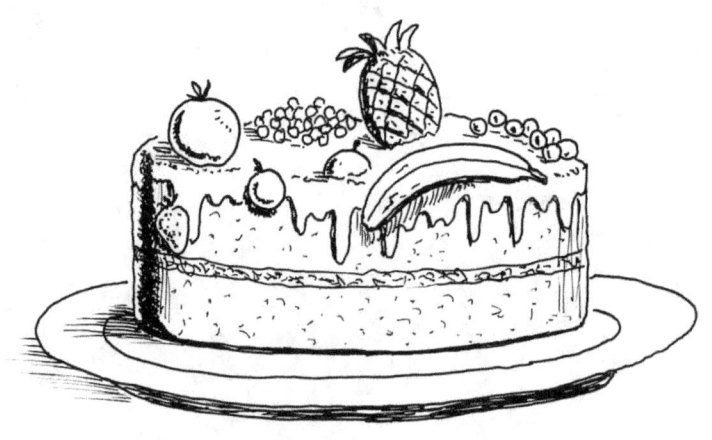

LADYBUG - ink - pen

FRUIT CAKE - ink - pen

Csontos ©

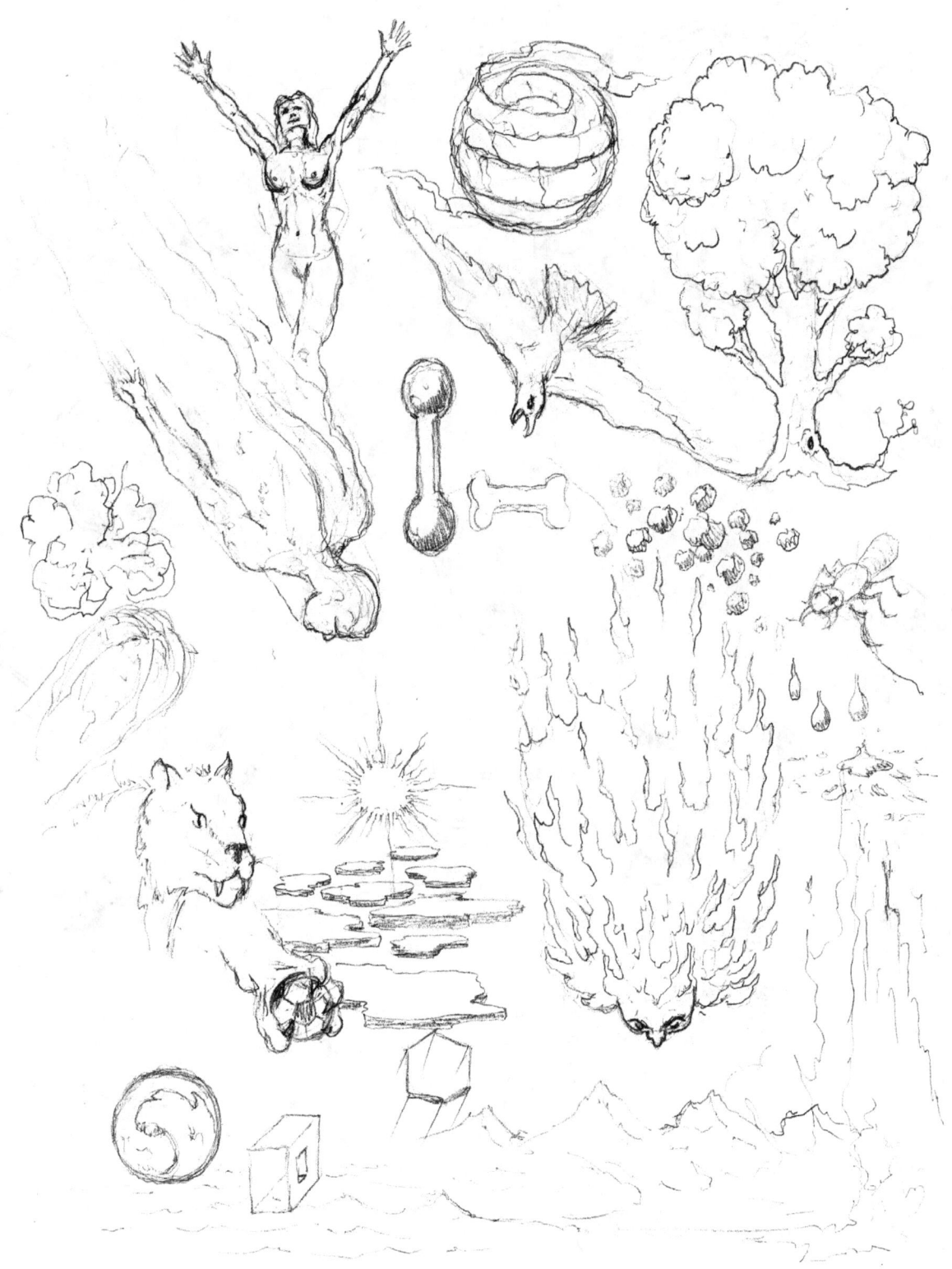

DOODLE - pencil - sometimes a particular composition will just not come out of the initial sketching. When that happens I will just continue to draw haphazardly and maybe something will come out of the randomness to give me an idea. For example; the fireball looking image midway on the left side gave me a starting thought when I began to sketch out 'Punching Through the Ozone'. And the flying man image gave me the idea for 'Rocket Man'. When painting in the past, I used to randomly and continually apply paint if I had artist's block, but most of the time with painting, the resulting imagery was not overly spectacular. But hopefully the painting procedure itself gave me needed practice. These days when painting, I try to focus on a theme that gives a more impressive emotional response.

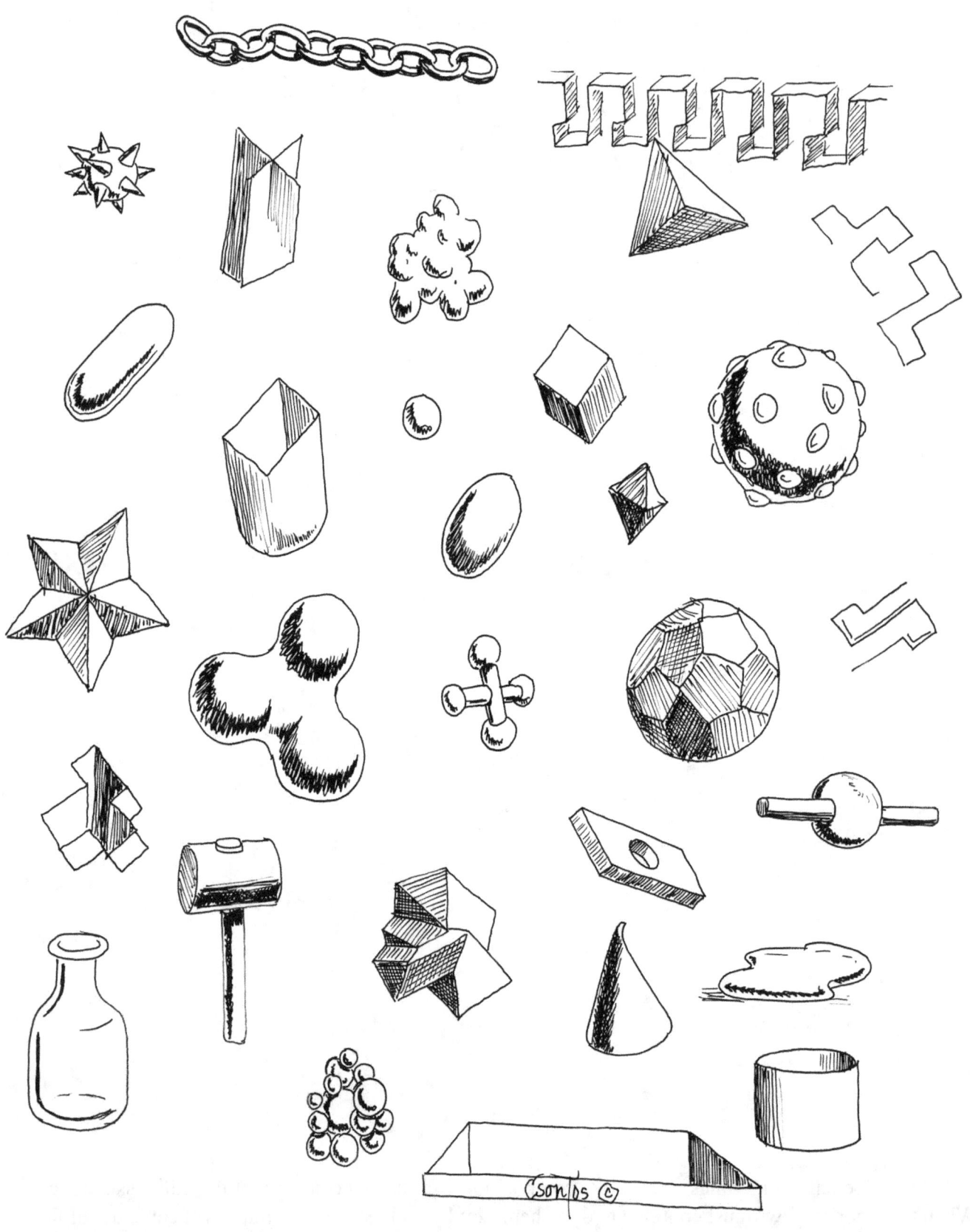

GEOMETRIC DOODLE - ink - pen

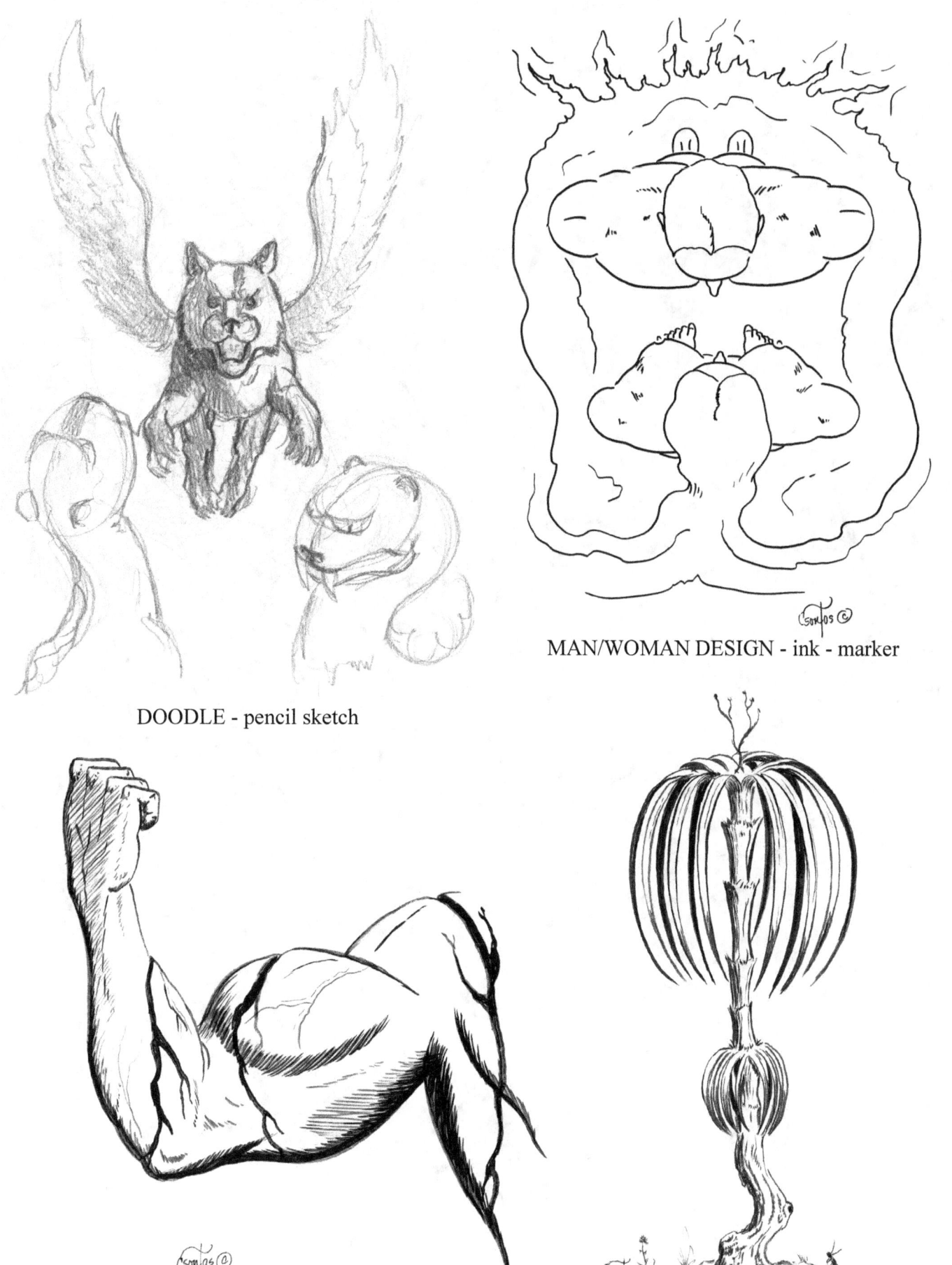

DOODLE - pencil sketch

MAN/WOMAN DESIGN - ink - marker

RIPPED - ink - brush

GROW LIKE A PUMPKIN - ink - brush

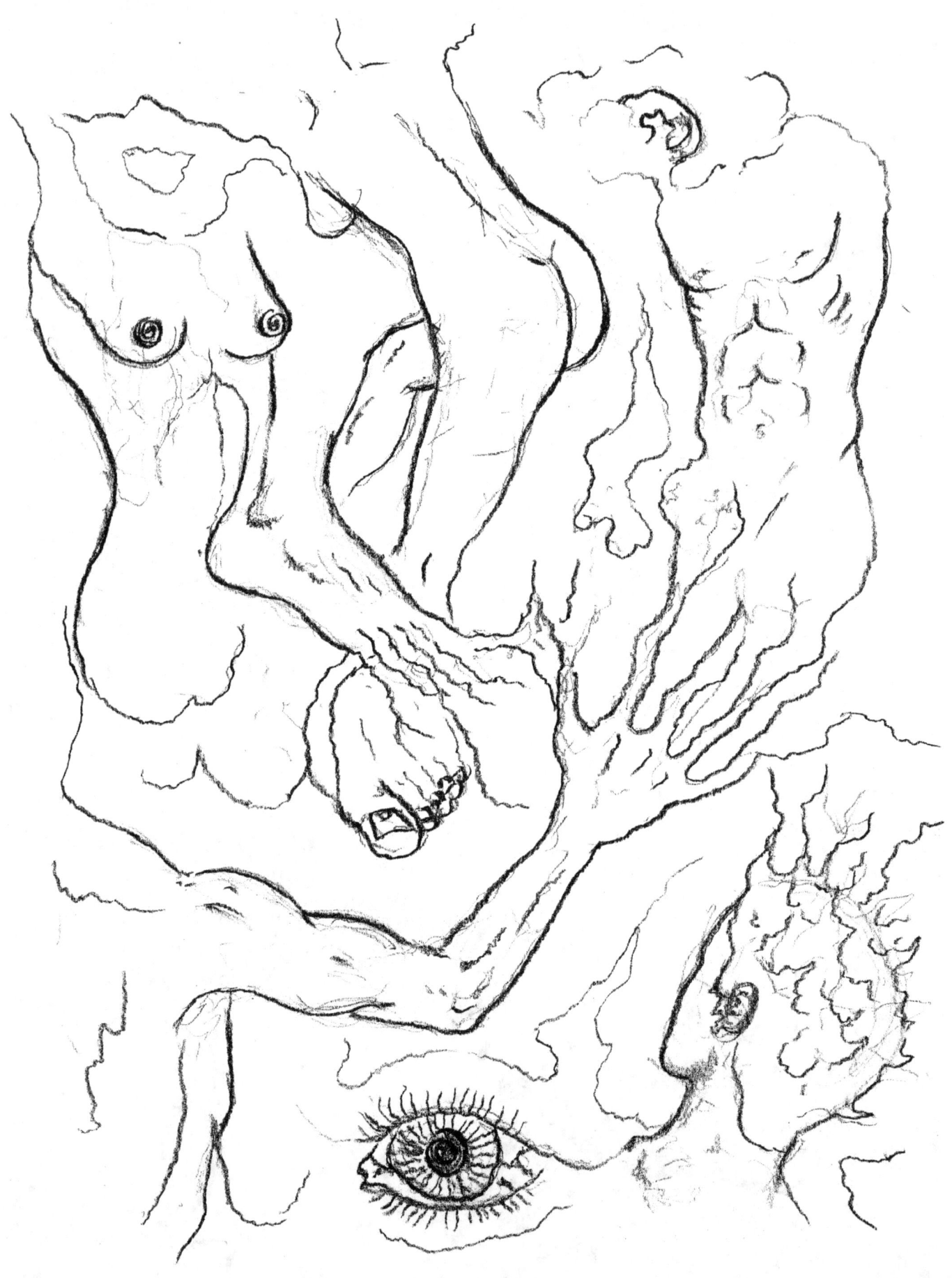

GROWING PARTS - pencil doodle

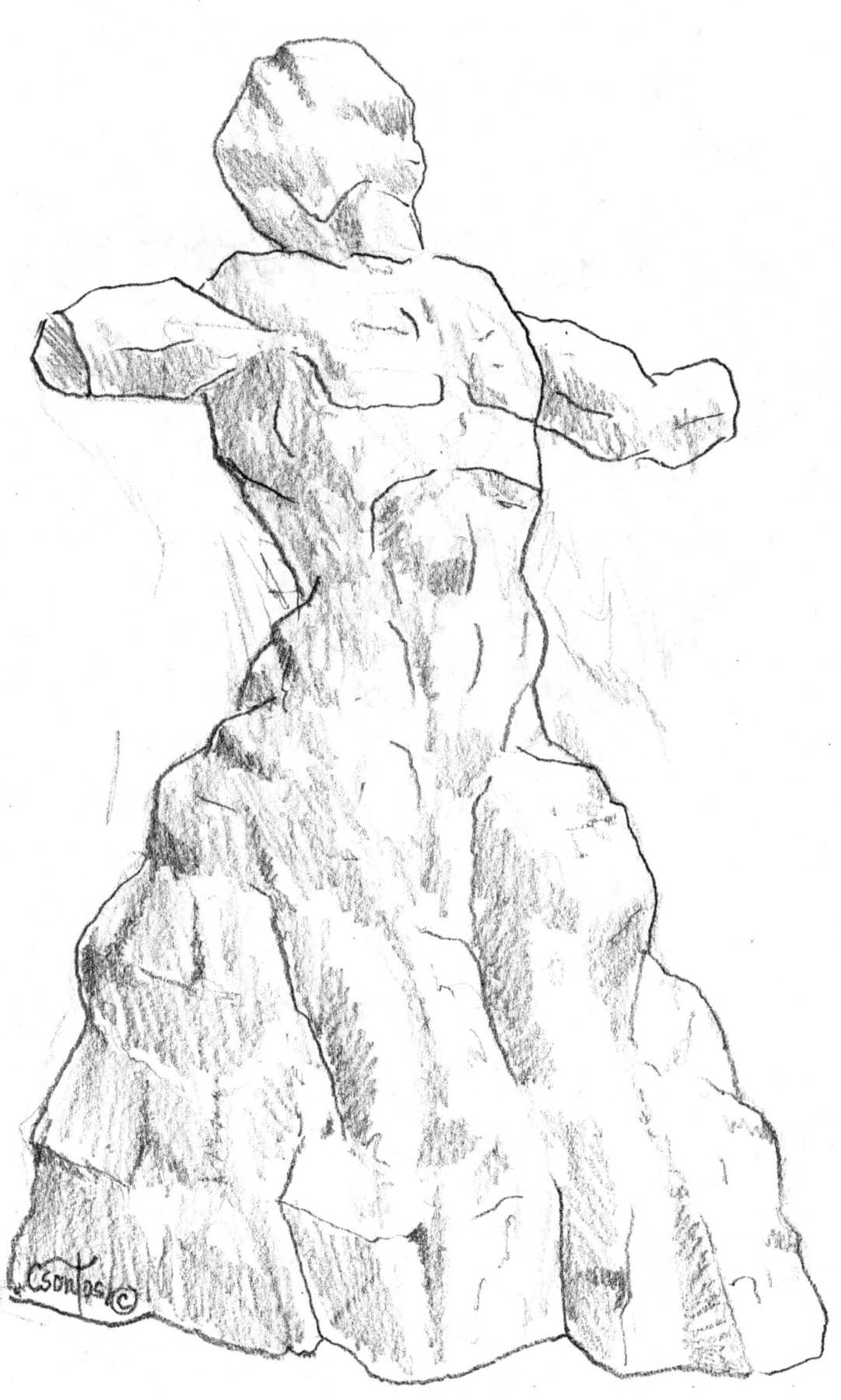

STONE MAN - pencil sketch

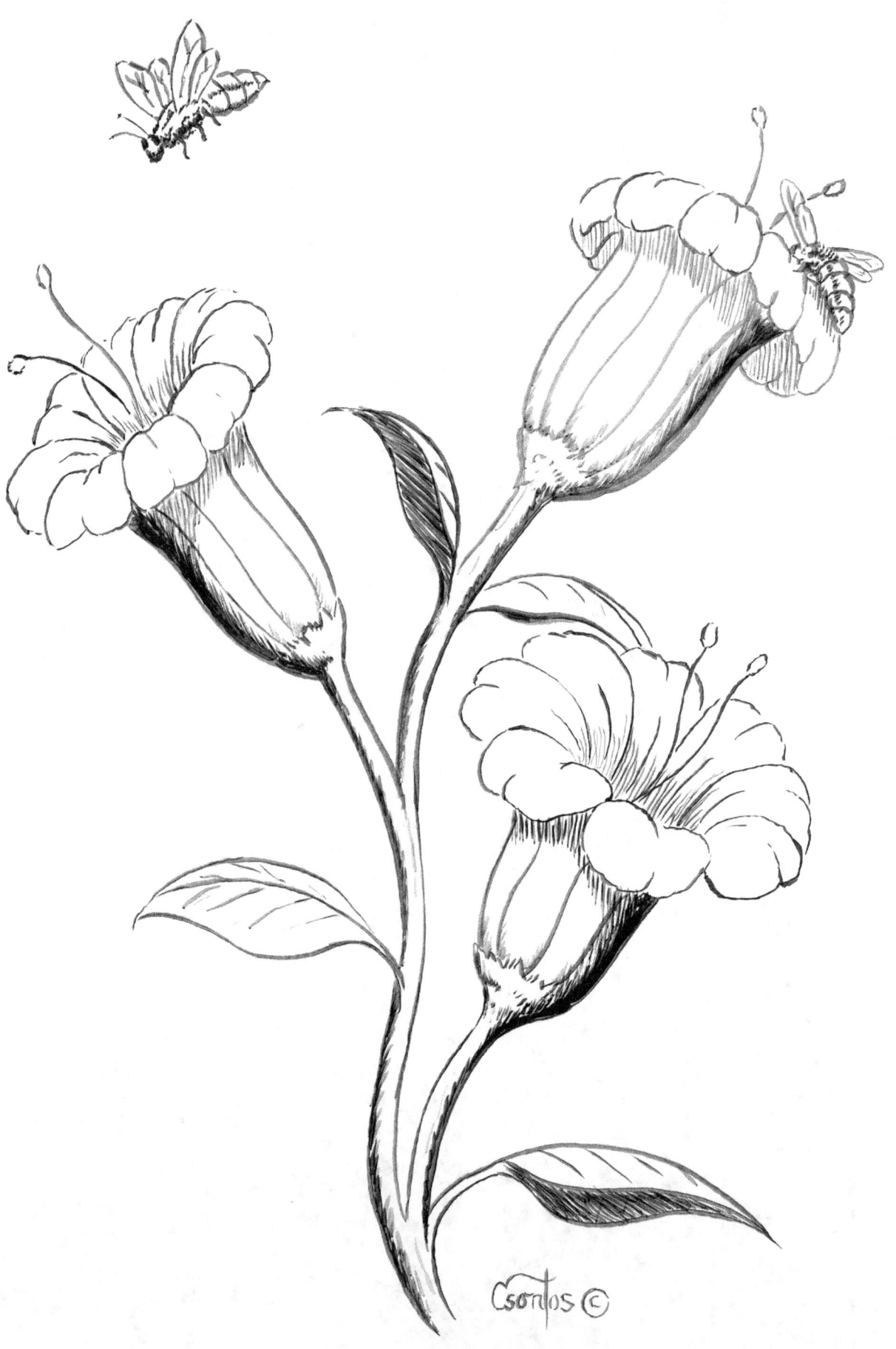

POLLINATION - ink - brush

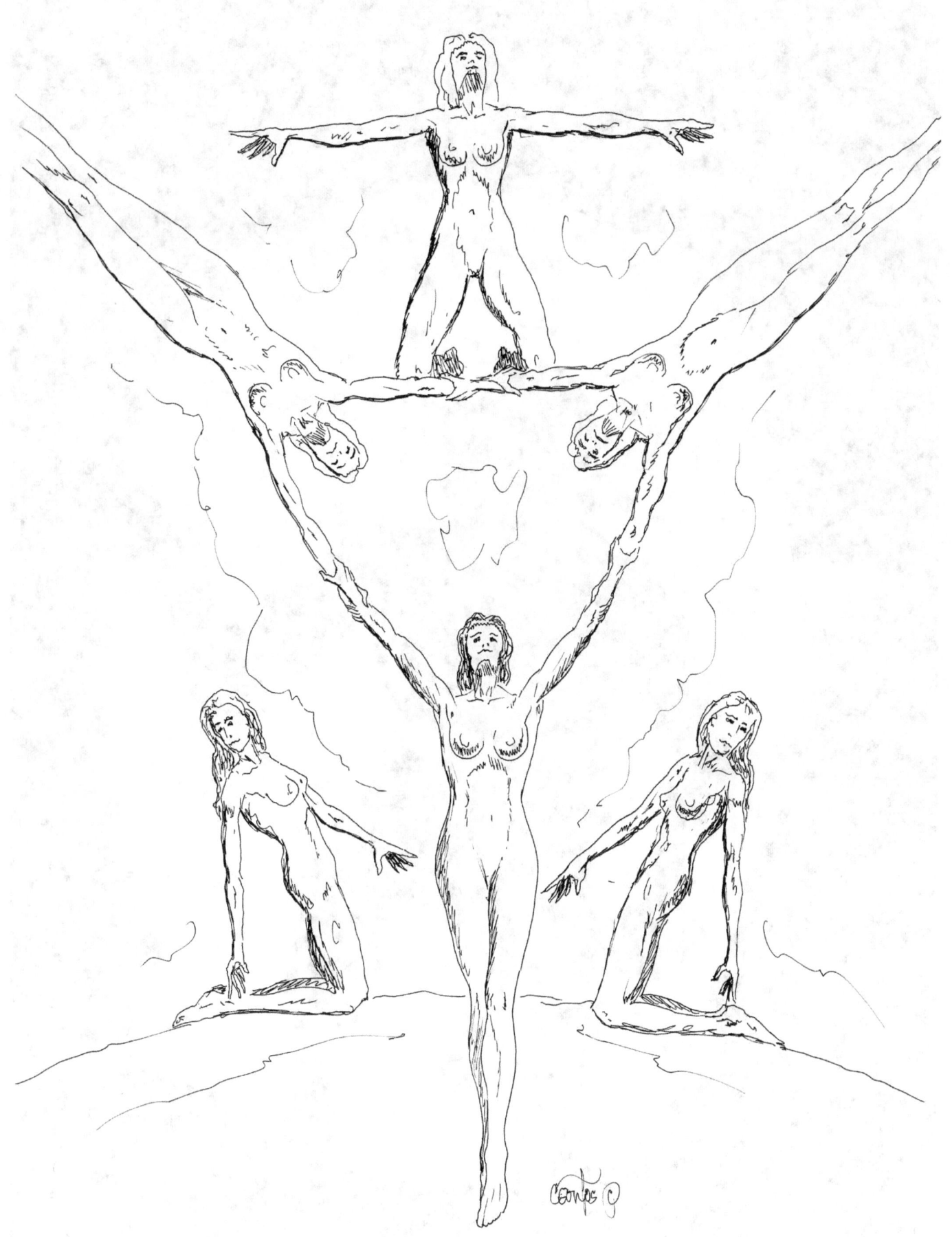

LADY DESIGN - pen sketch

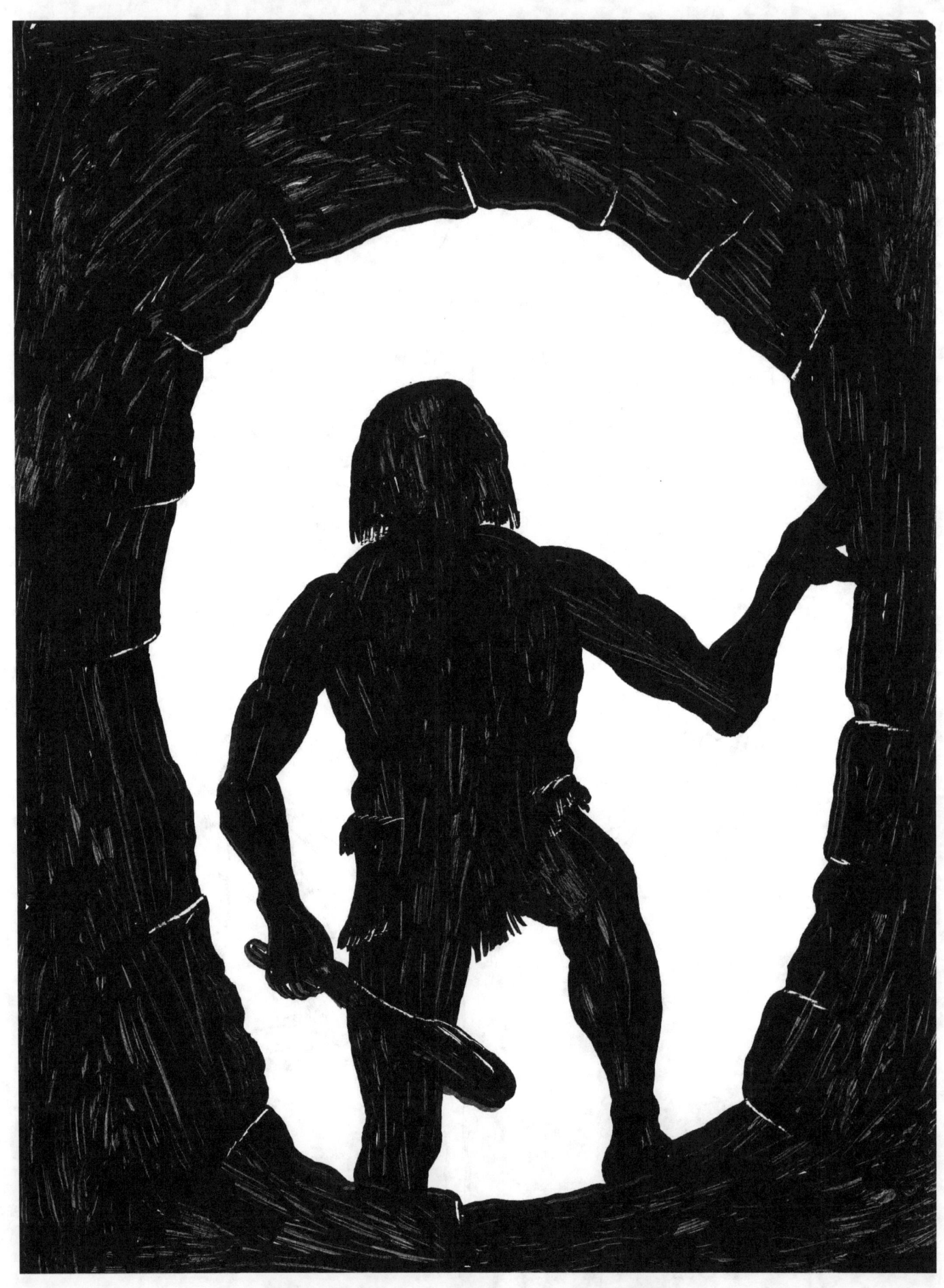

NEANDERTHAL SILHOUETTE - ink - brush

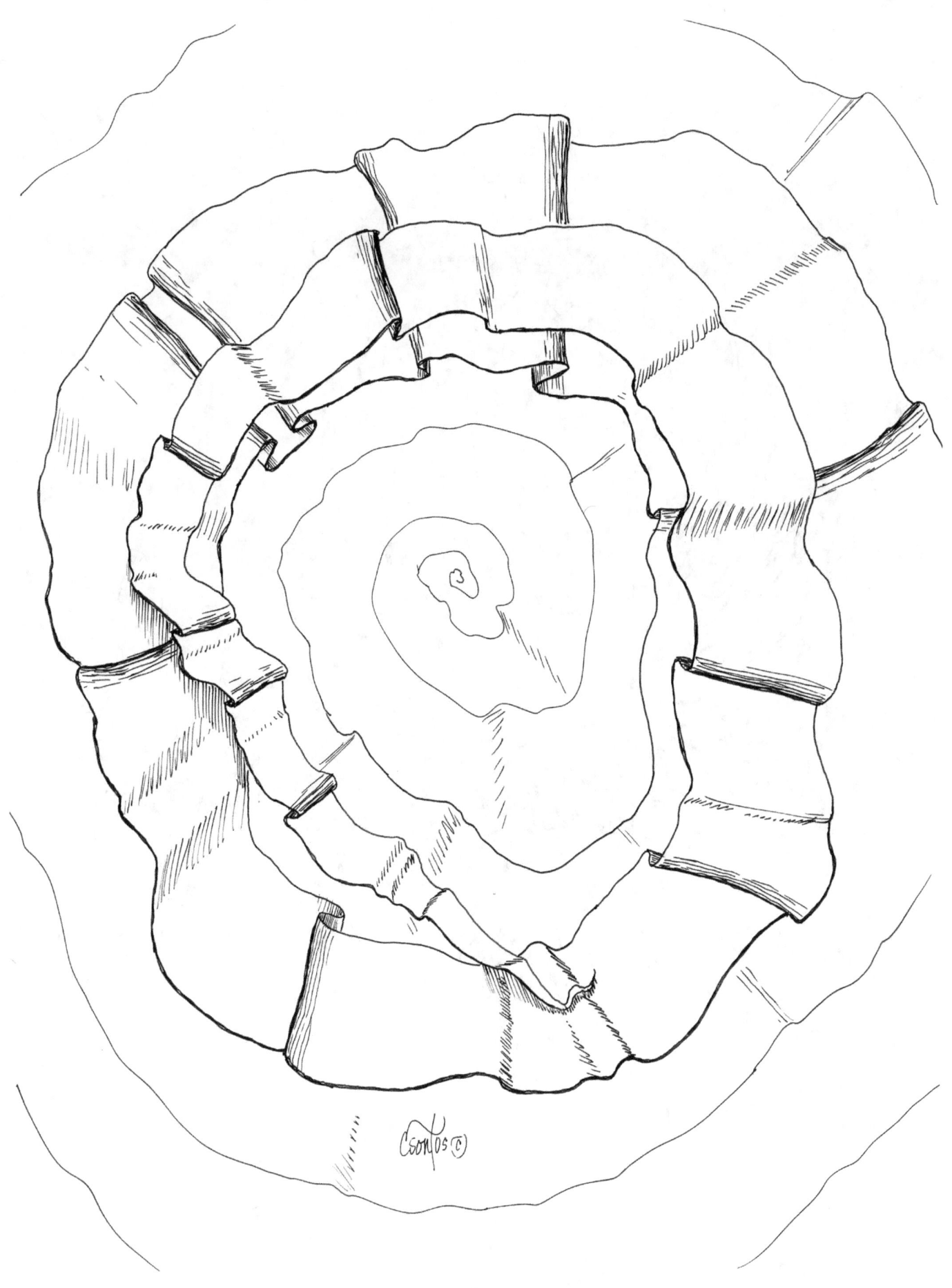

THE RIBBON - ink - pen

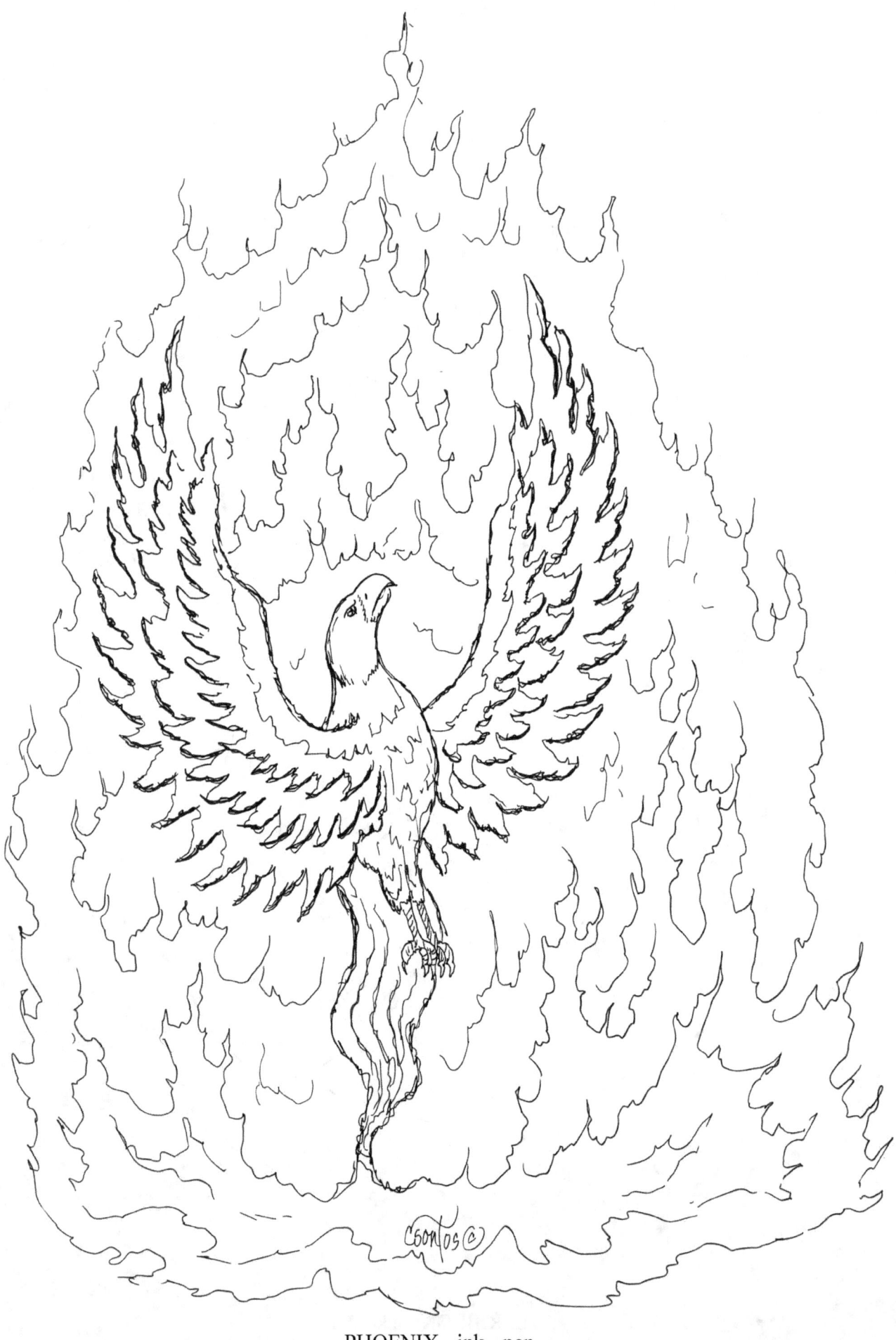

PHOENIX - ink - pen

Critters

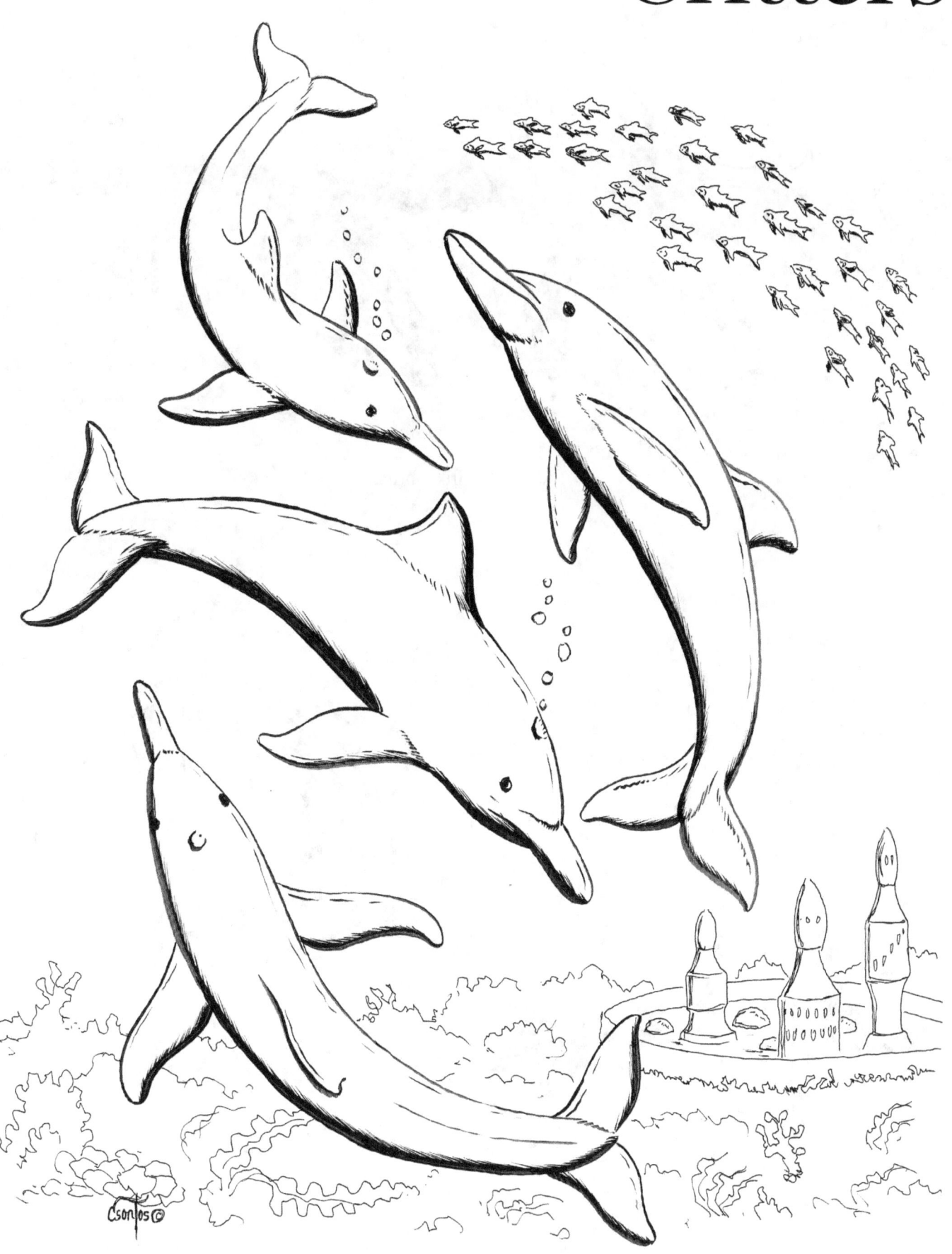

DOLPHINS - ink - pen & brush

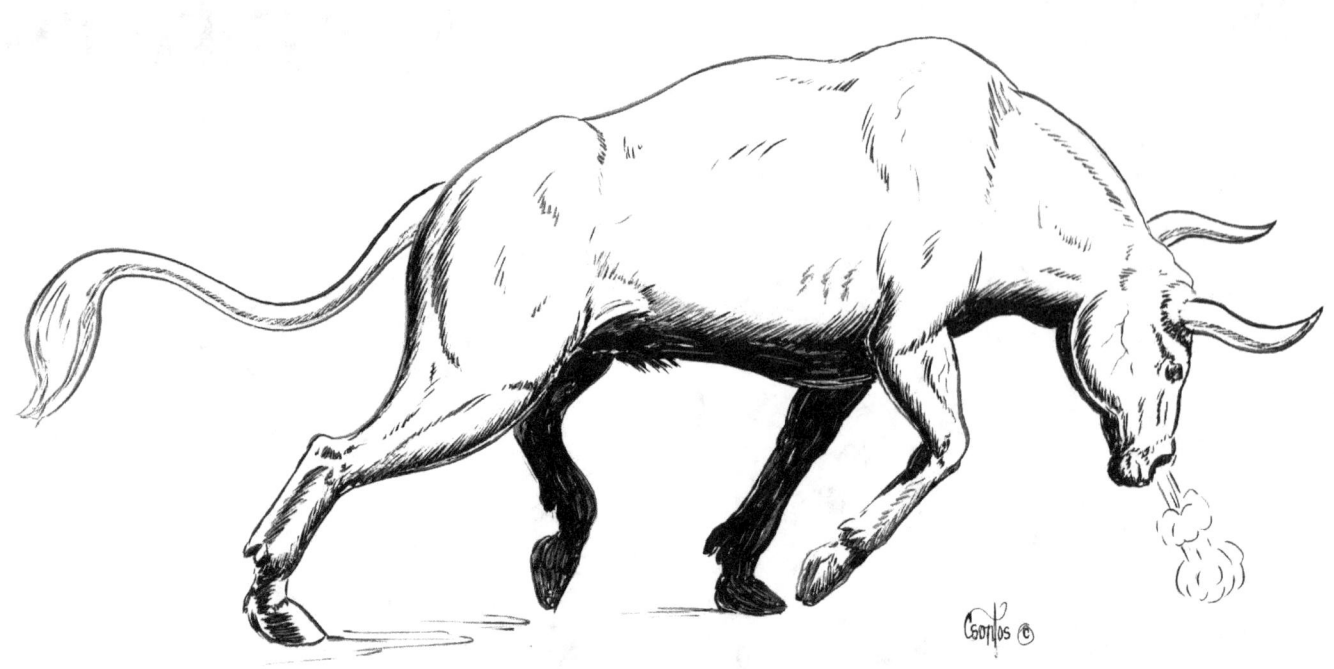

TAURUS - ink - brush

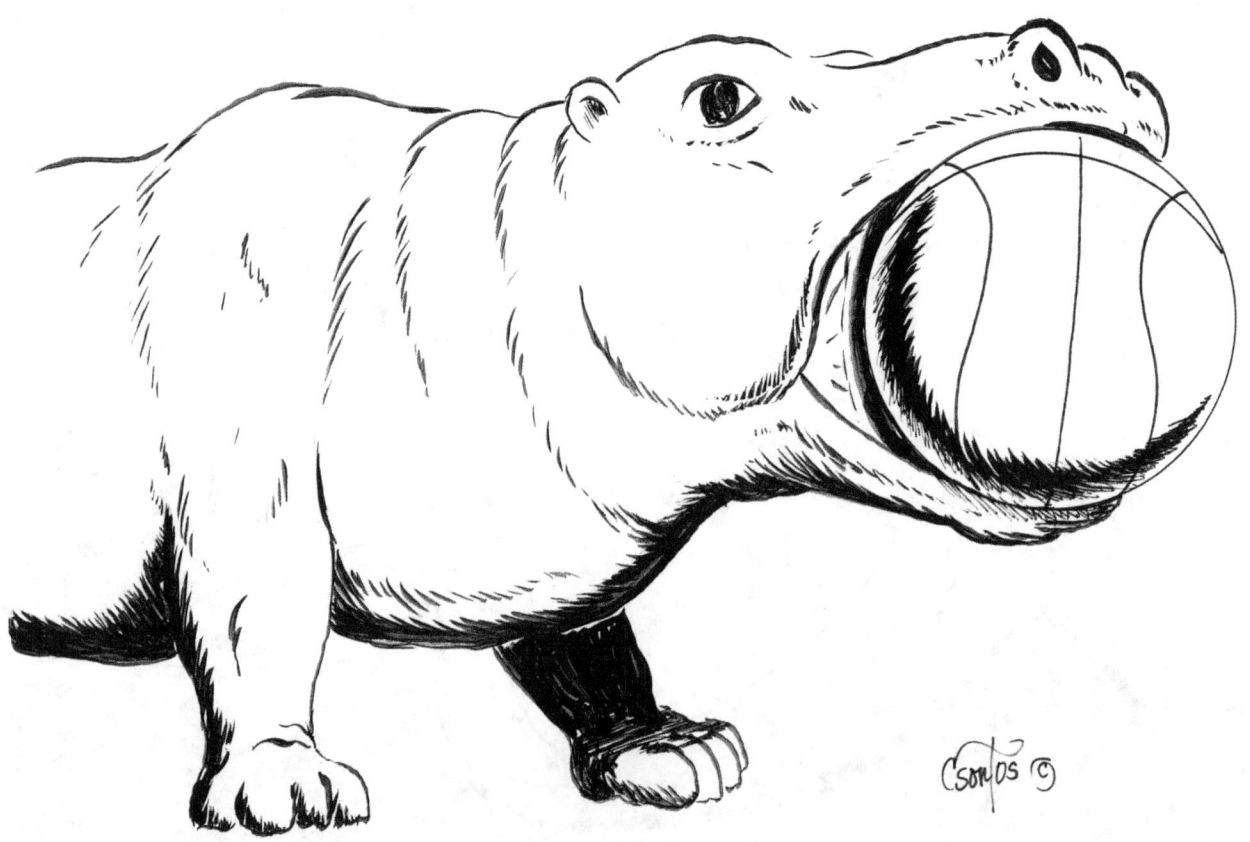

PLAYING BALL - ink - pen & brush

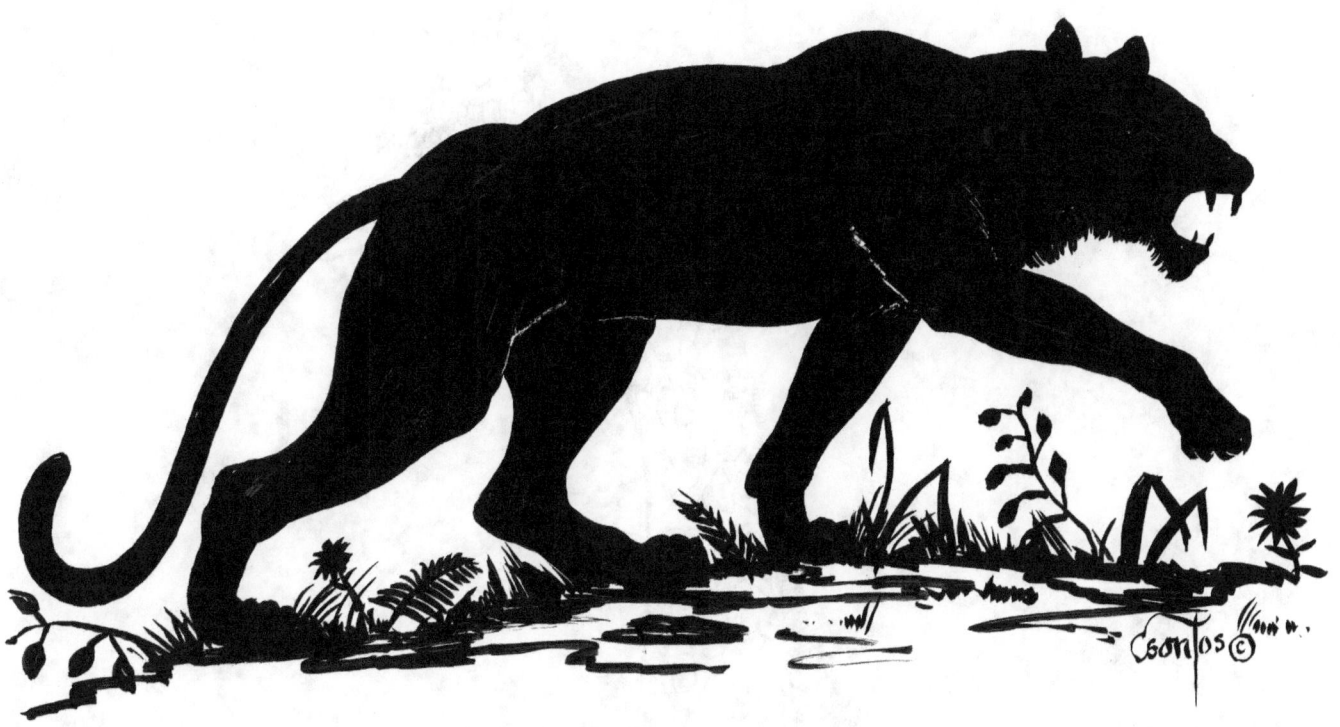

CAT SILHOUETTE - ink - brush

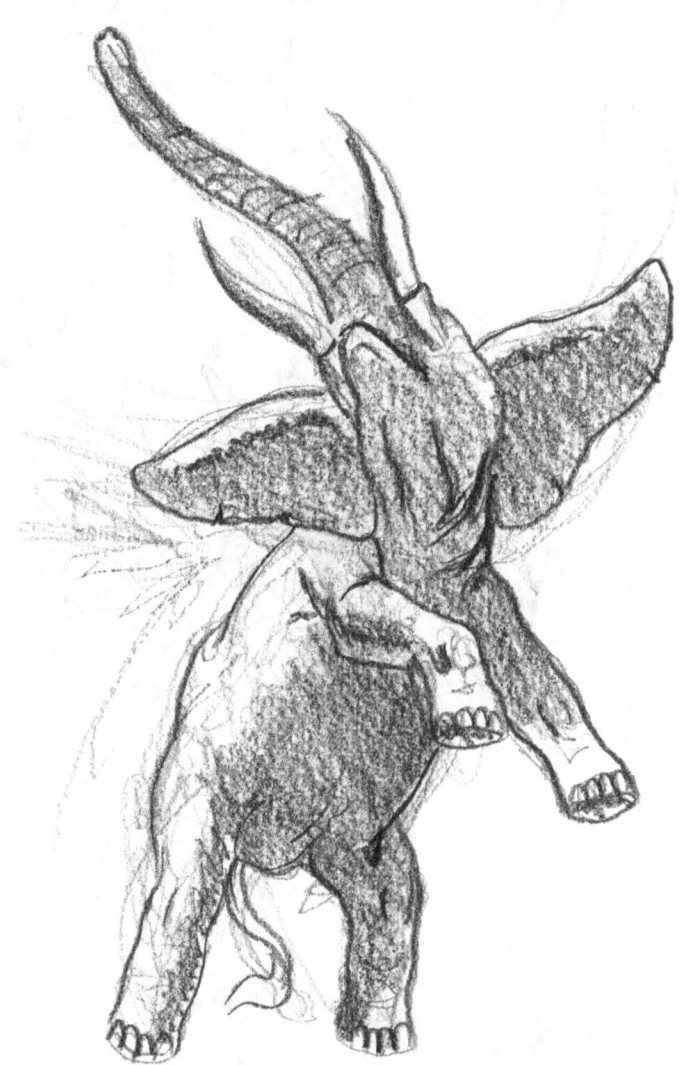

STUDY - pencil - this study was for the painting 'Raising the Colossus'. After I saw the image come out of the abstract umber paint sketch
I did this study to get a better feel for the pose
I saw in my head and on the panel. This pose is
actually reversed from the pose in the painting.
That painting was also the very first painting that
inspired my third book 'Perceptions II'.

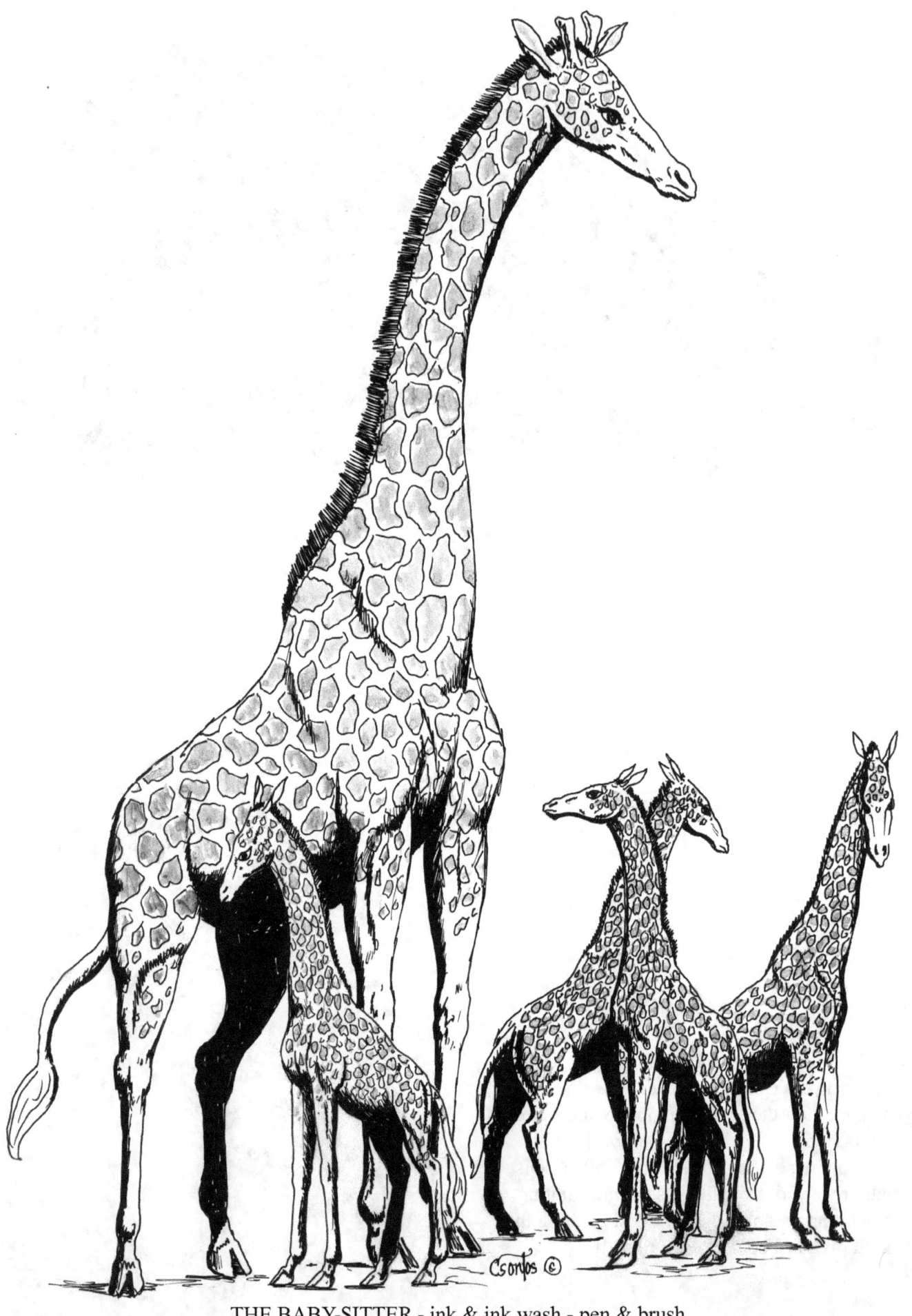

THE BABY-SITTER - ink & ink wash - pen & brush

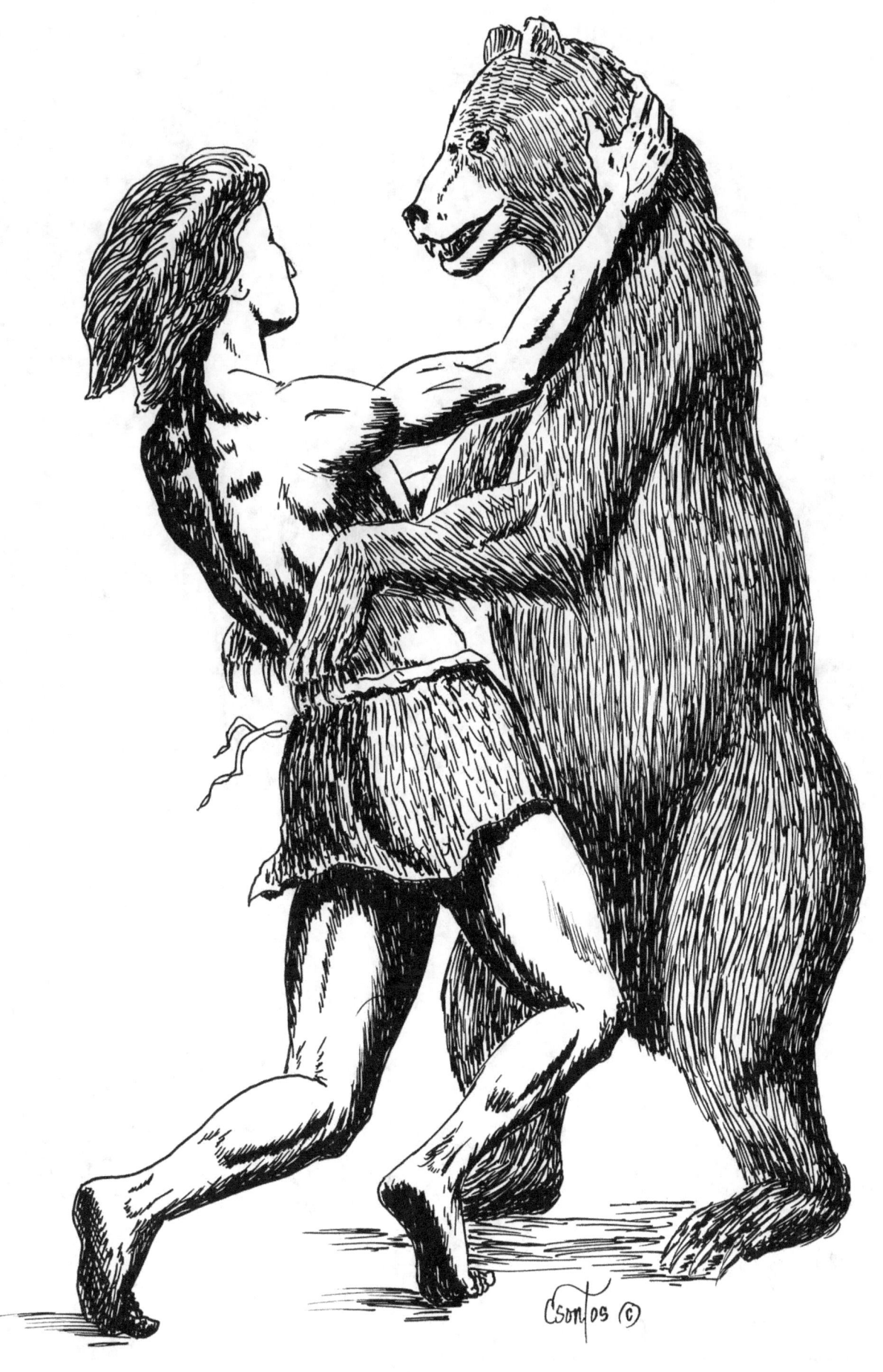

BEAR HUG - ink - pen & brush

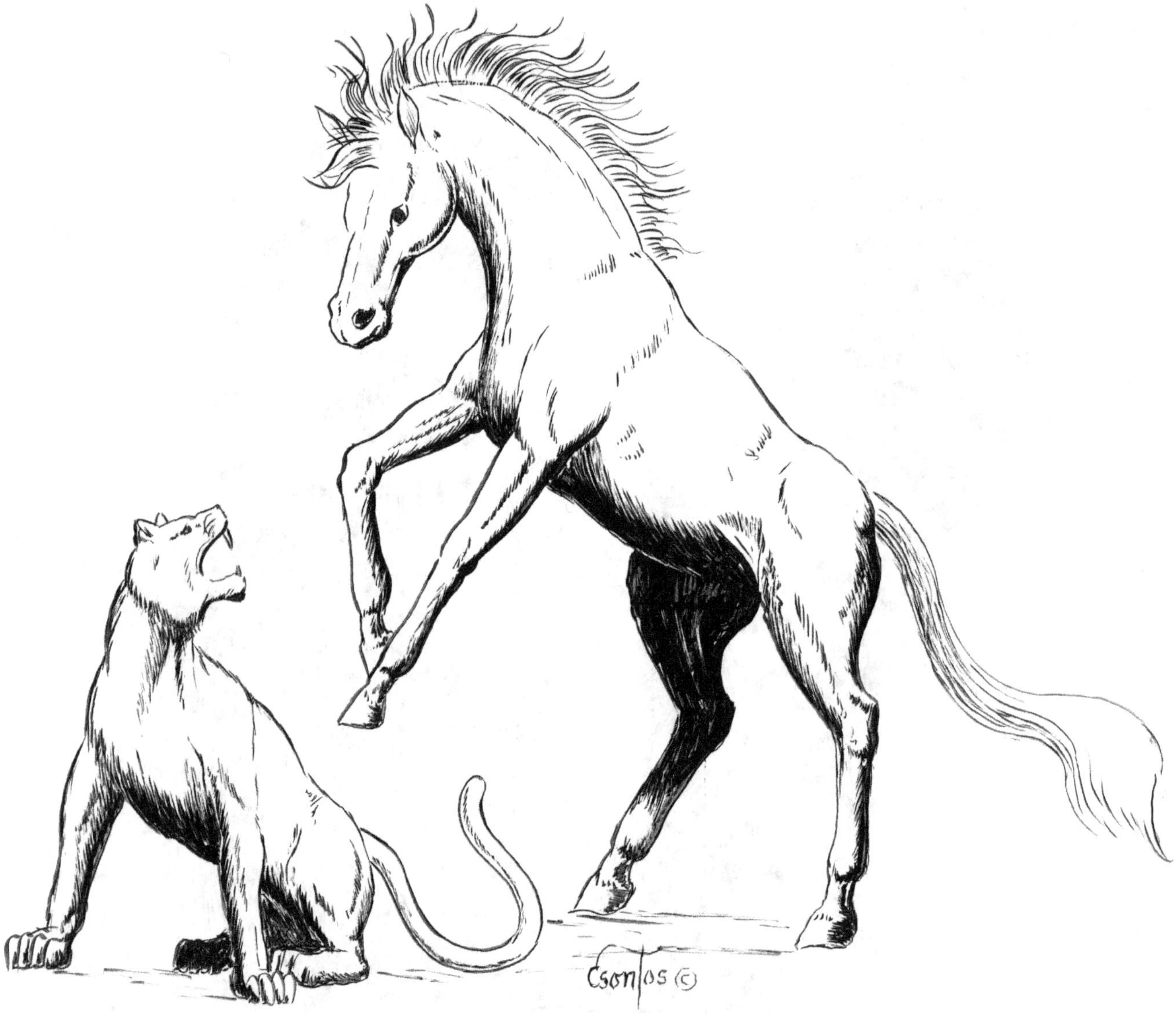

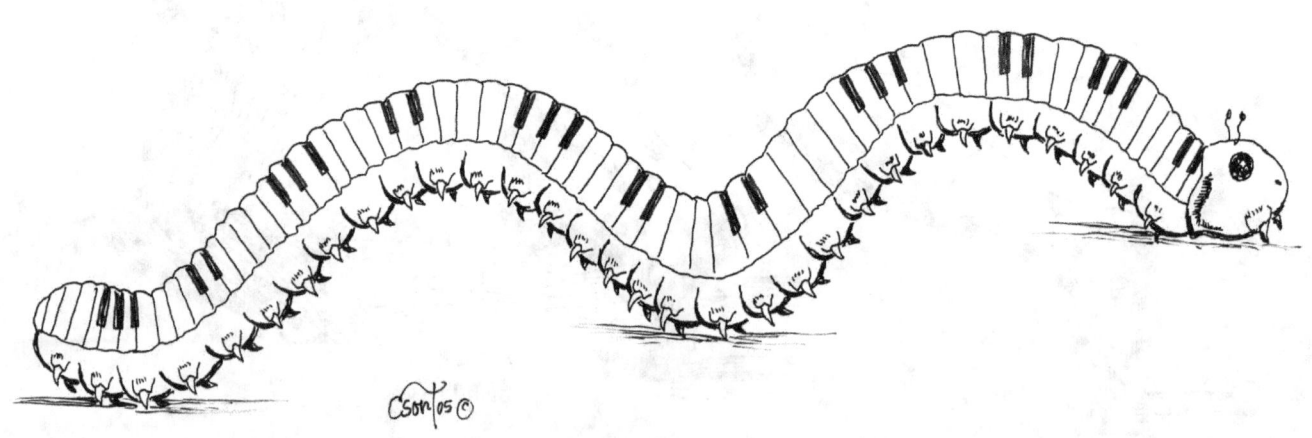

CONFRONTATION - ink - brush

CATERPIANO - ink - pen

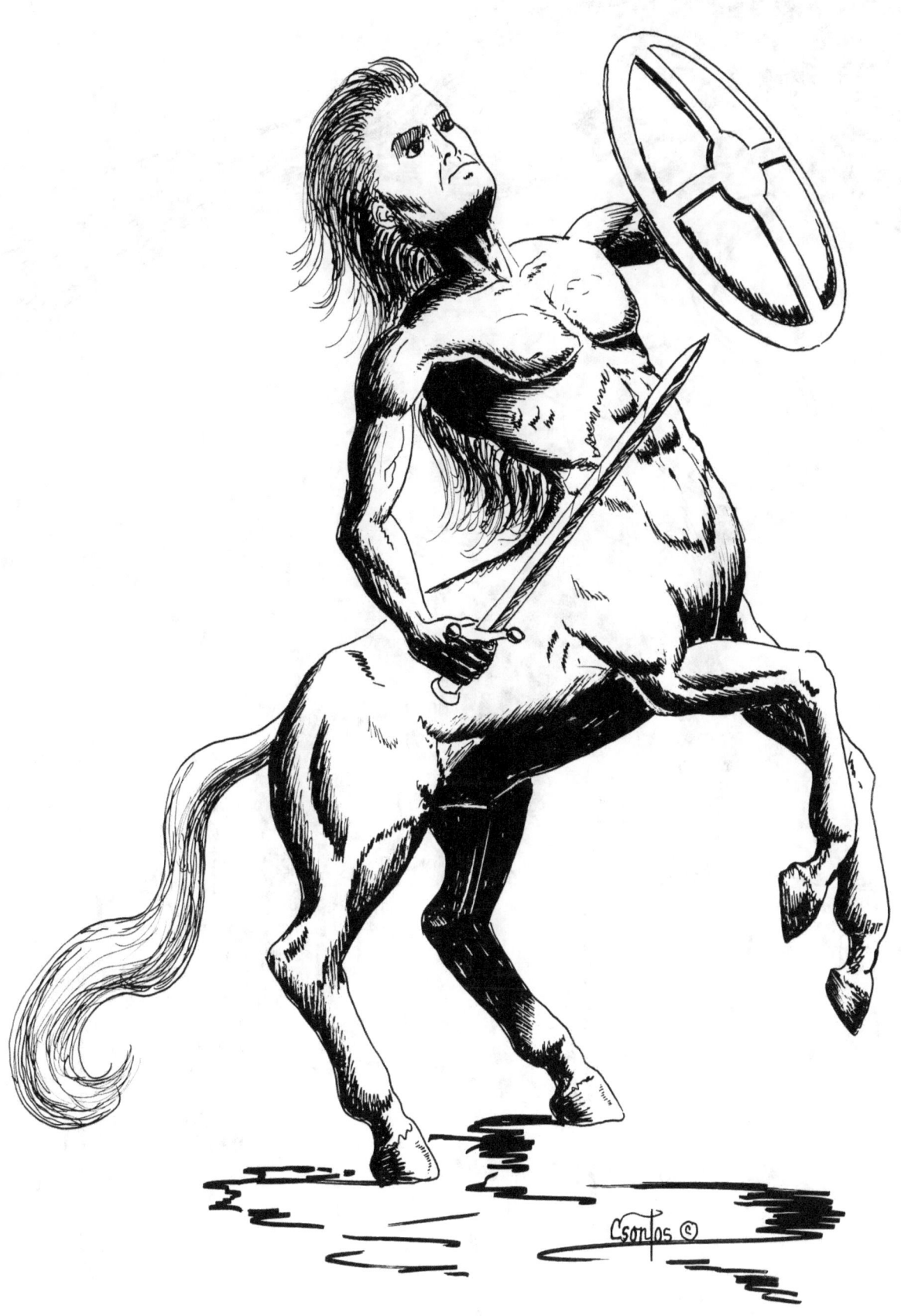

CENTAUR - ink - pen & brush

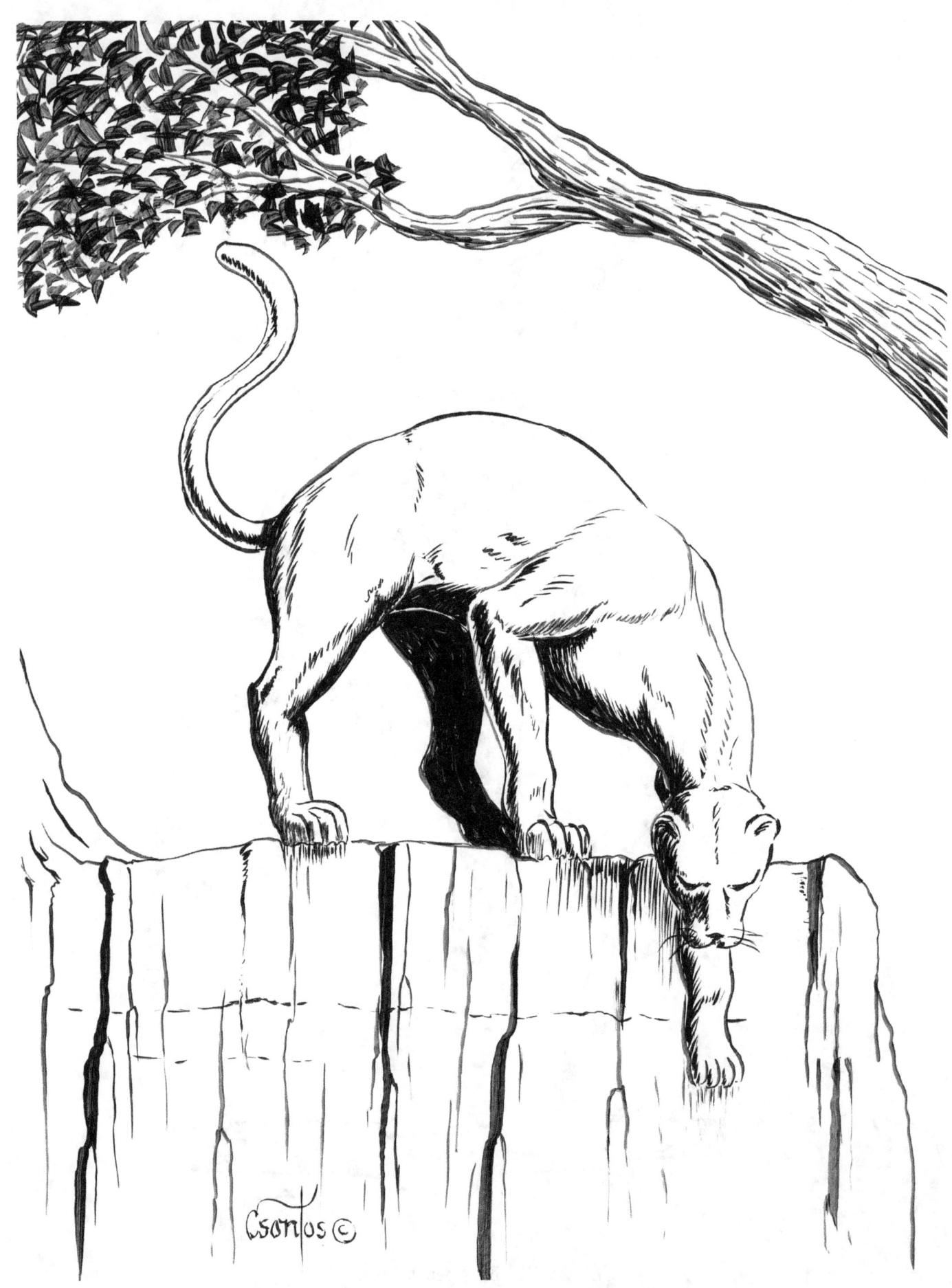

THINKING ABOUT A JUMP - ink - brush

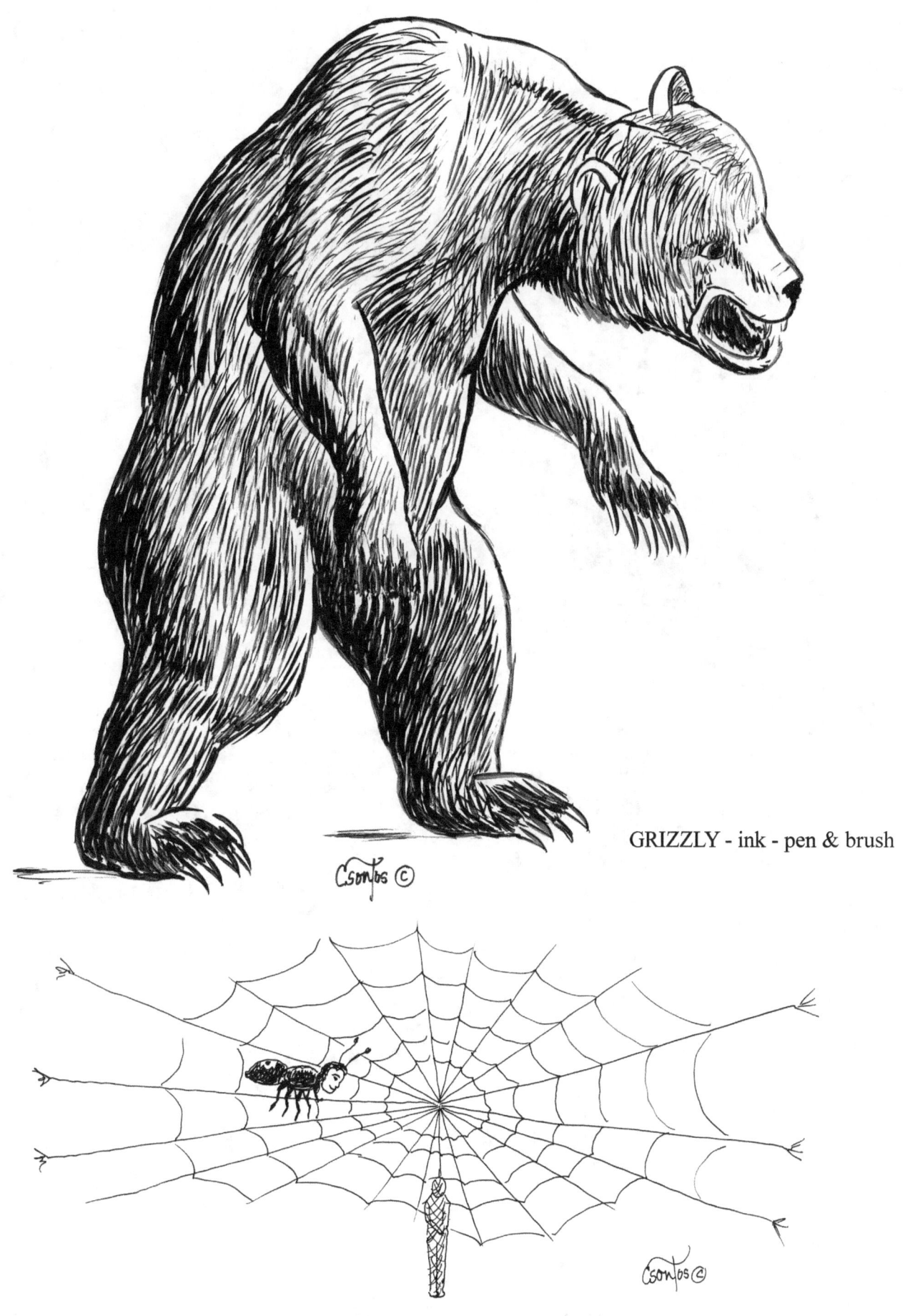

GRIZZLY - ink - pen & brush

BLACK WIDOW - ink - pen

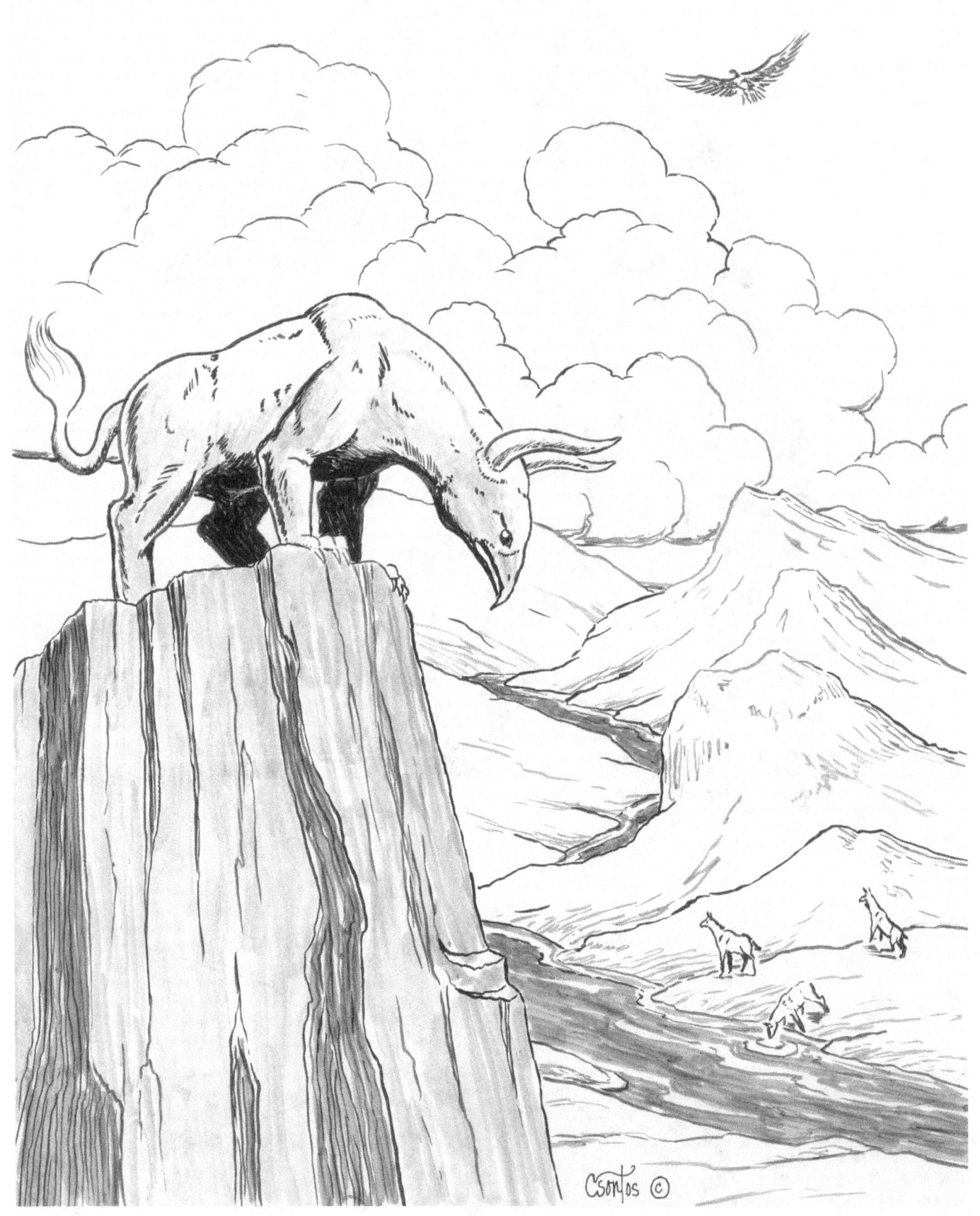

THINKING ABOUT LUNCH - ink & ink wash - pen & brush

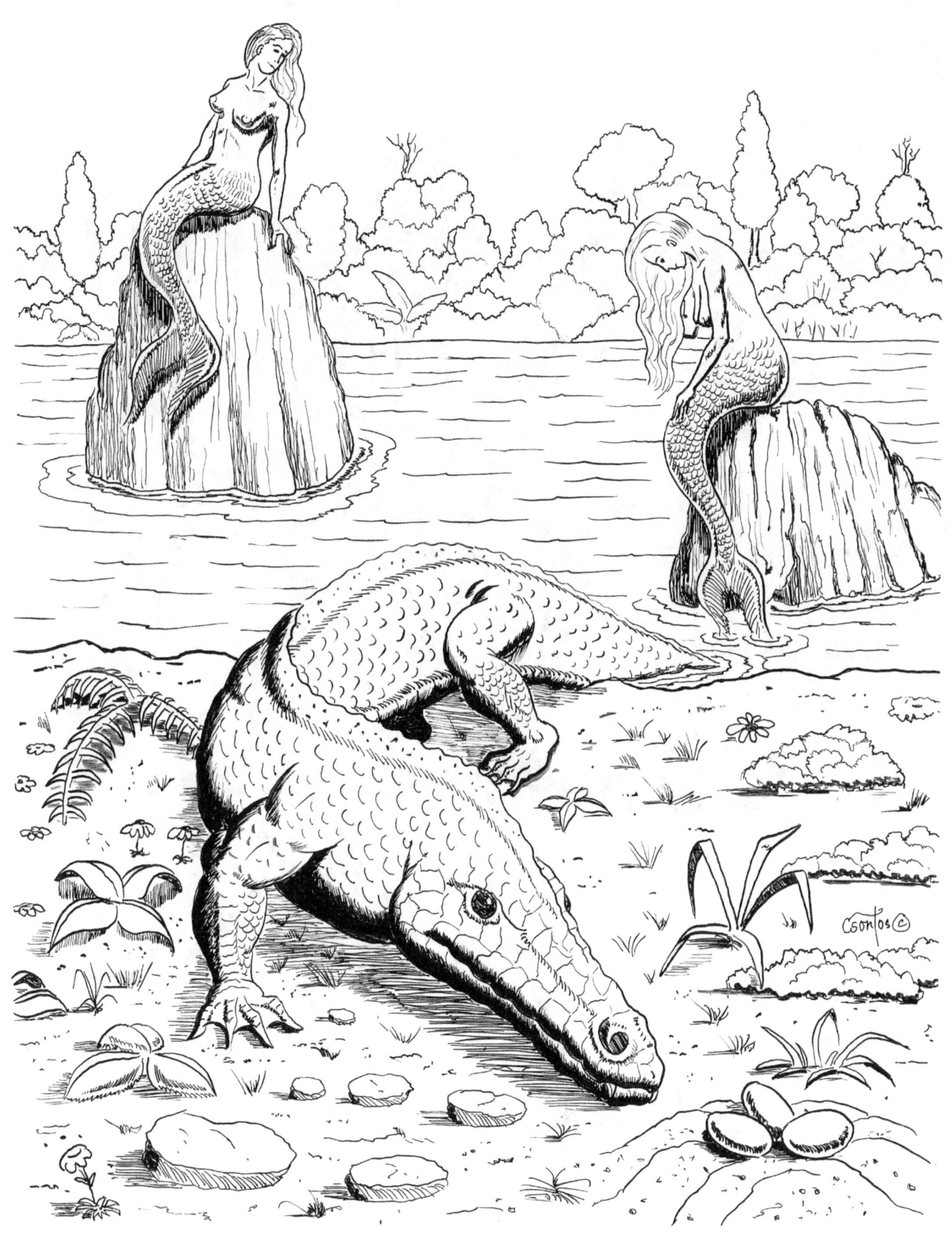

WATER'S EDGE - ink - pen & brush

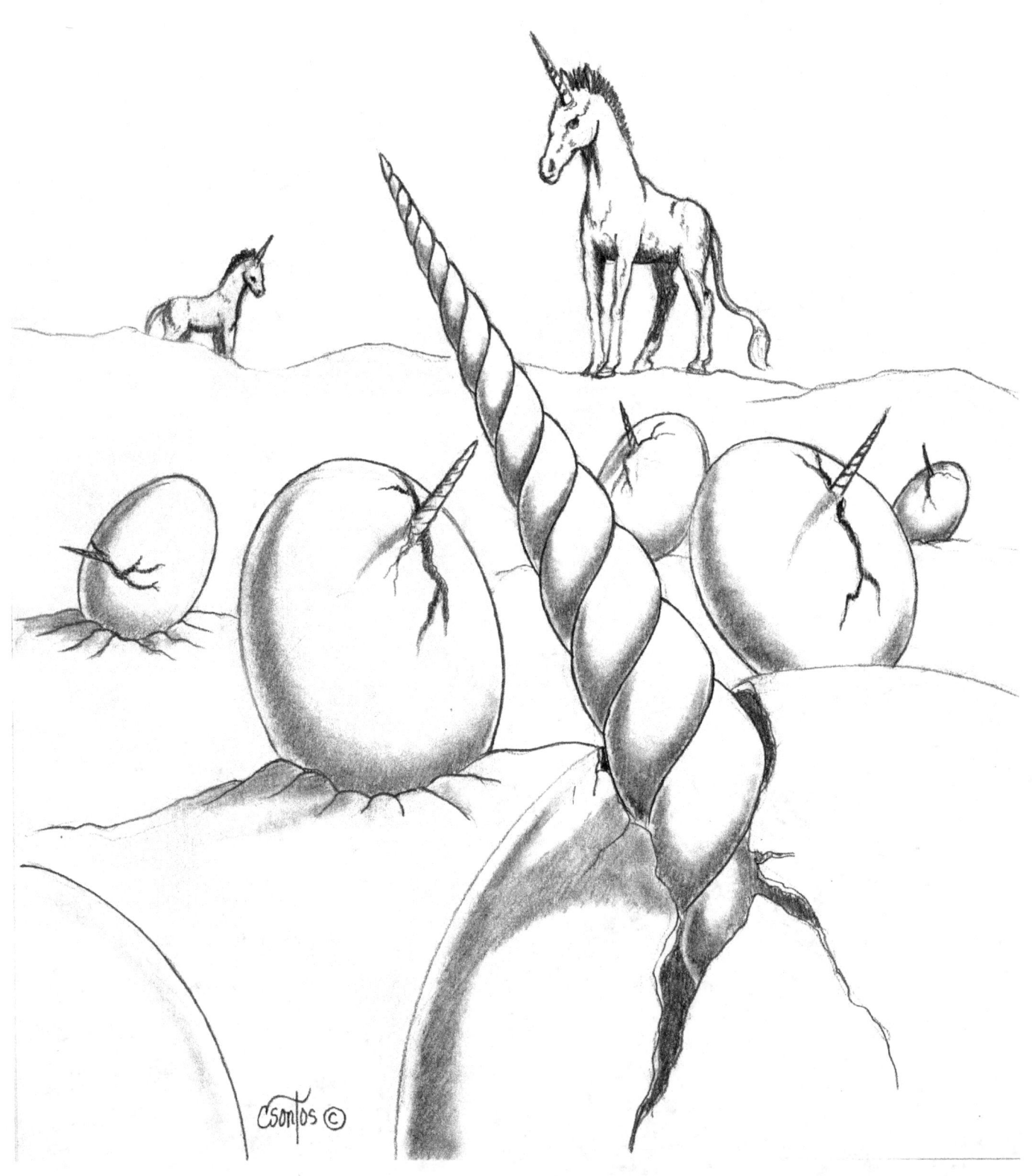

UNICORN HATCHLINGS - pencil

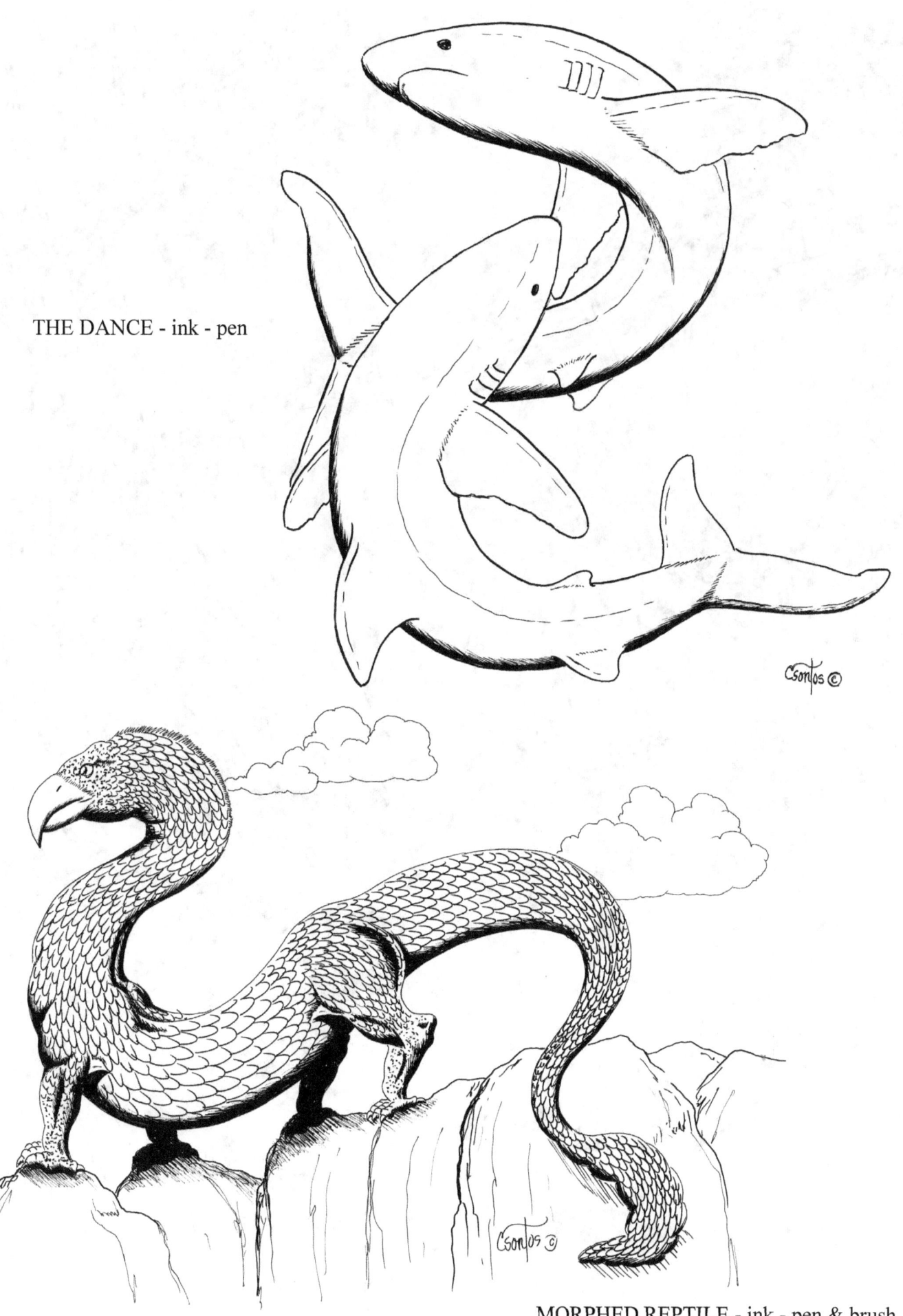

THE DANCE - ink - pen

MORPHED REPTILE - ink - pen & brush

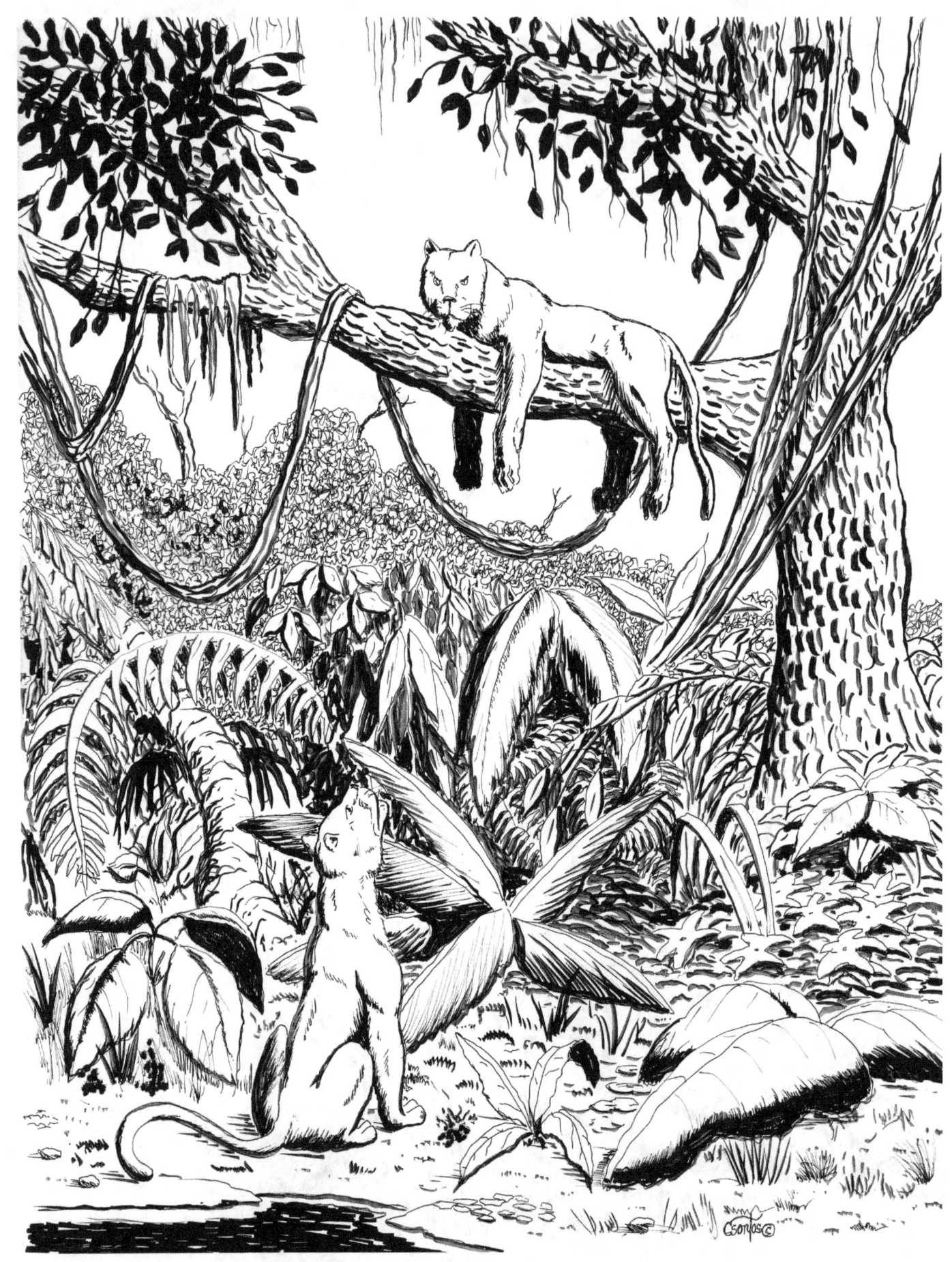

WANNA PLAY? - ink - pen & brush

Idiosyncrasy

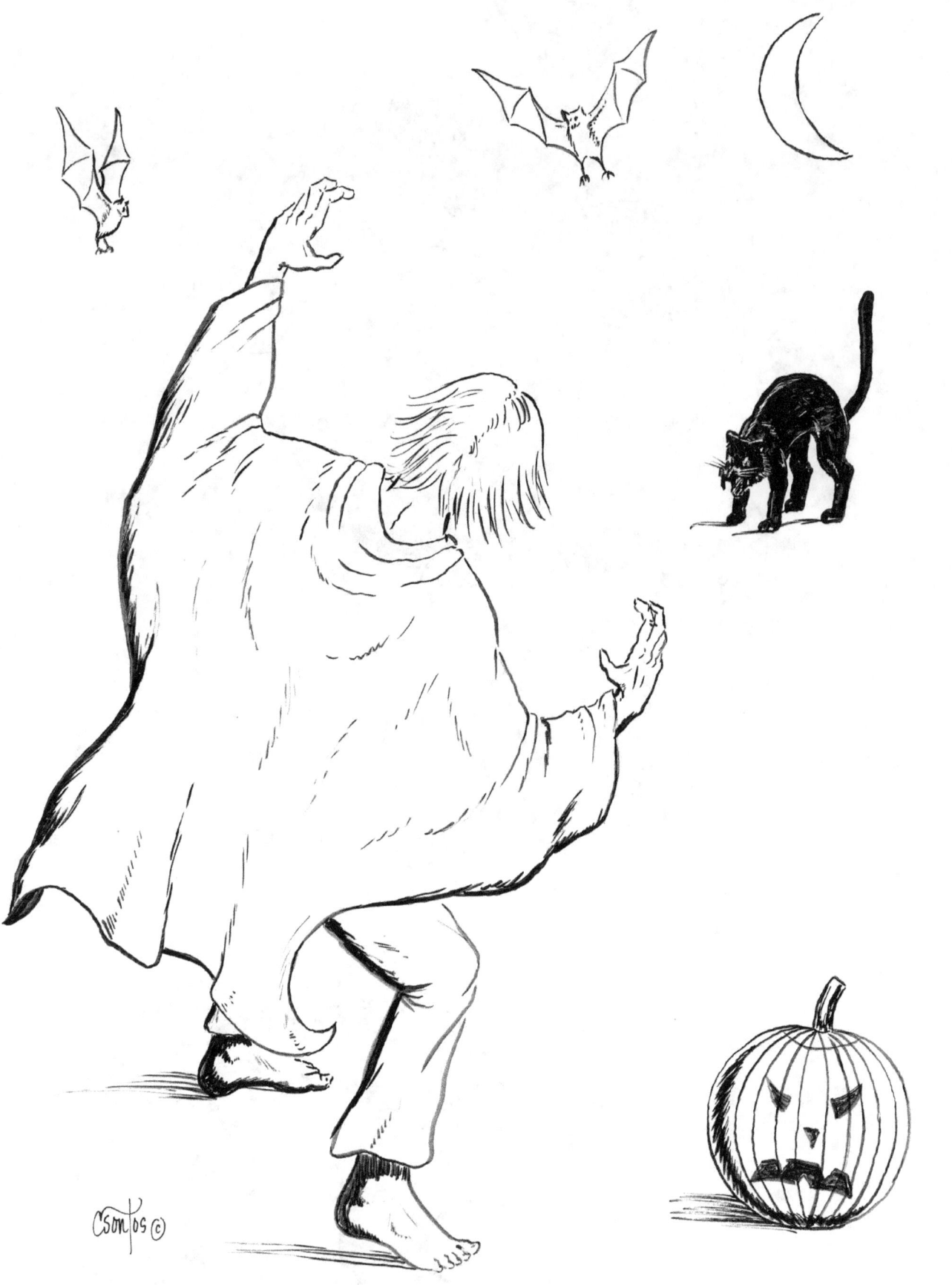

HALLOWEEN - ink - pen & brush

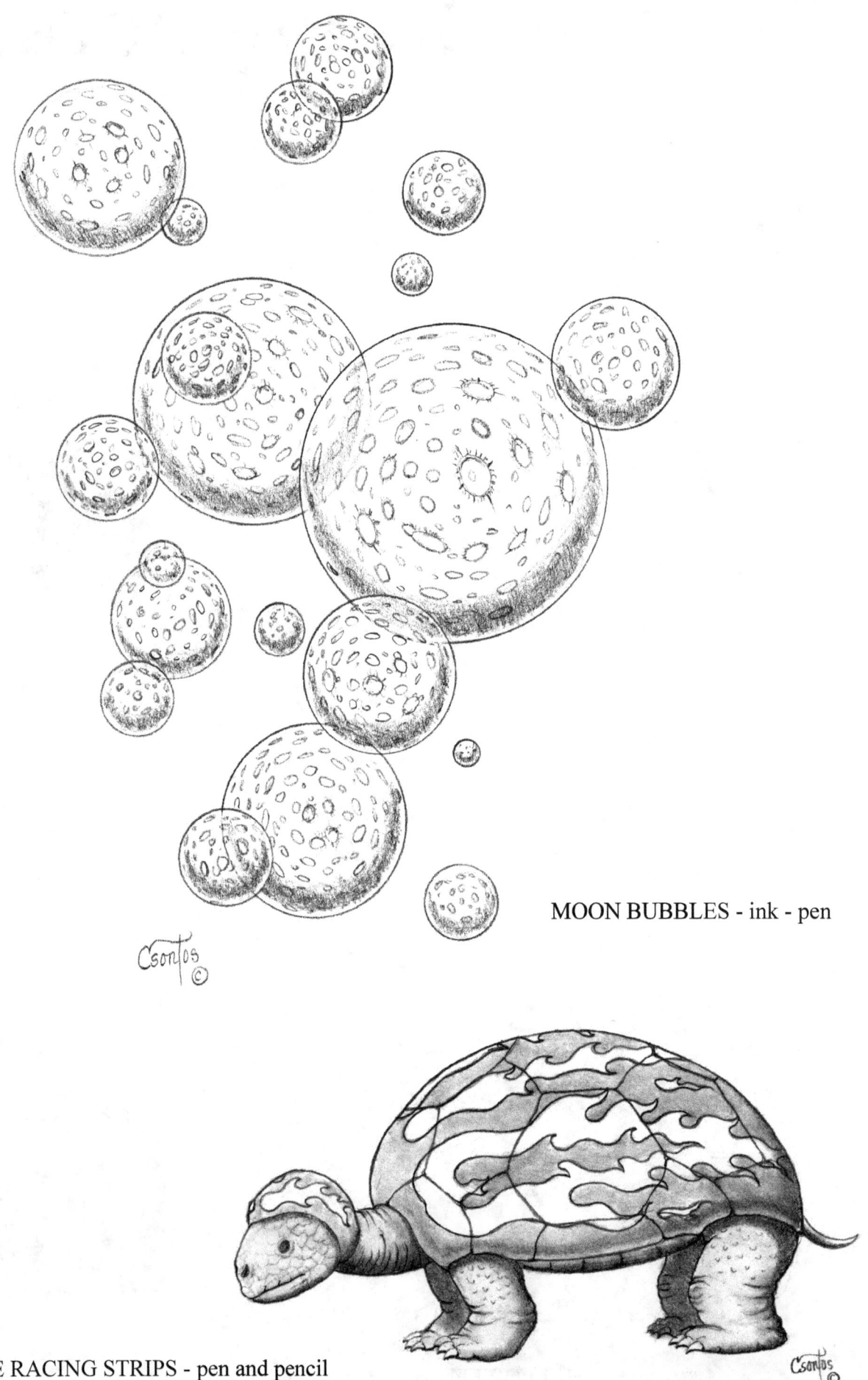

MOON BUBBLES - ink - pen

FLAME RACING STRIPS - pen and pencil

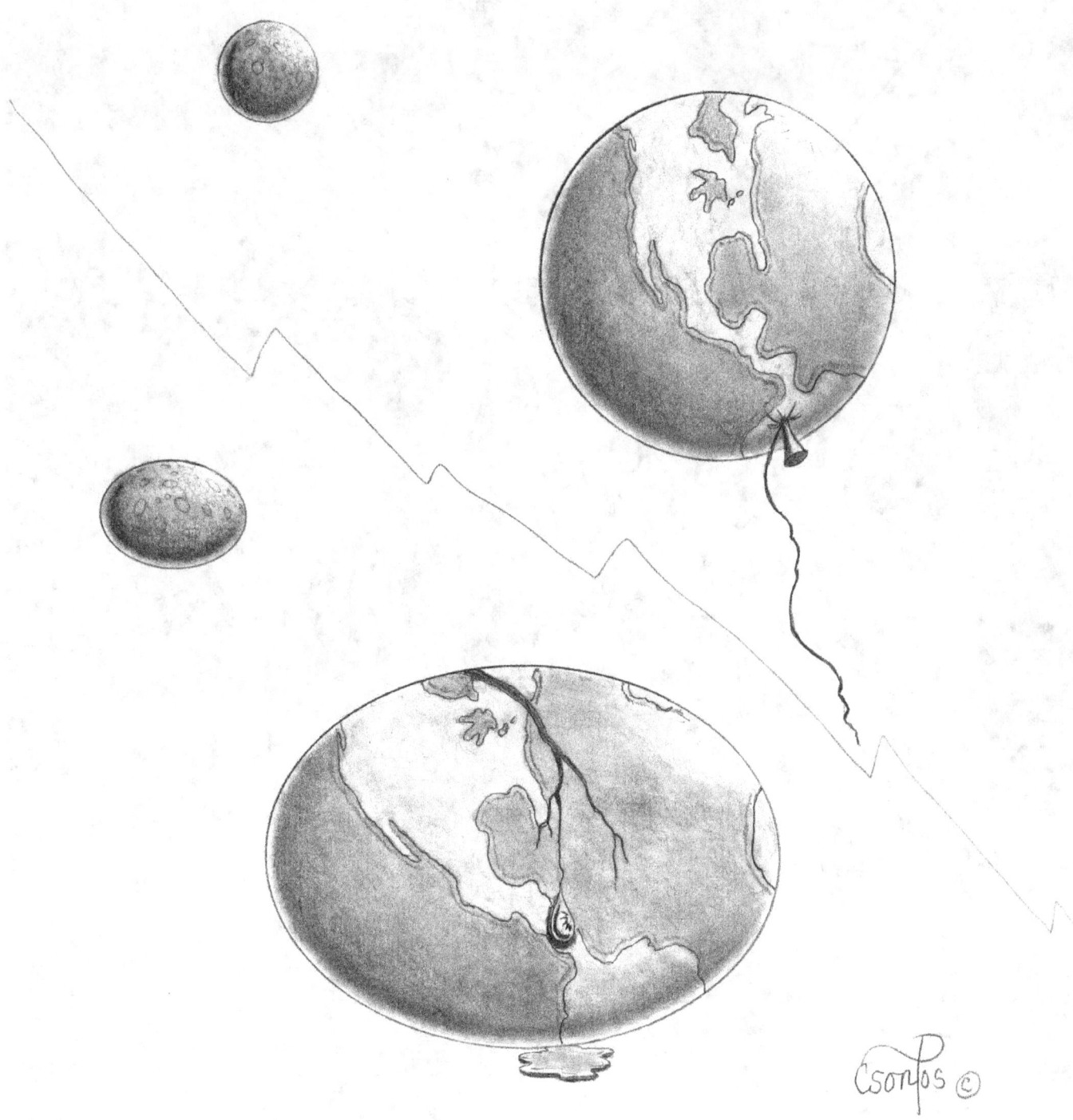

A COUPLE OF EARTHS - pen and pencil

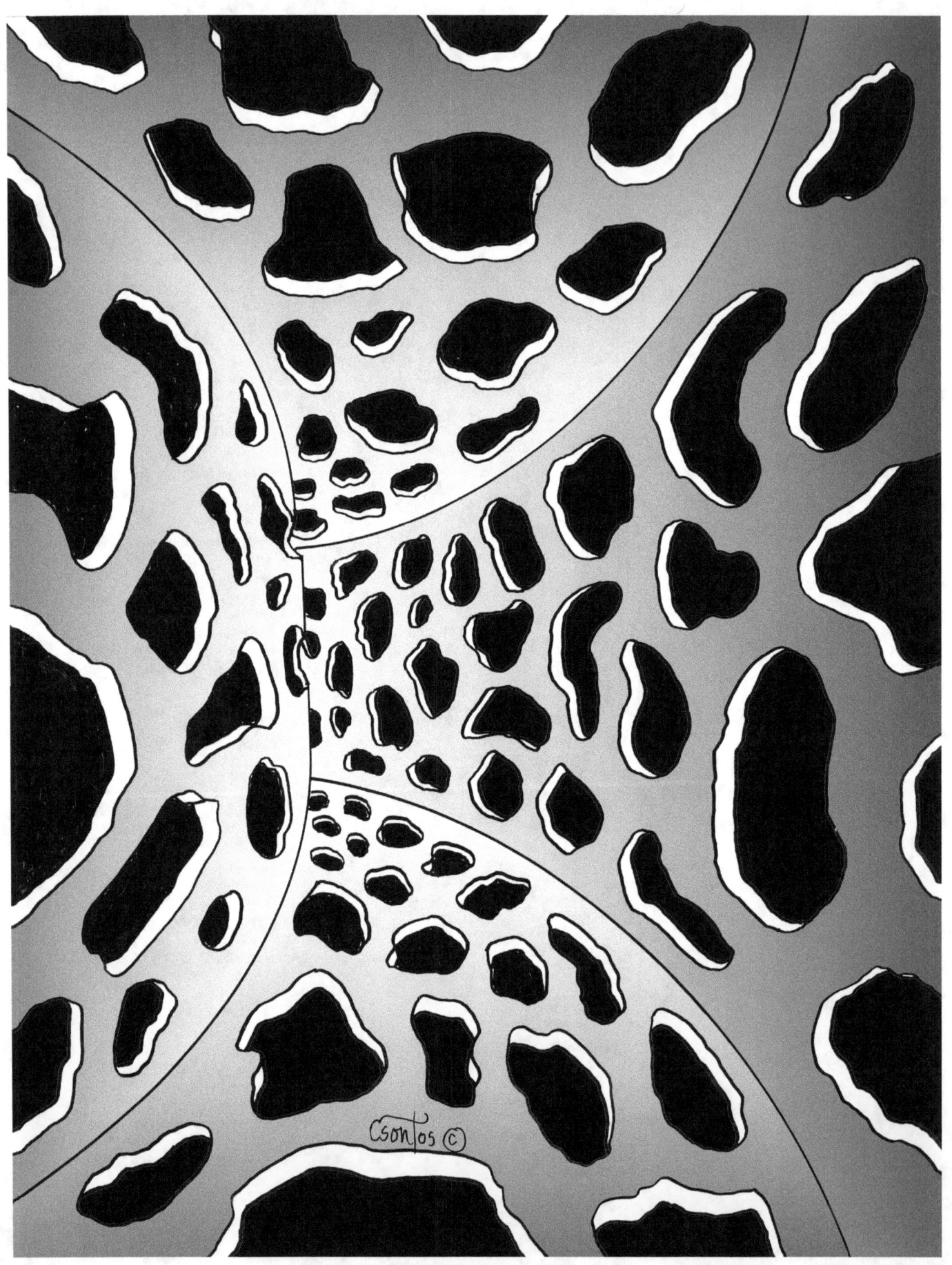

CURVED PERSPECTIVE - ink - pen & brush - toned with Photoshop

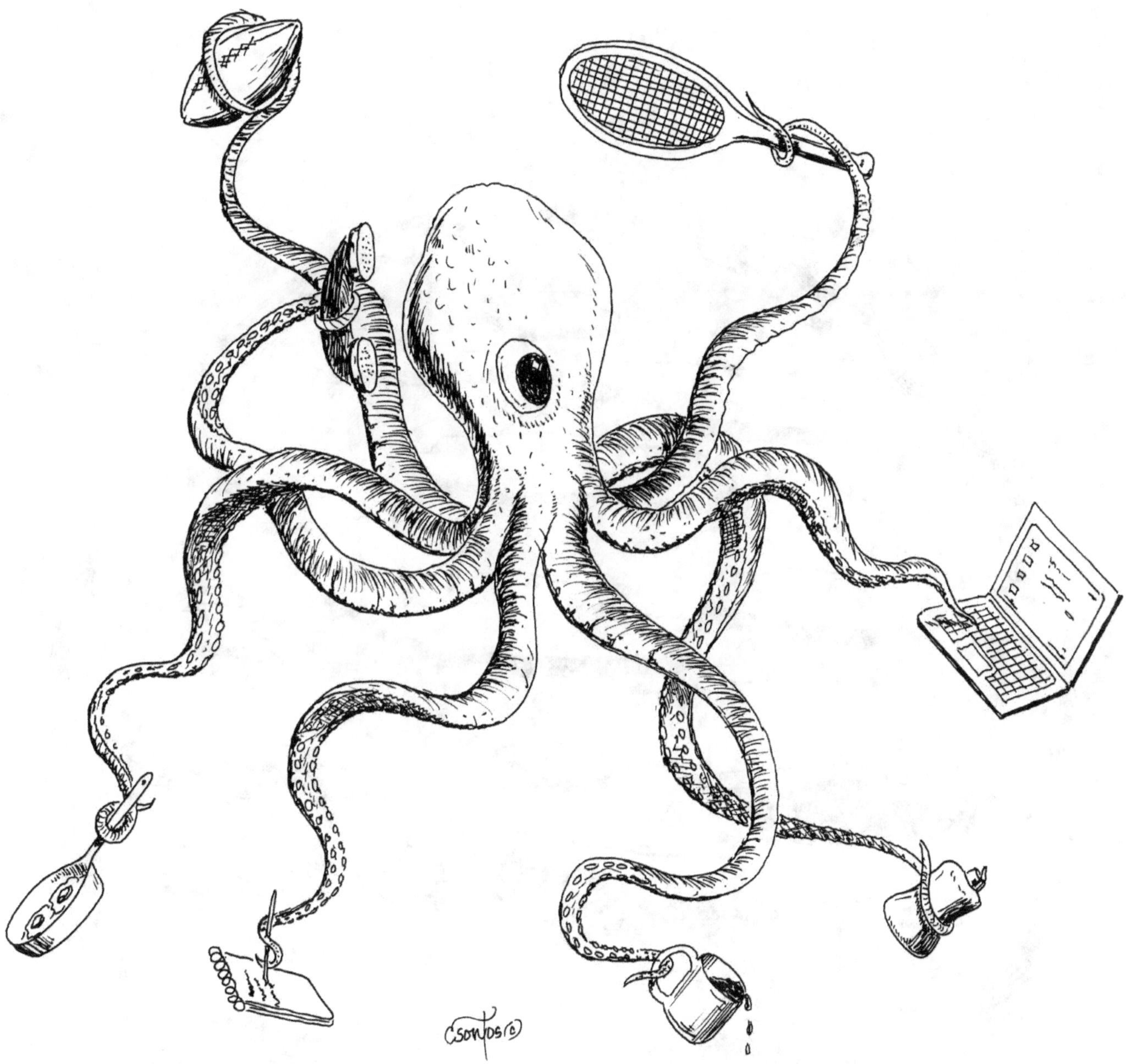

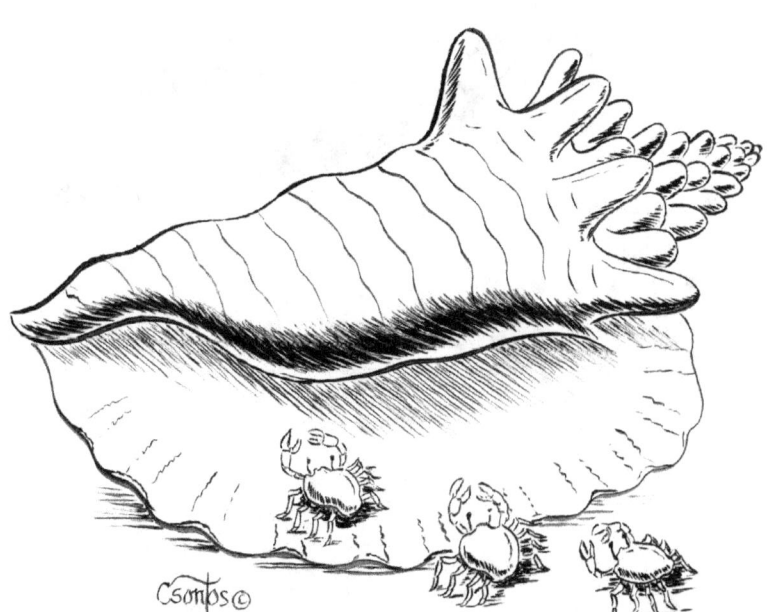

MULTI-TASKING - ink - pen

CONDO - ink - pen & brush

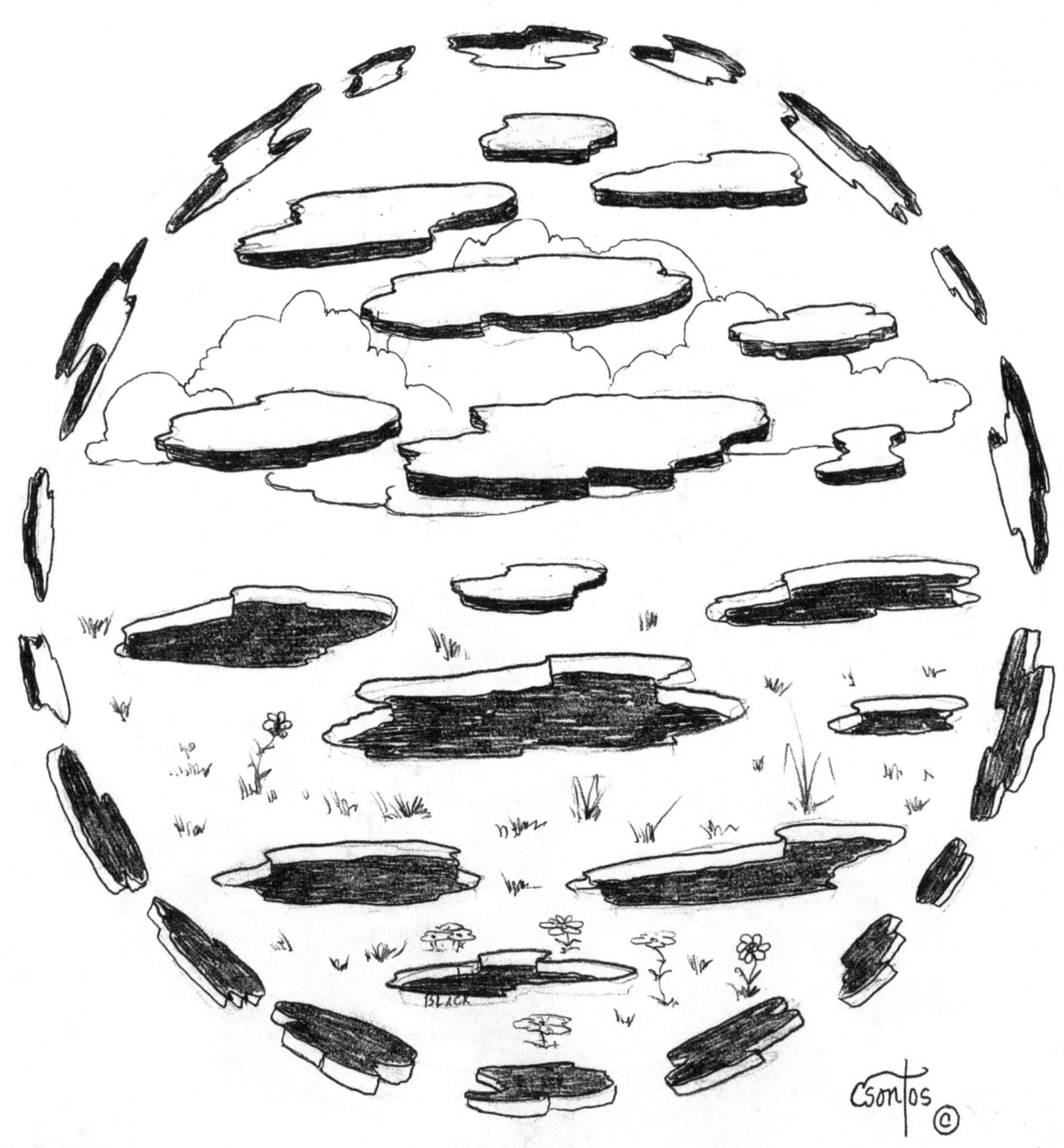

CONVOLUTED METAMORPHOSIS - pencil

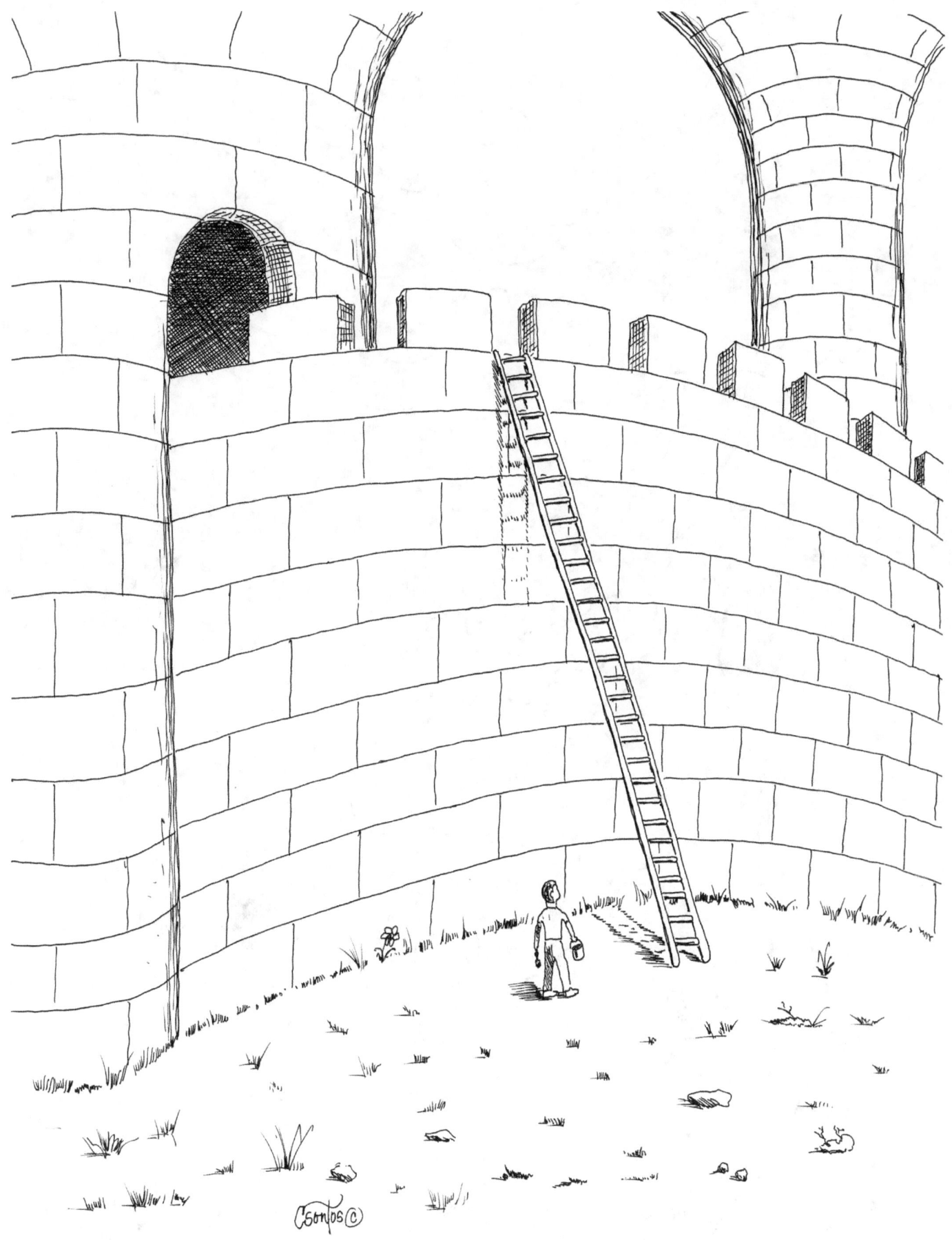

PAINT JOB - ink - pen

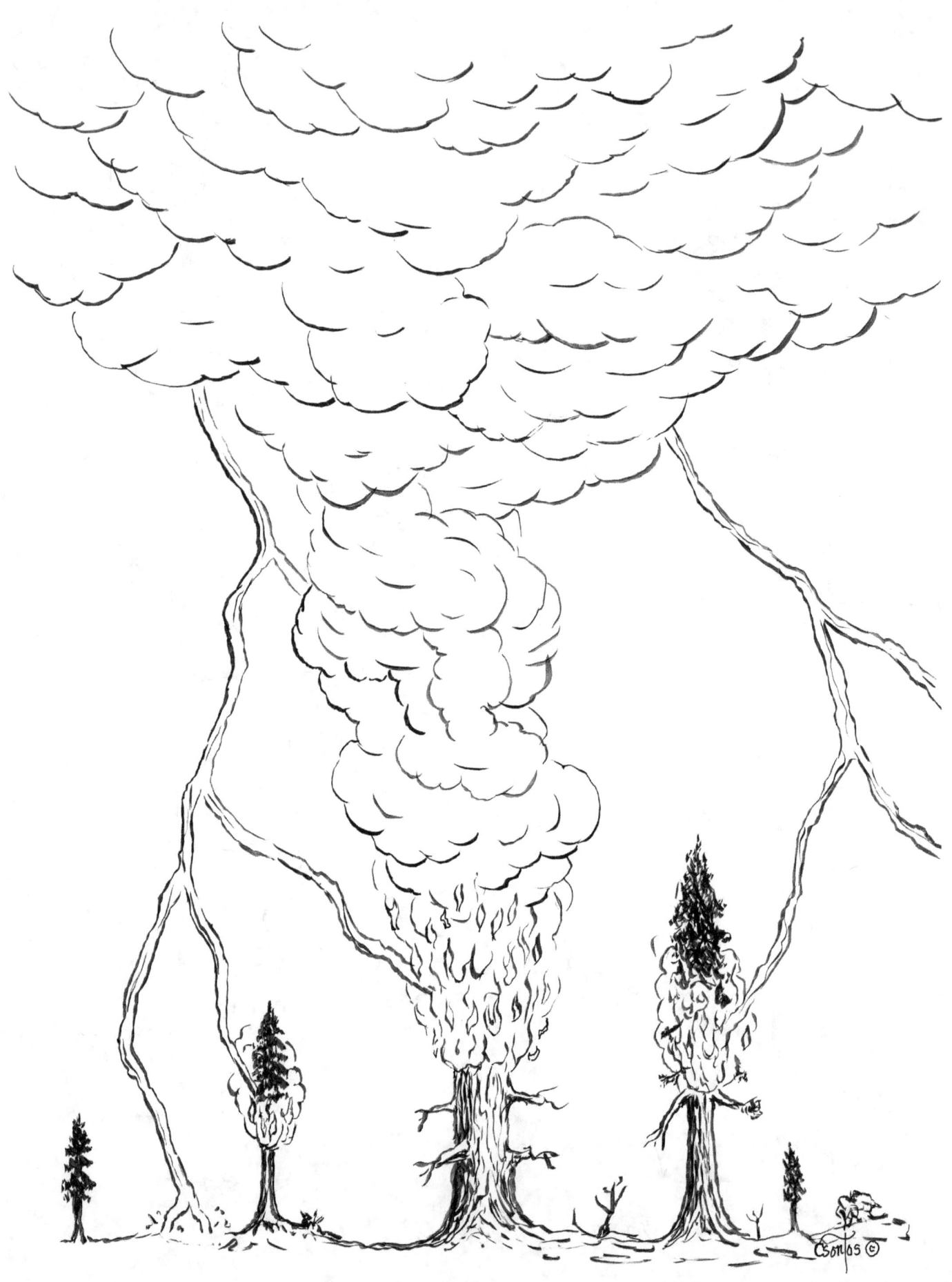

PERPETUAL WILDFIRE - ink - brush

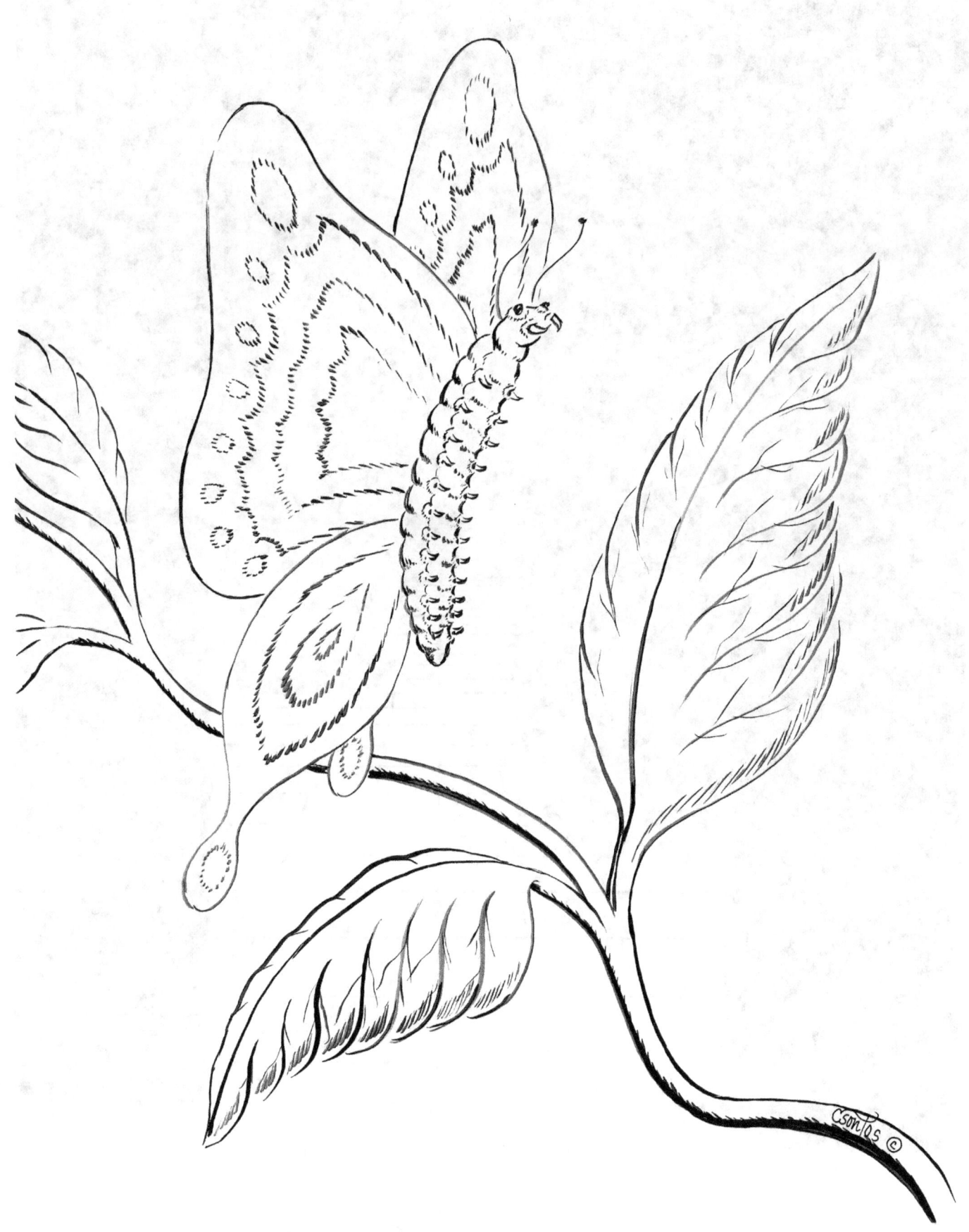

WHO NEEDS TO CHANGE? - ink - brush

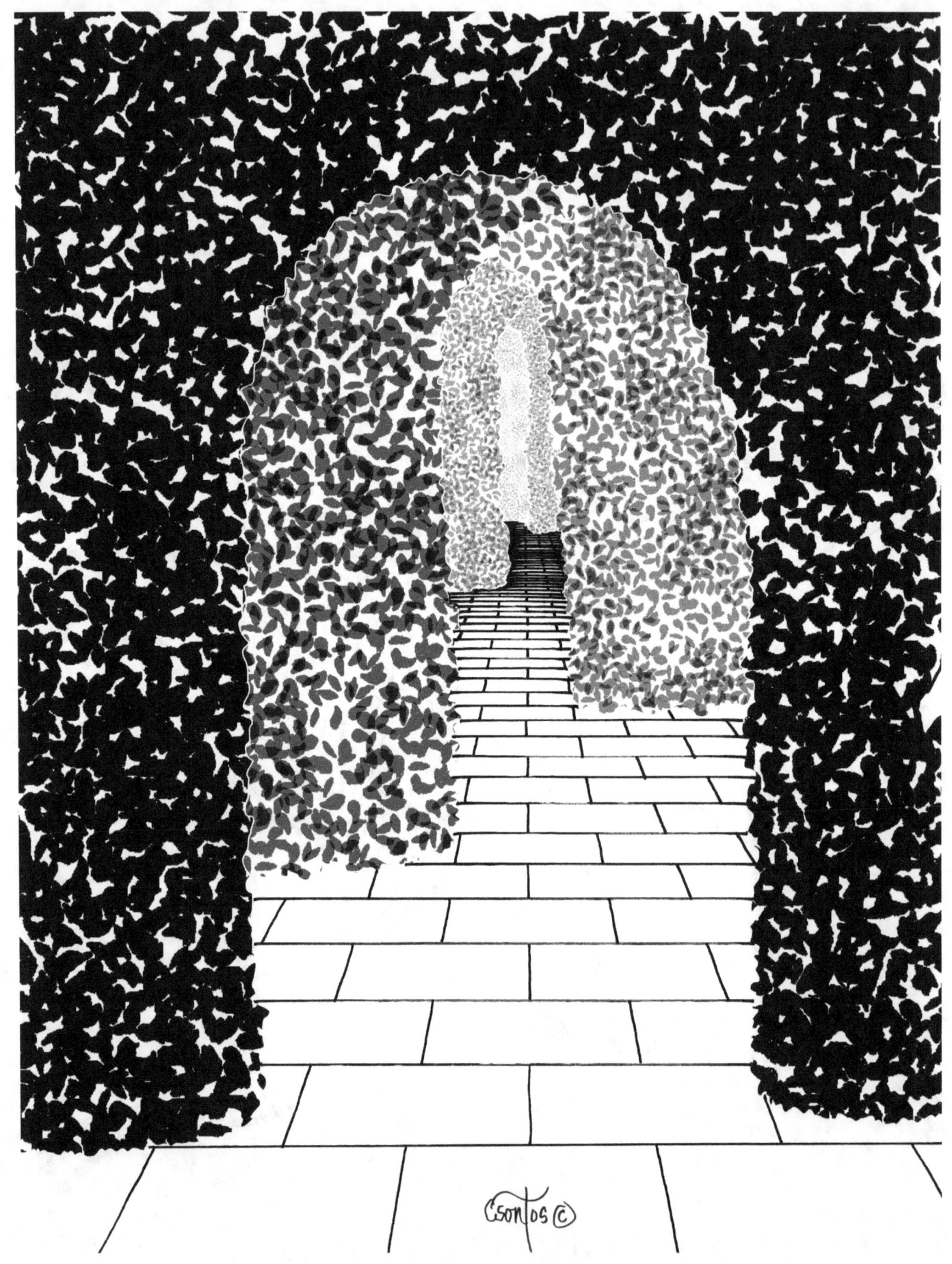

ENTER THE MAZE - ink - pen - Photoshop

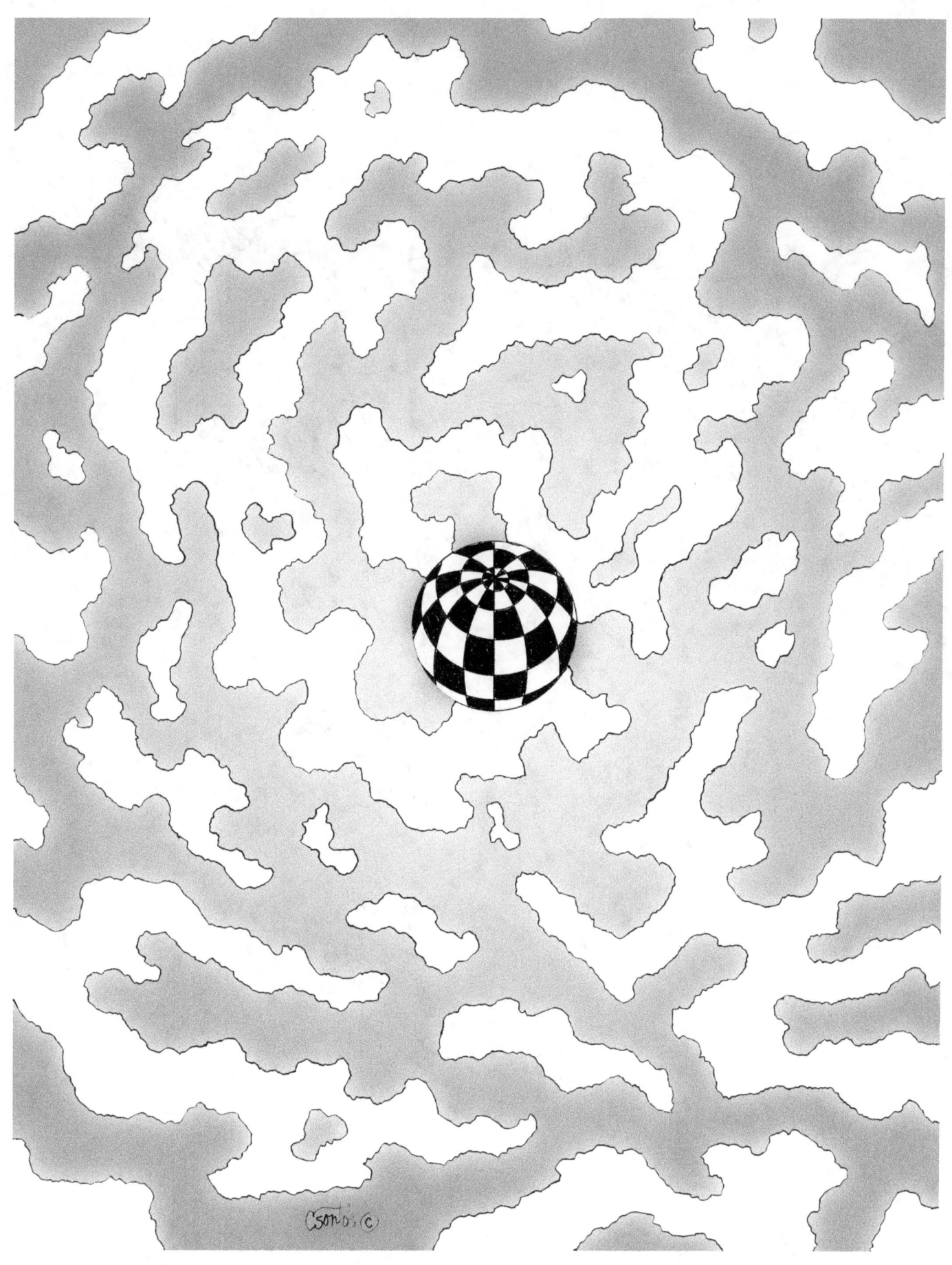

ORDER/CHAOS - ink - pen & brush - toned in Photoshop

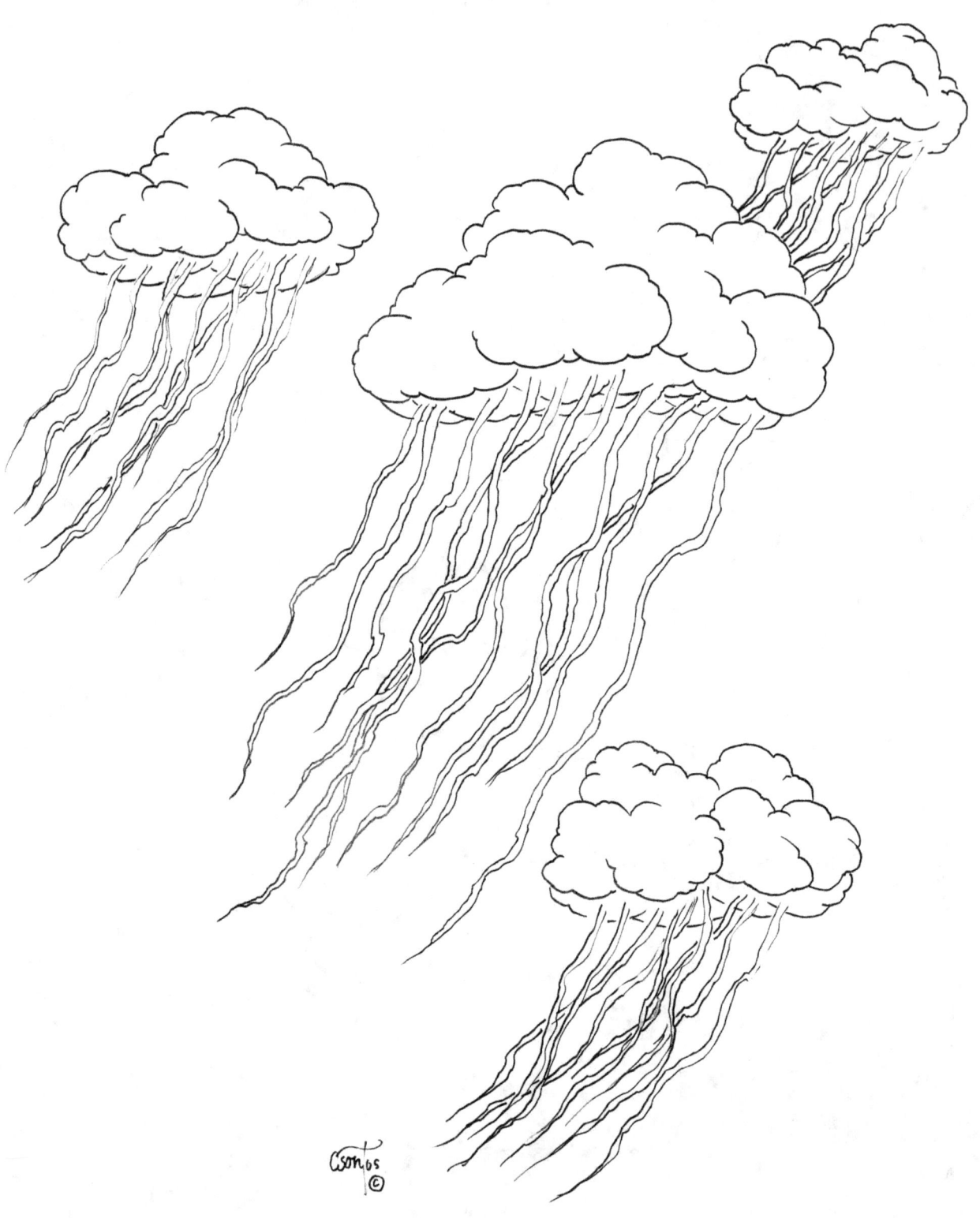

JELLYFISH CLOUDS - ink - pen

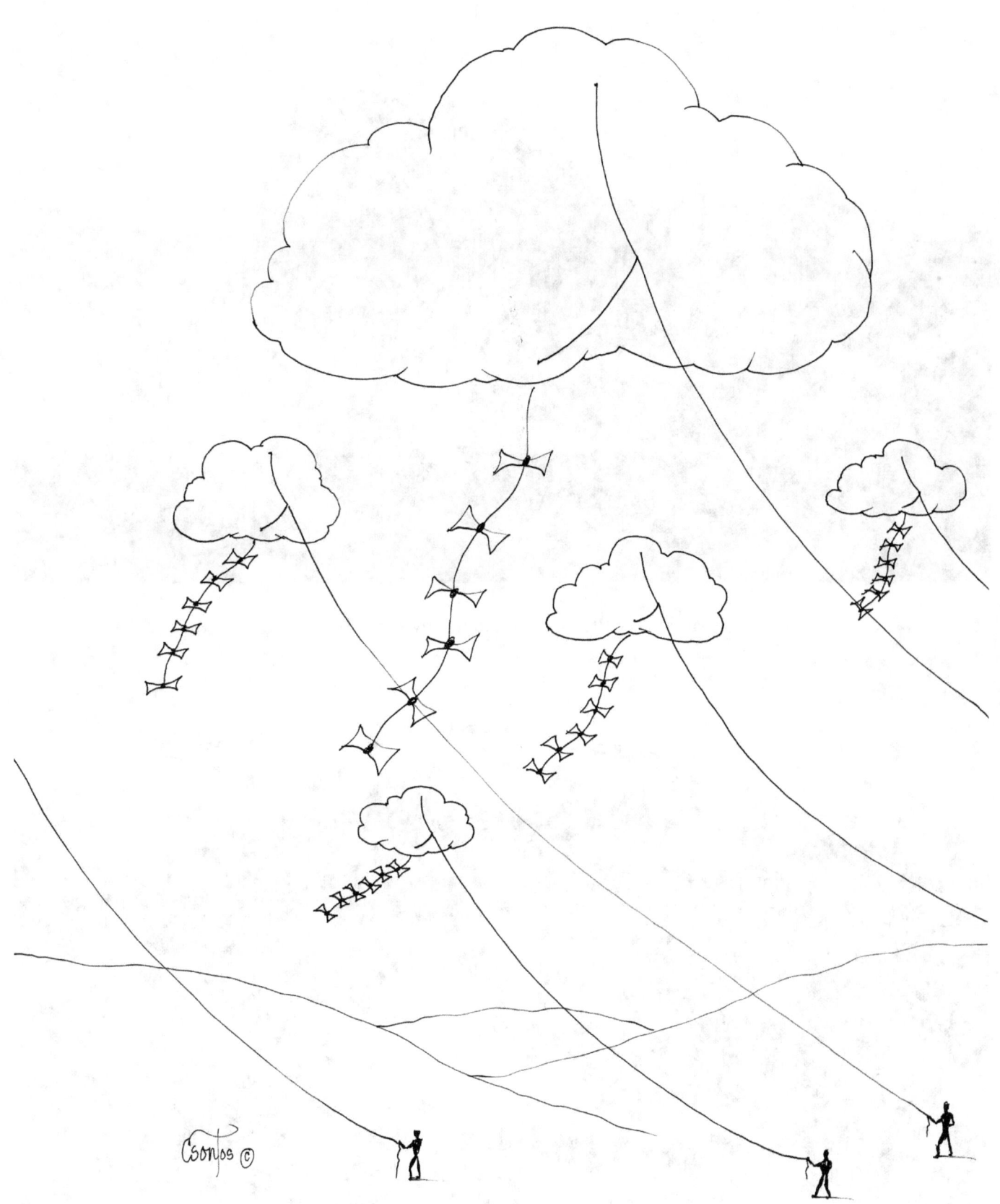

CLOUD KITES - ink - pen

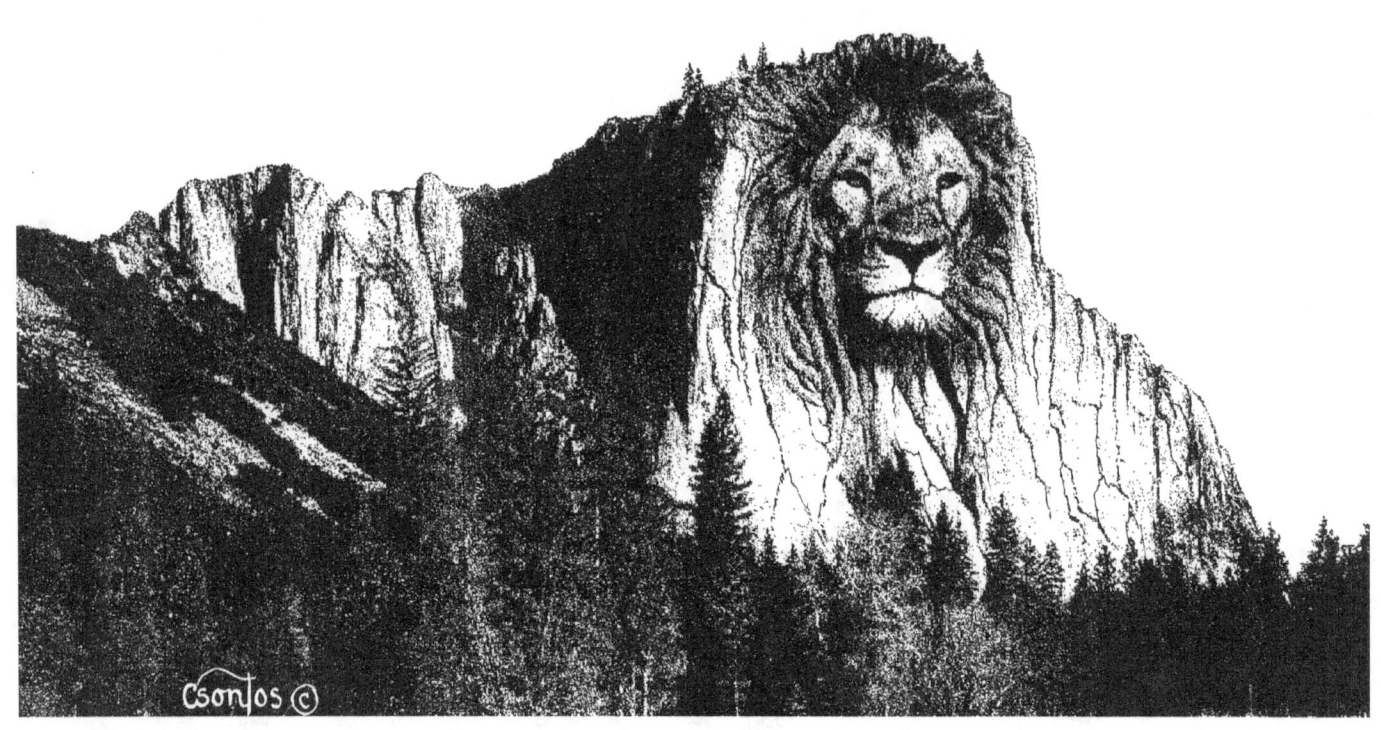

MOUNT SPHINX - photography - Photoshop

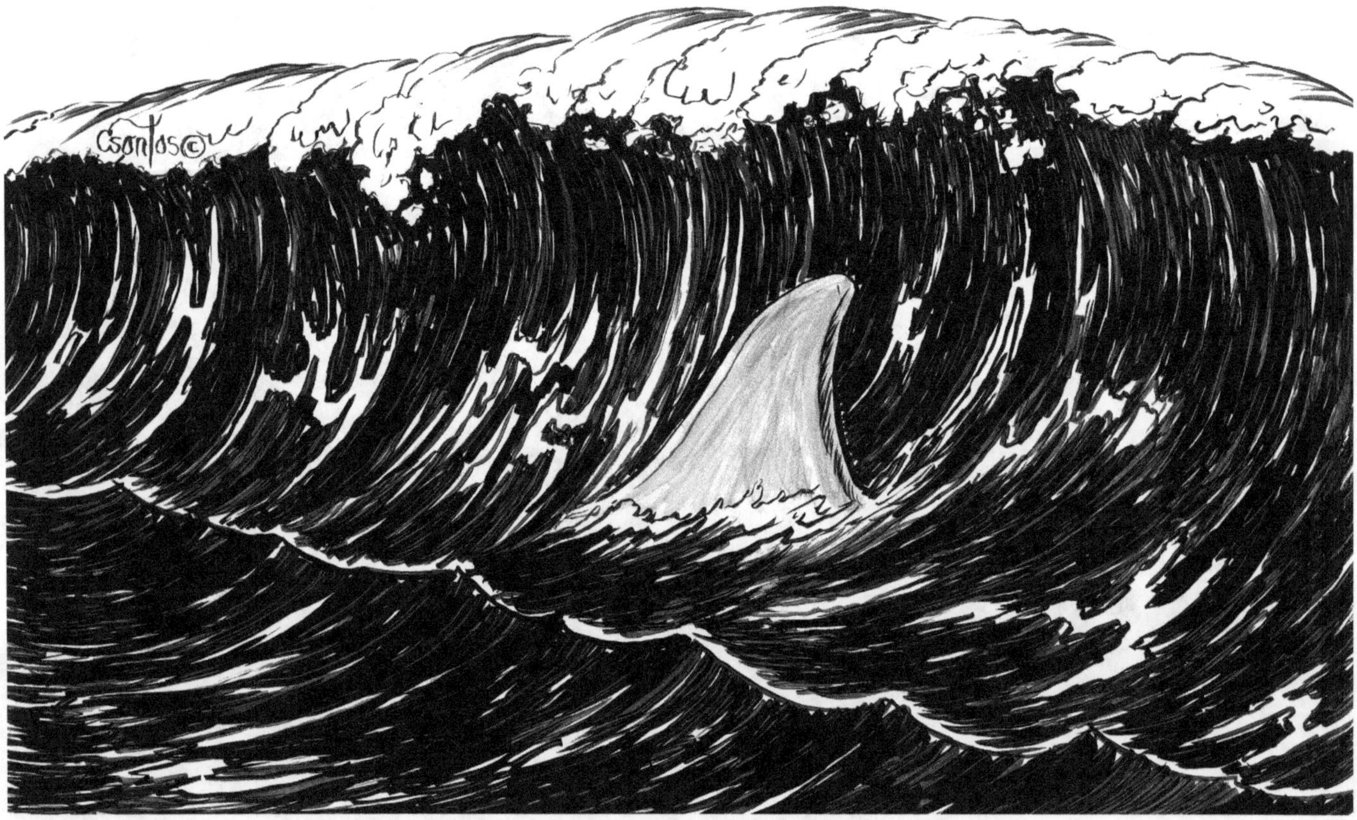

CRUISING THE SURF - ink & ink wash - brush

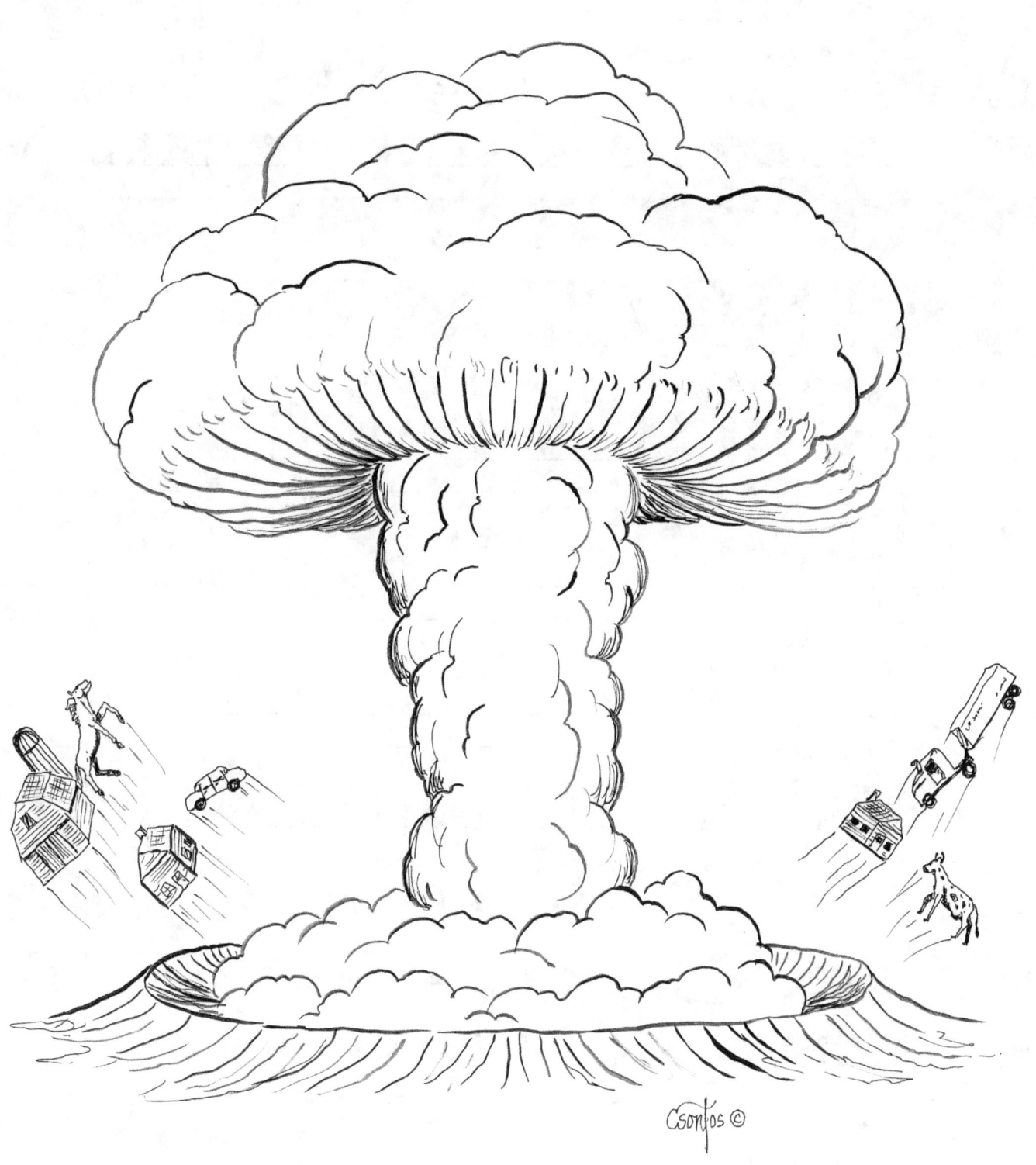

THE MUSHROOM EFFECT - ink - pen & brush

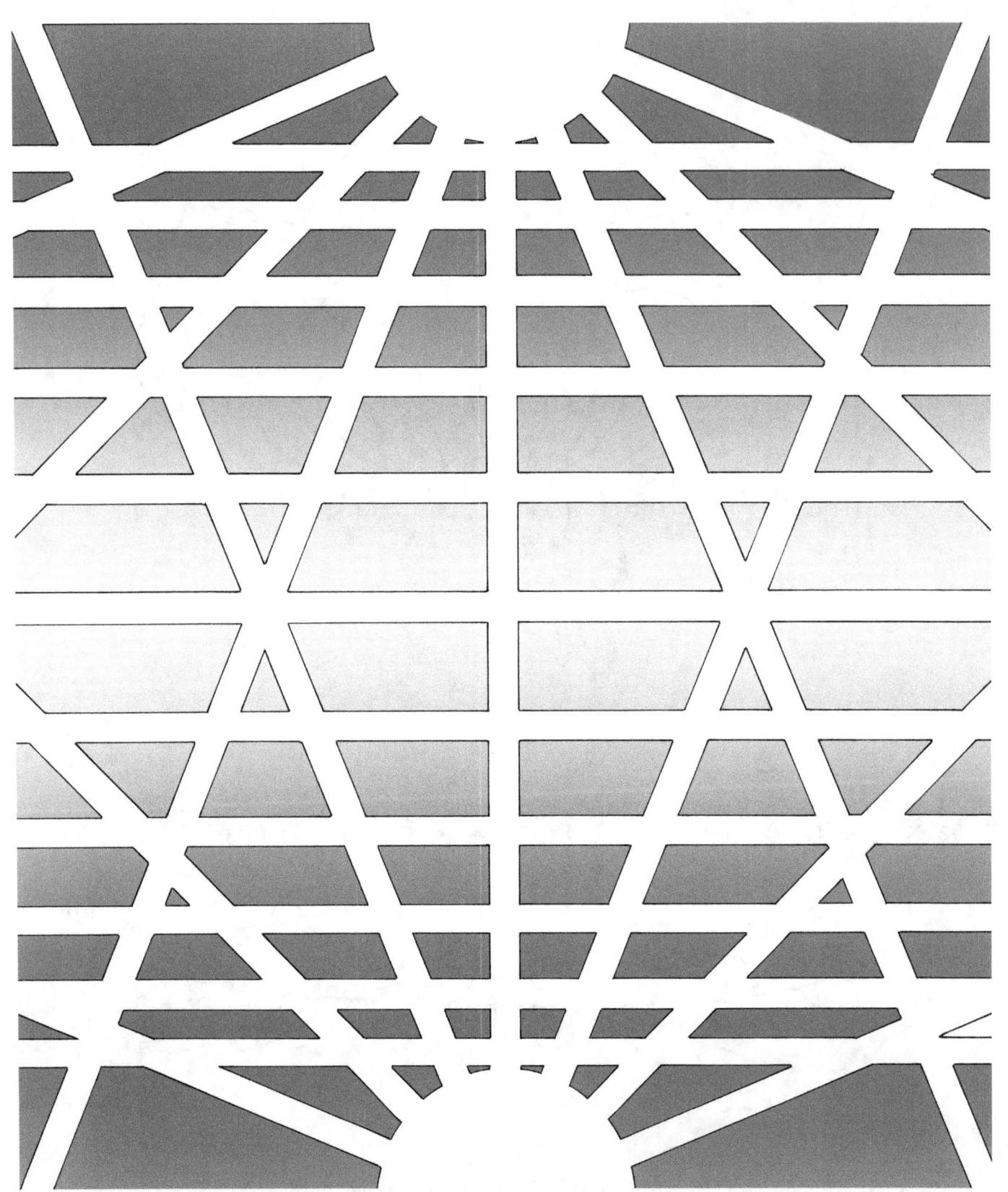

OP-ART - ink - pen - toned in Photoshop

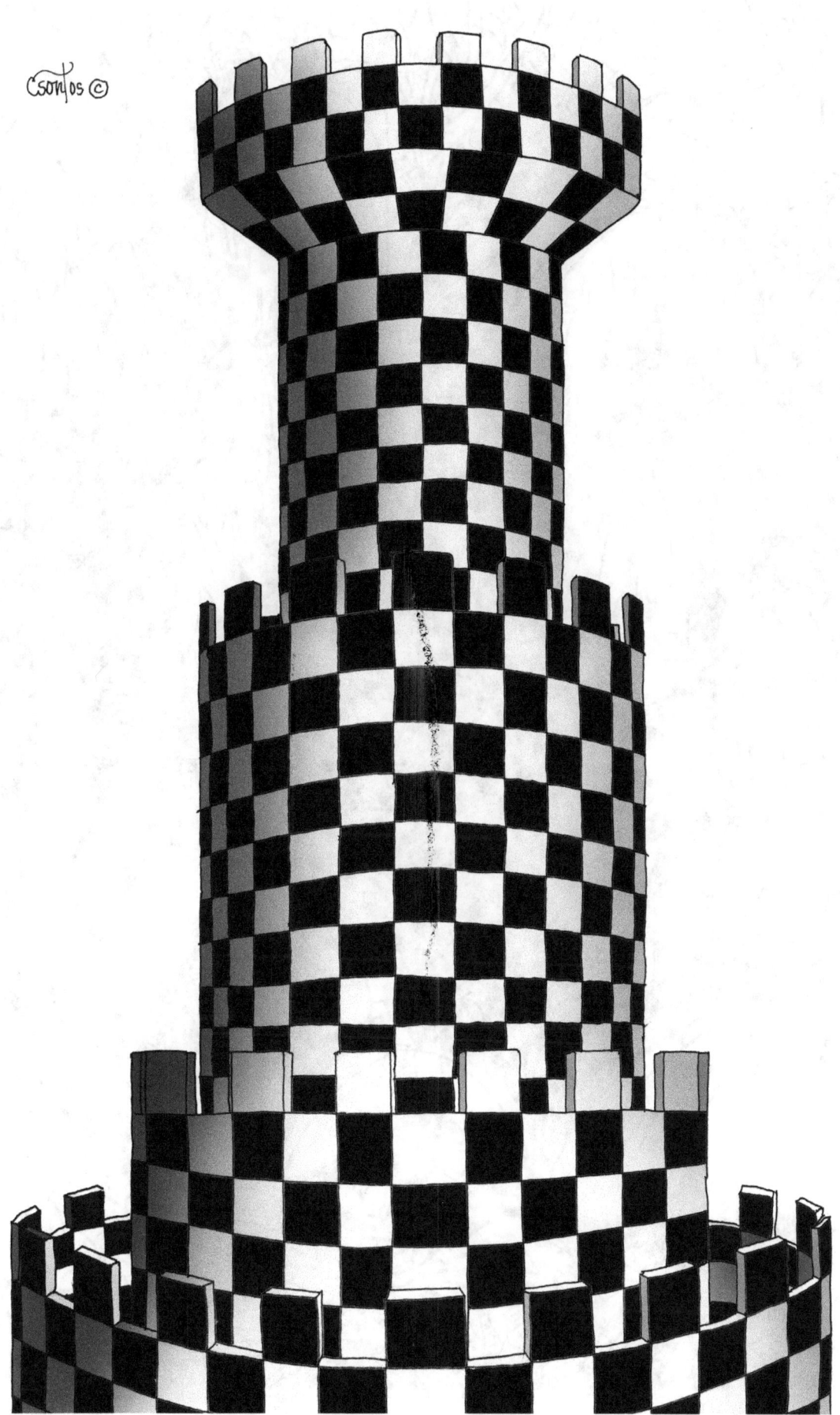

THE CASTLE WHERE THEY PLAY CHESS - ink - pen - Photoshop

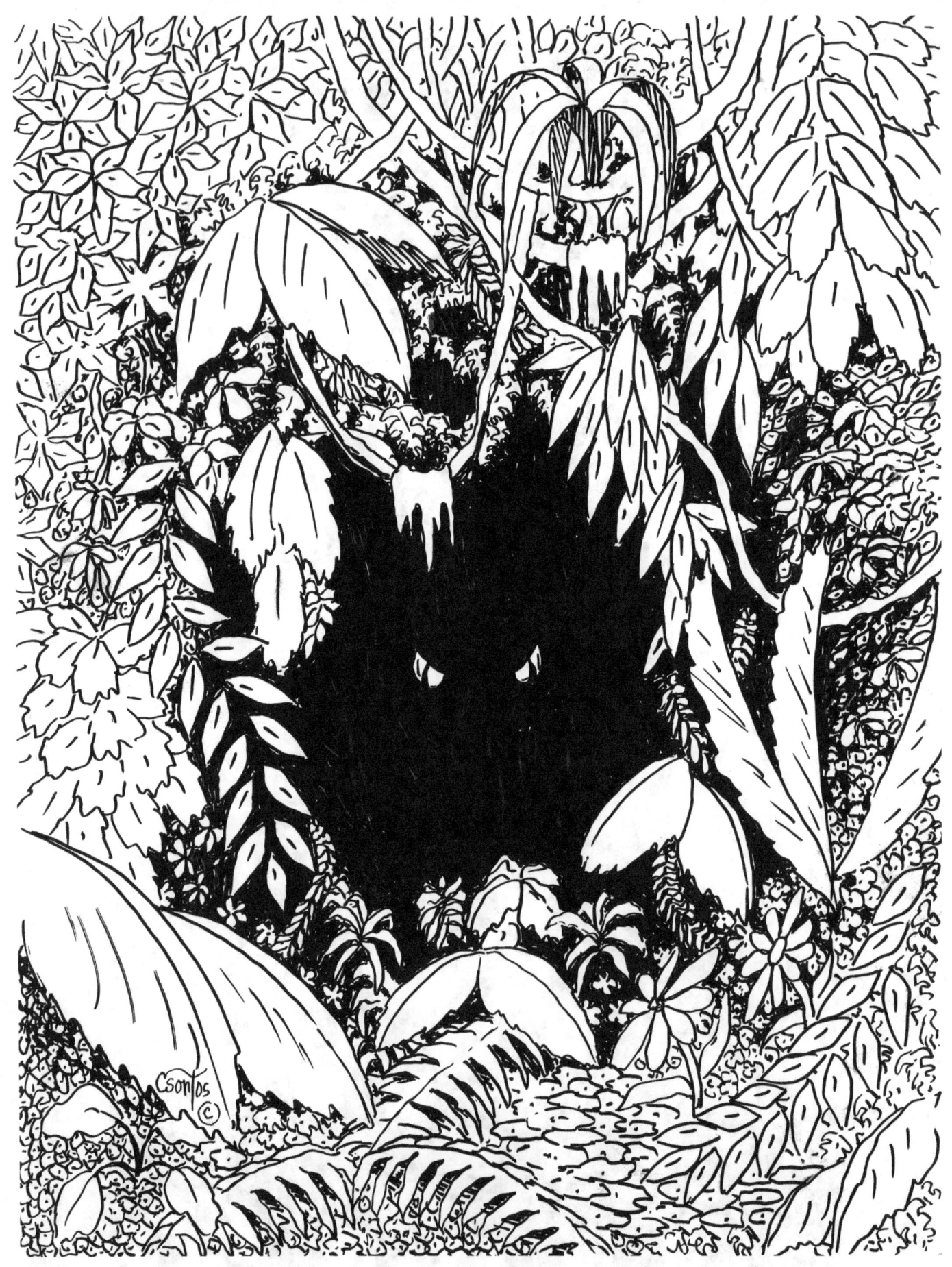

PEEK A BOO - ink - fine tip marker & brush

Landscapes & Seascapes

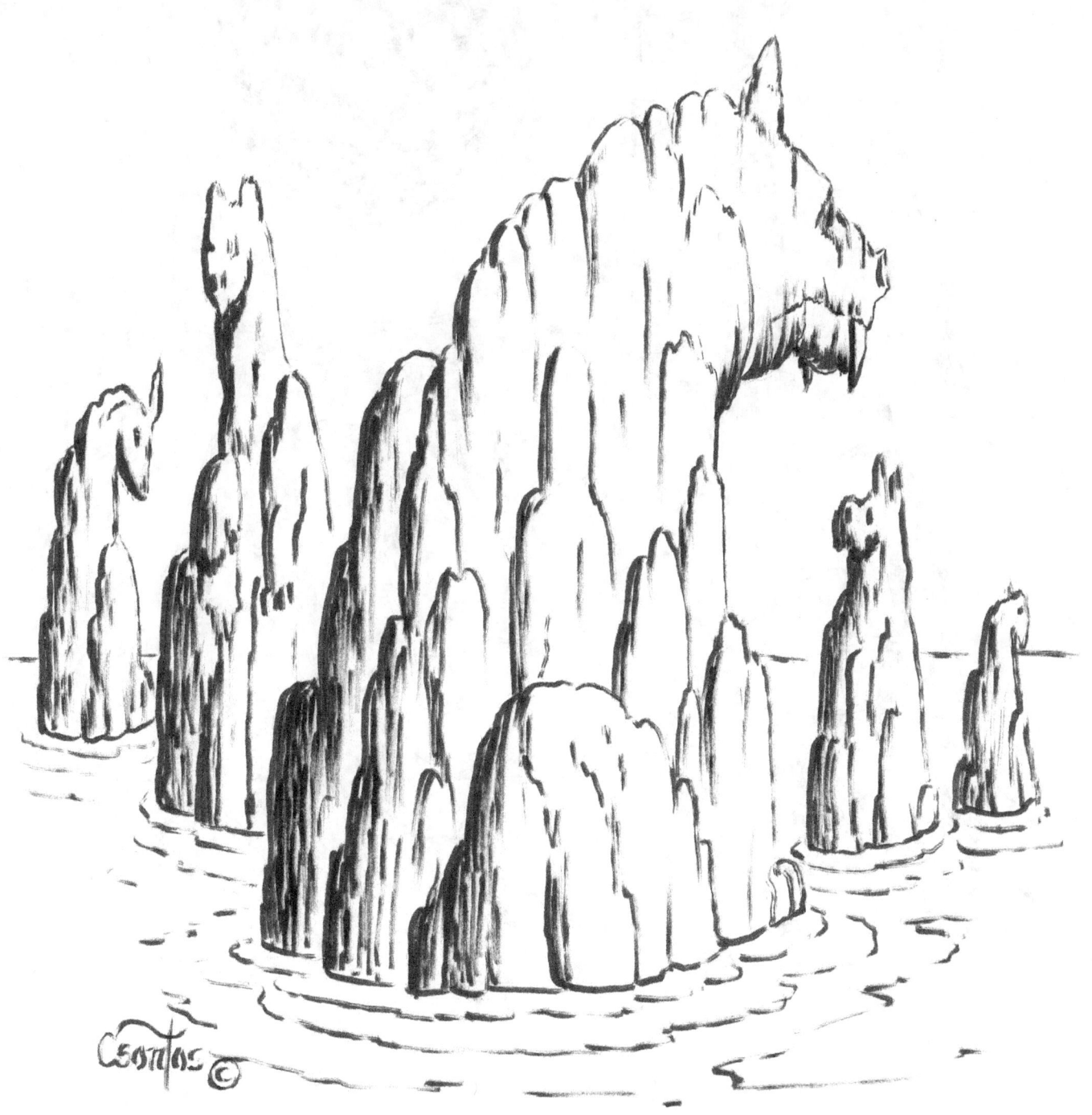

STONE CRITTERS - ink - brush

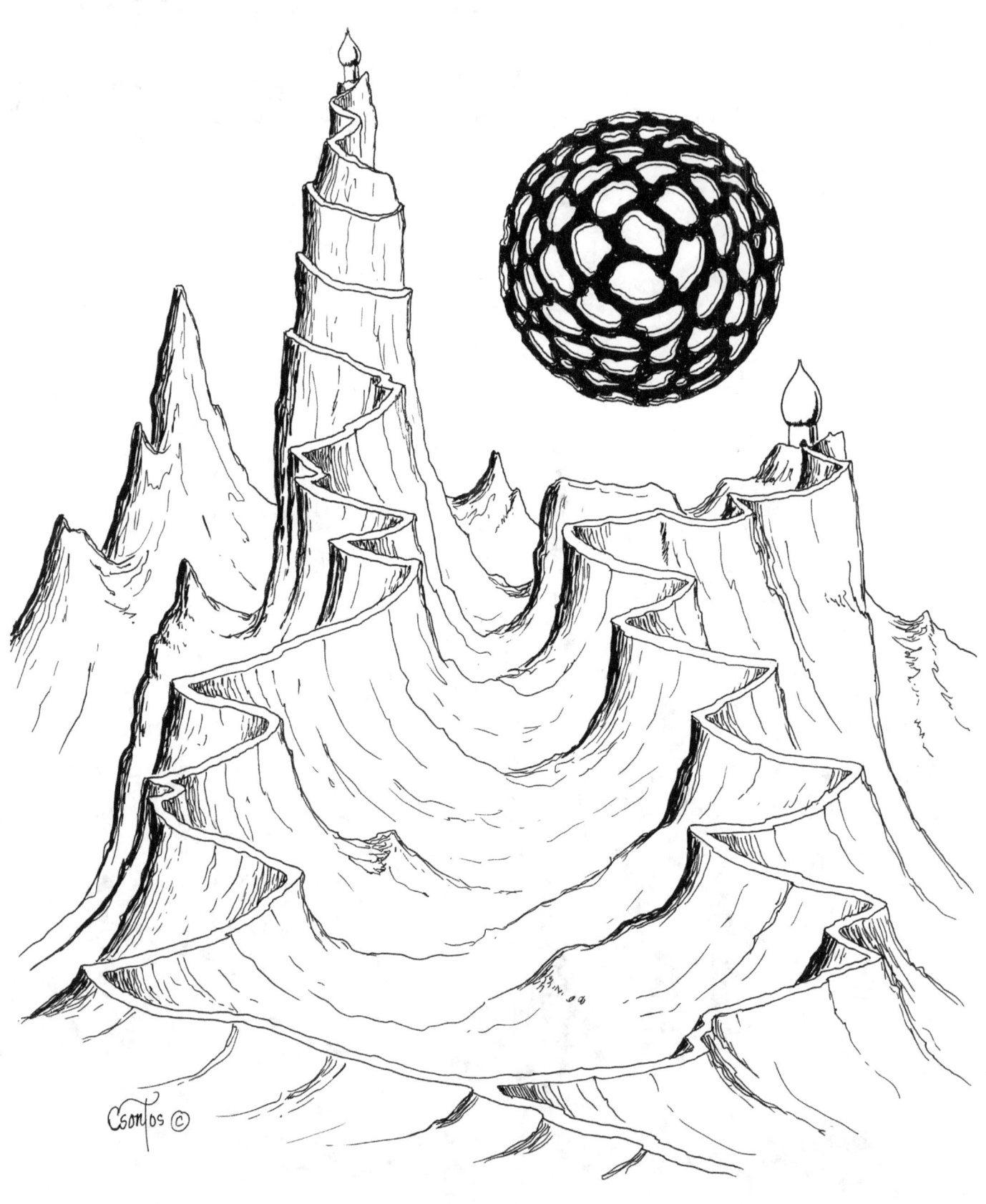

SWITCHBACKS - ink - pen & fine tip marker

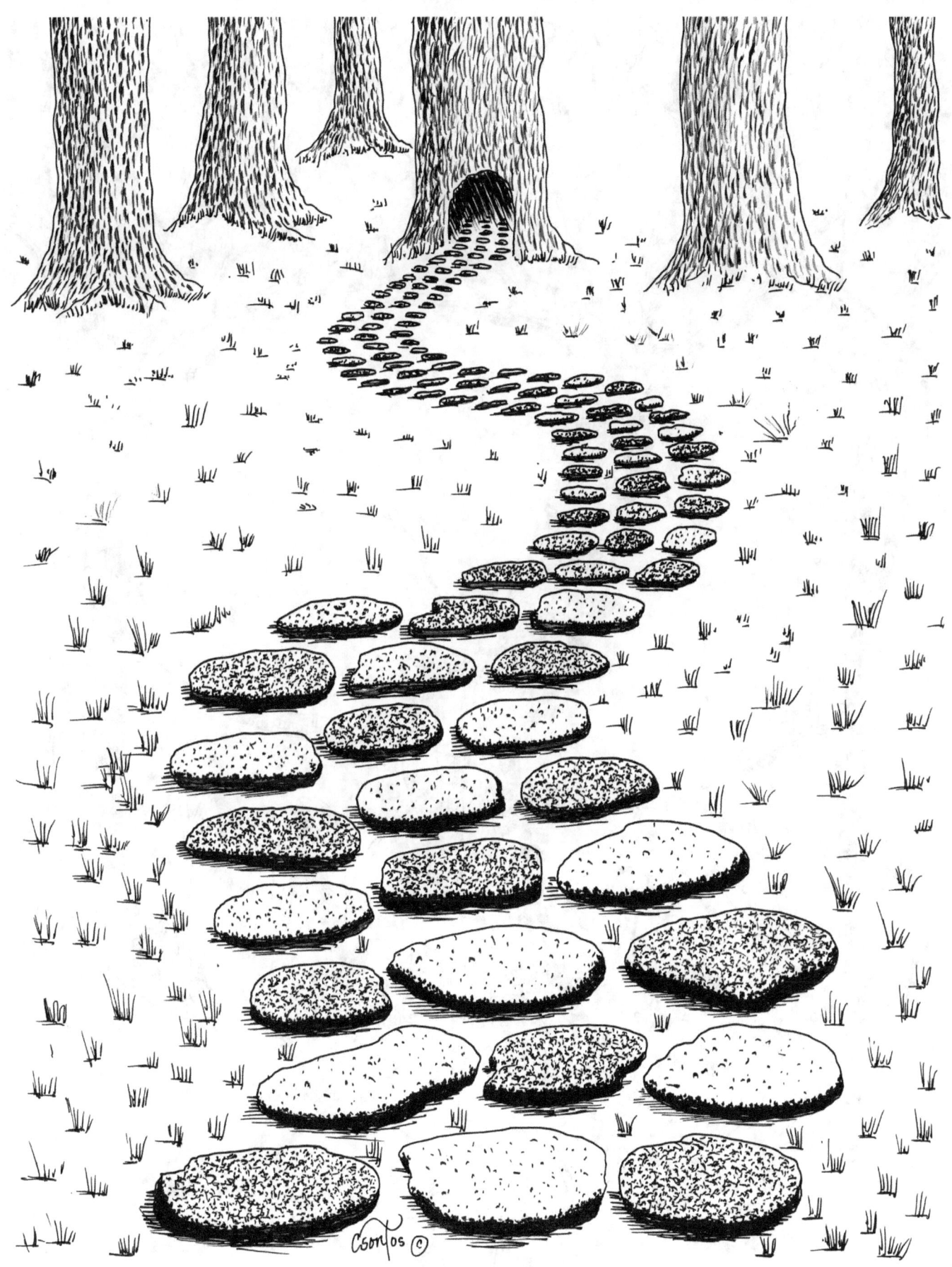

THE PATH - ink - pen & brush

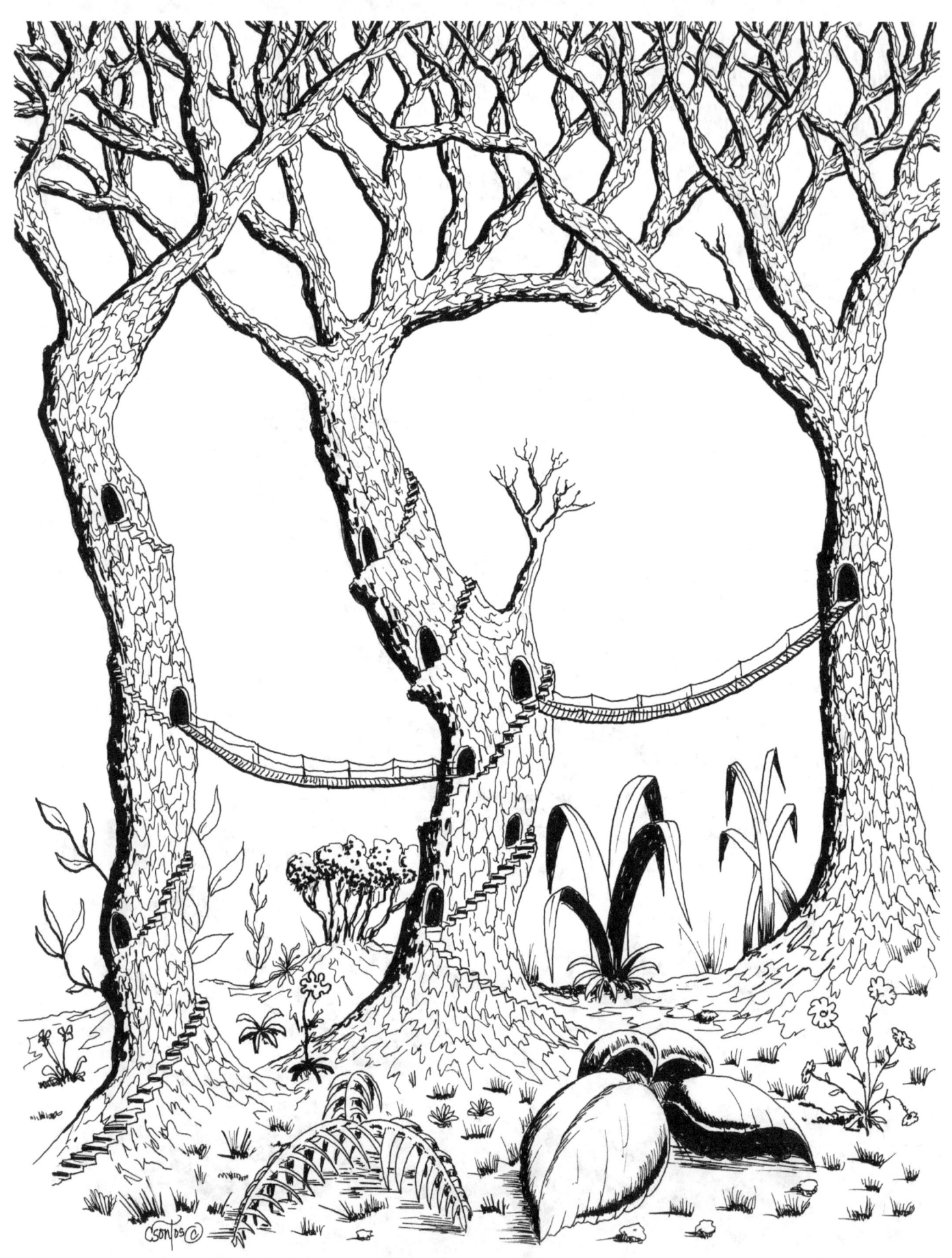

TREE DWELLERS - ink - pen & brush

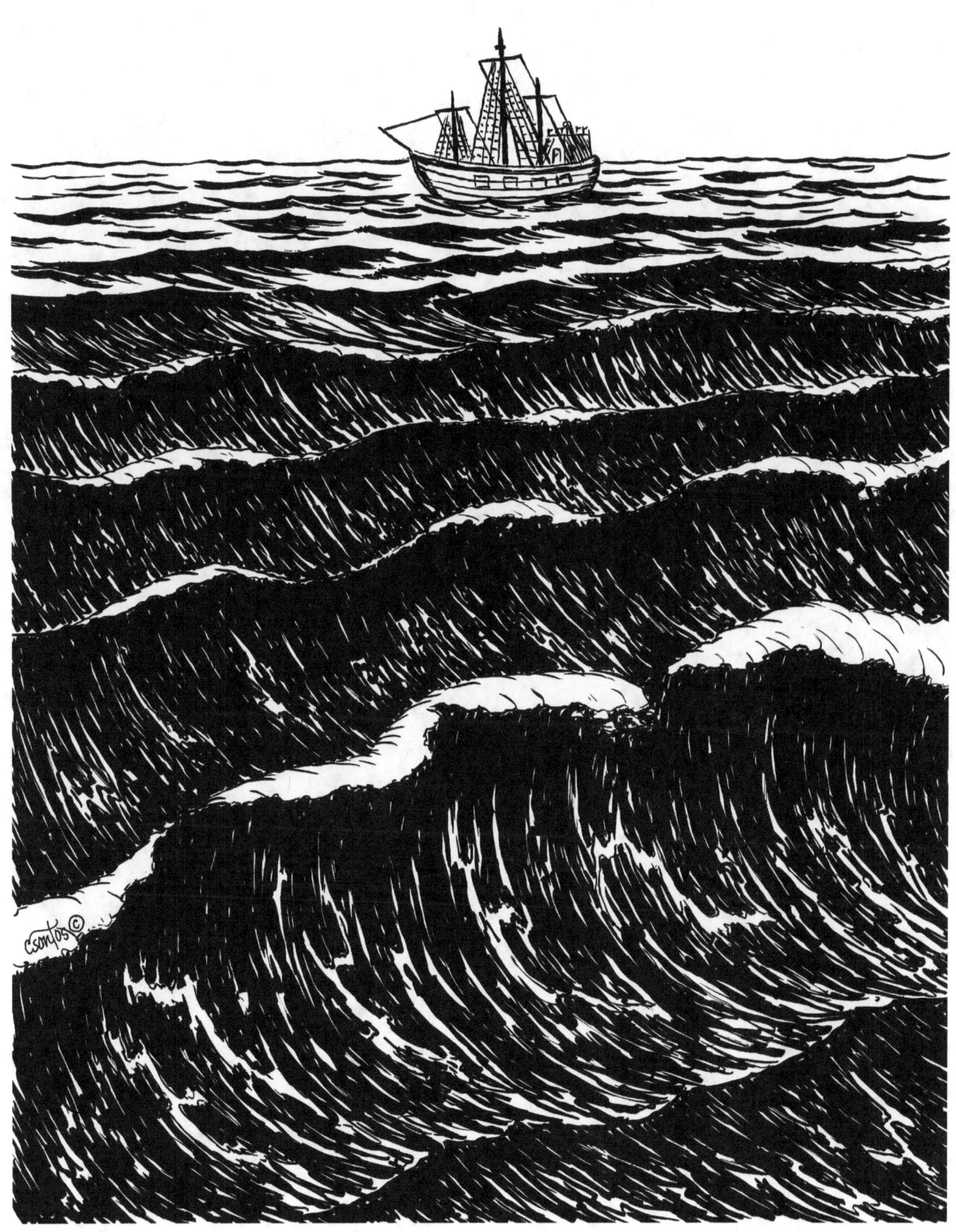

ANCHORED OFFSHORE - ink - pen & brush

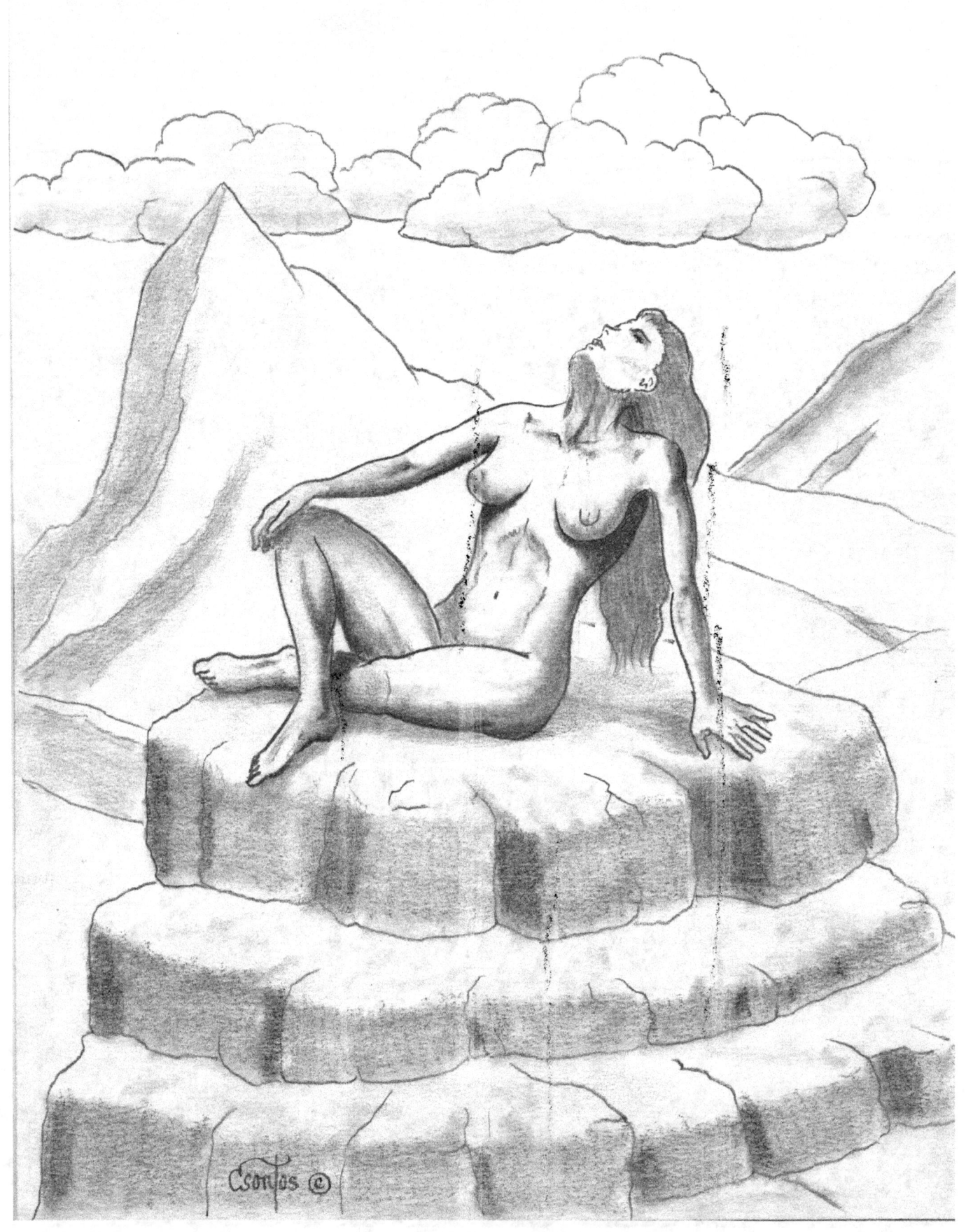

SUN BATHING ROCK - pencil

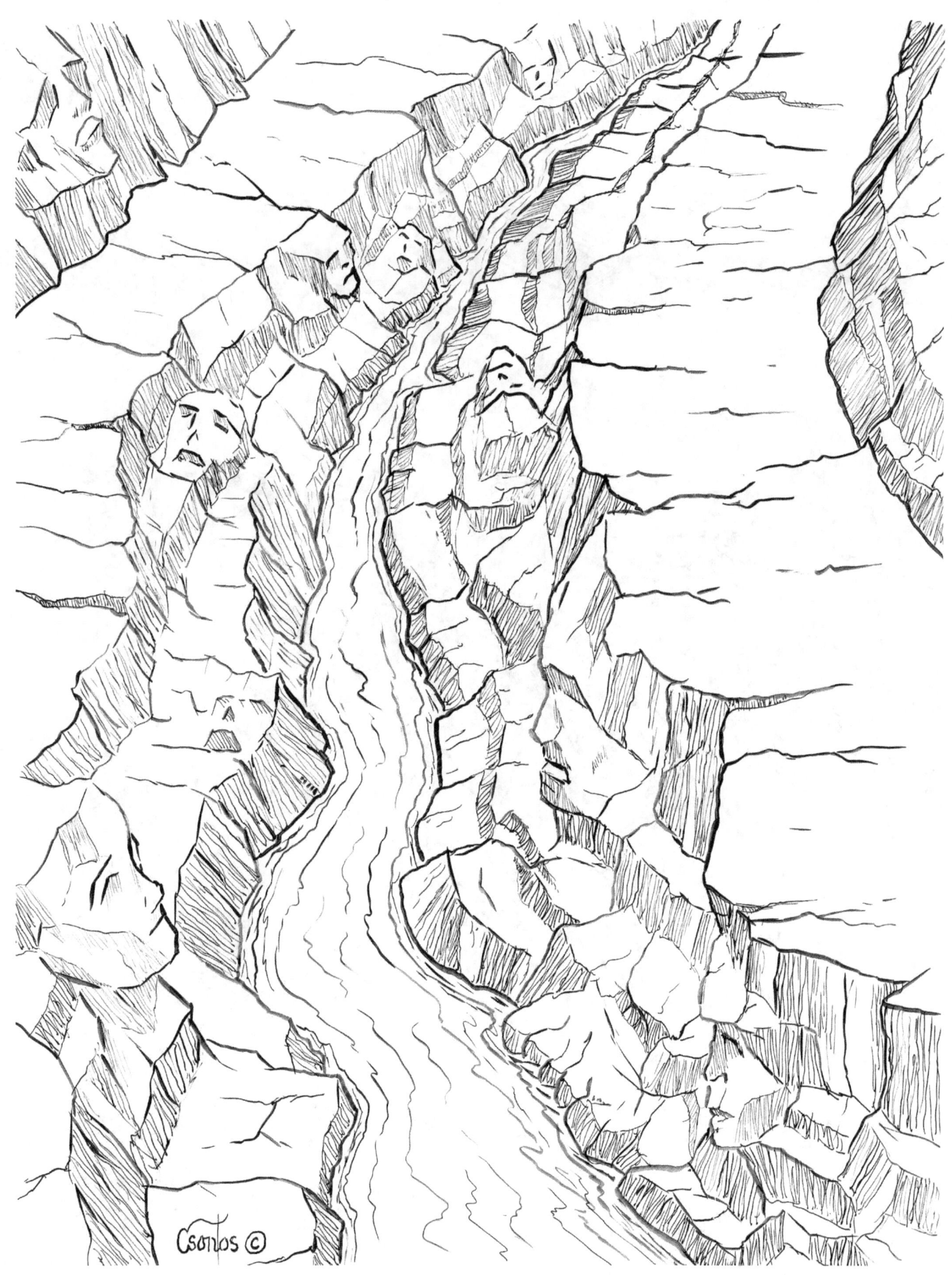

FACES IN THE CANYON - ink - pen

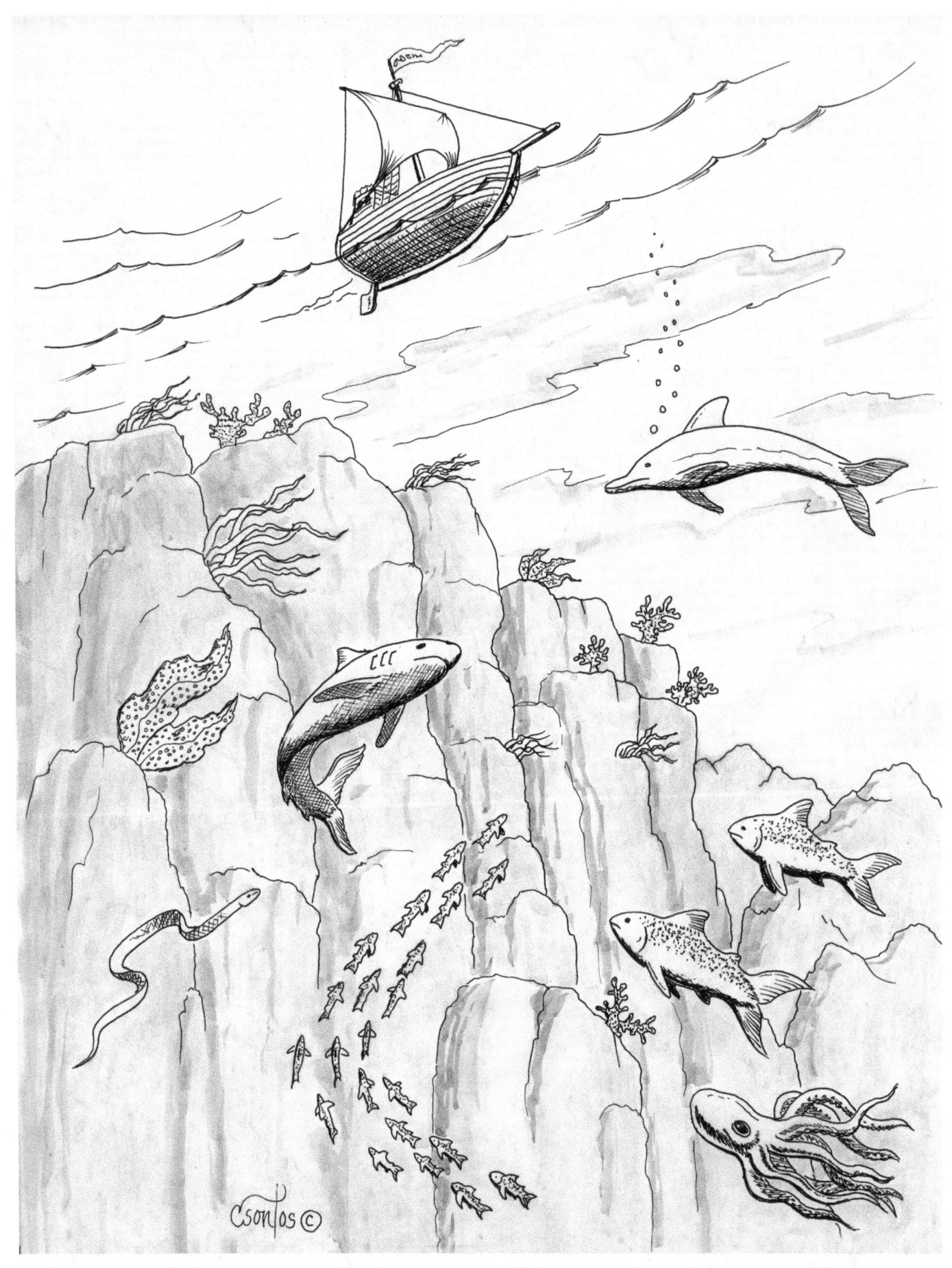

VIEW FROM BELOW - ink & ink wash - pen & brush

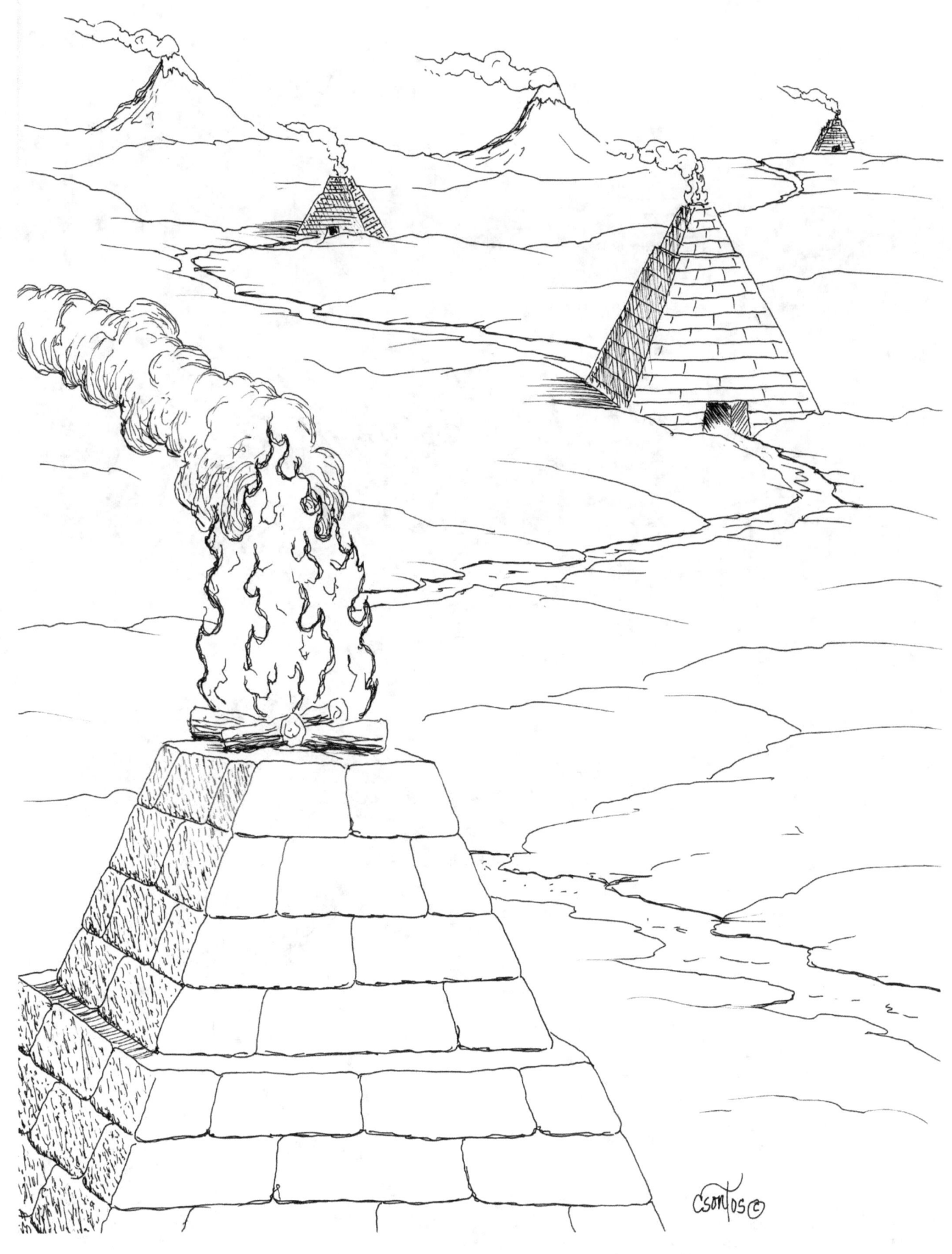

SIGNAL FIRES - ink - pen

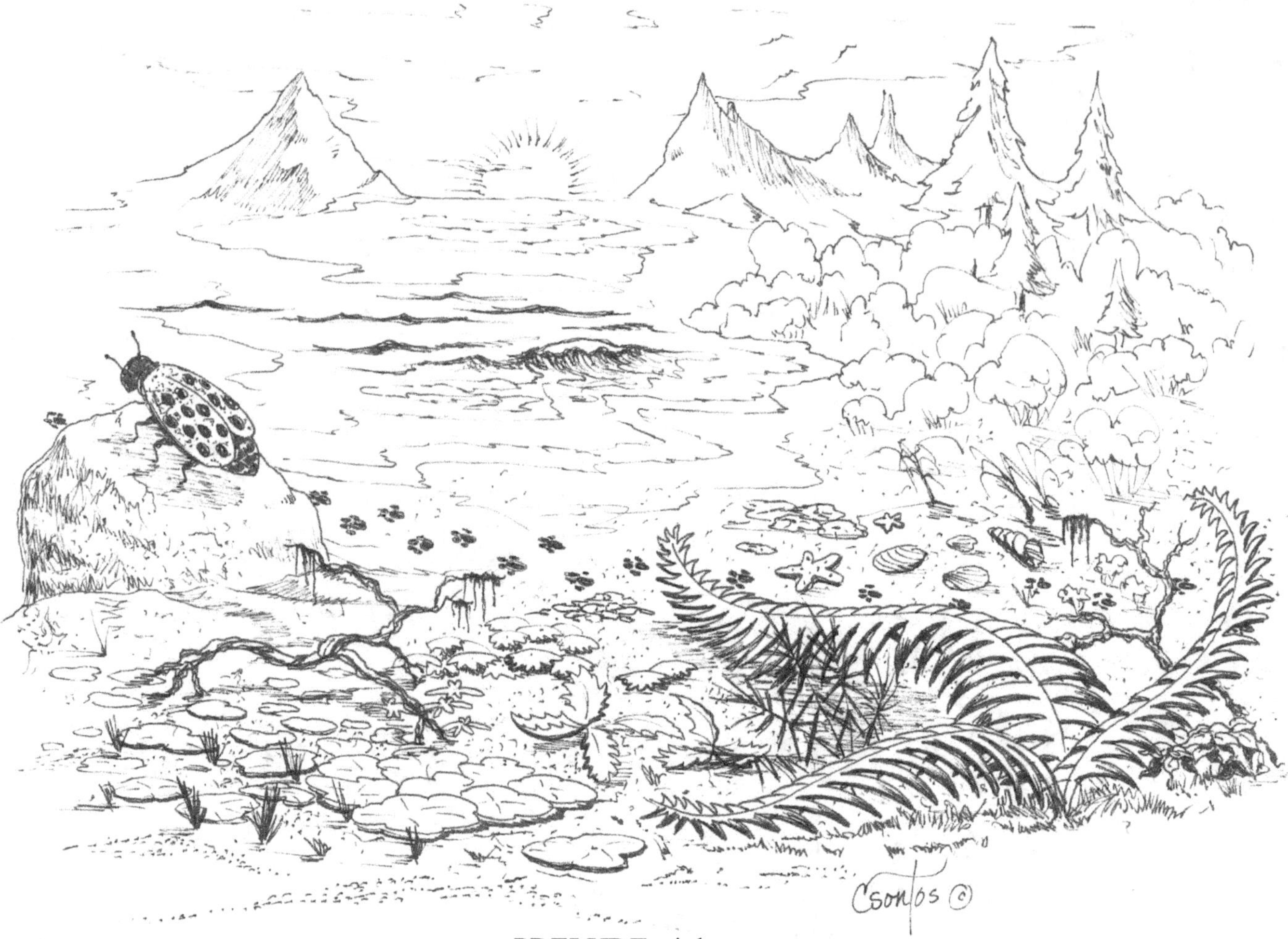

PRELUDE - ink - pen

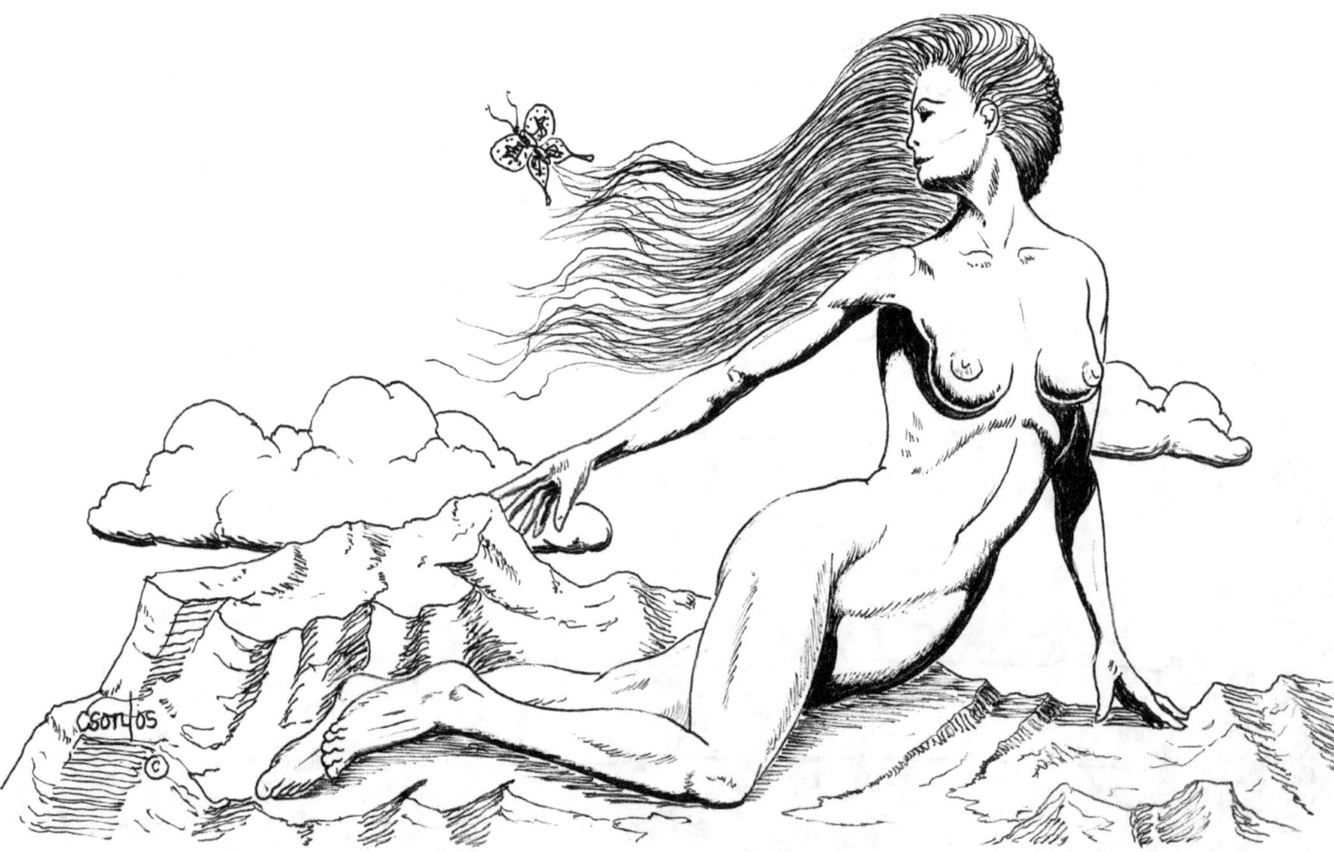

TAKING IN THE BREEZE - ink - pen

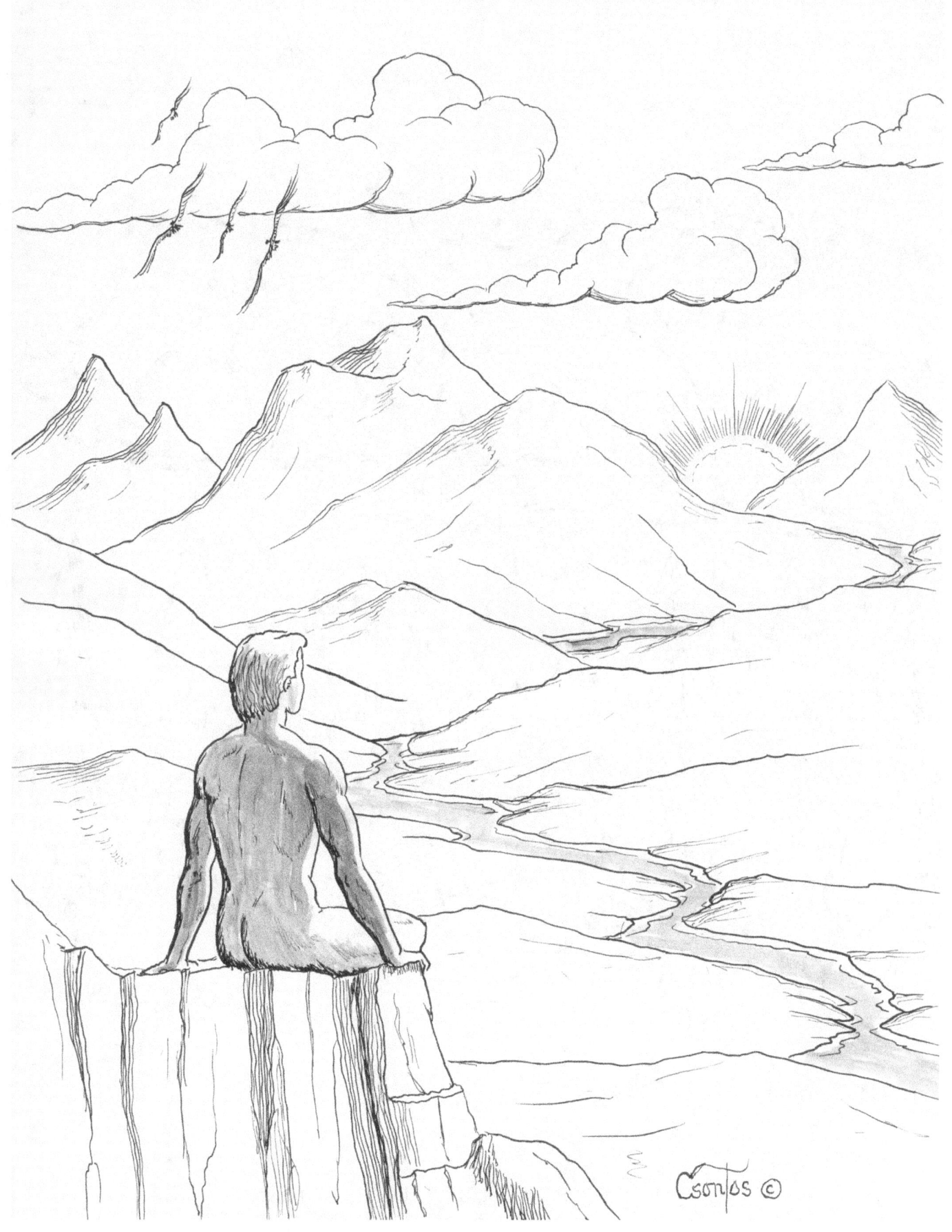

WATCHING THE SUNSET - ink & ink wash - pen & brush

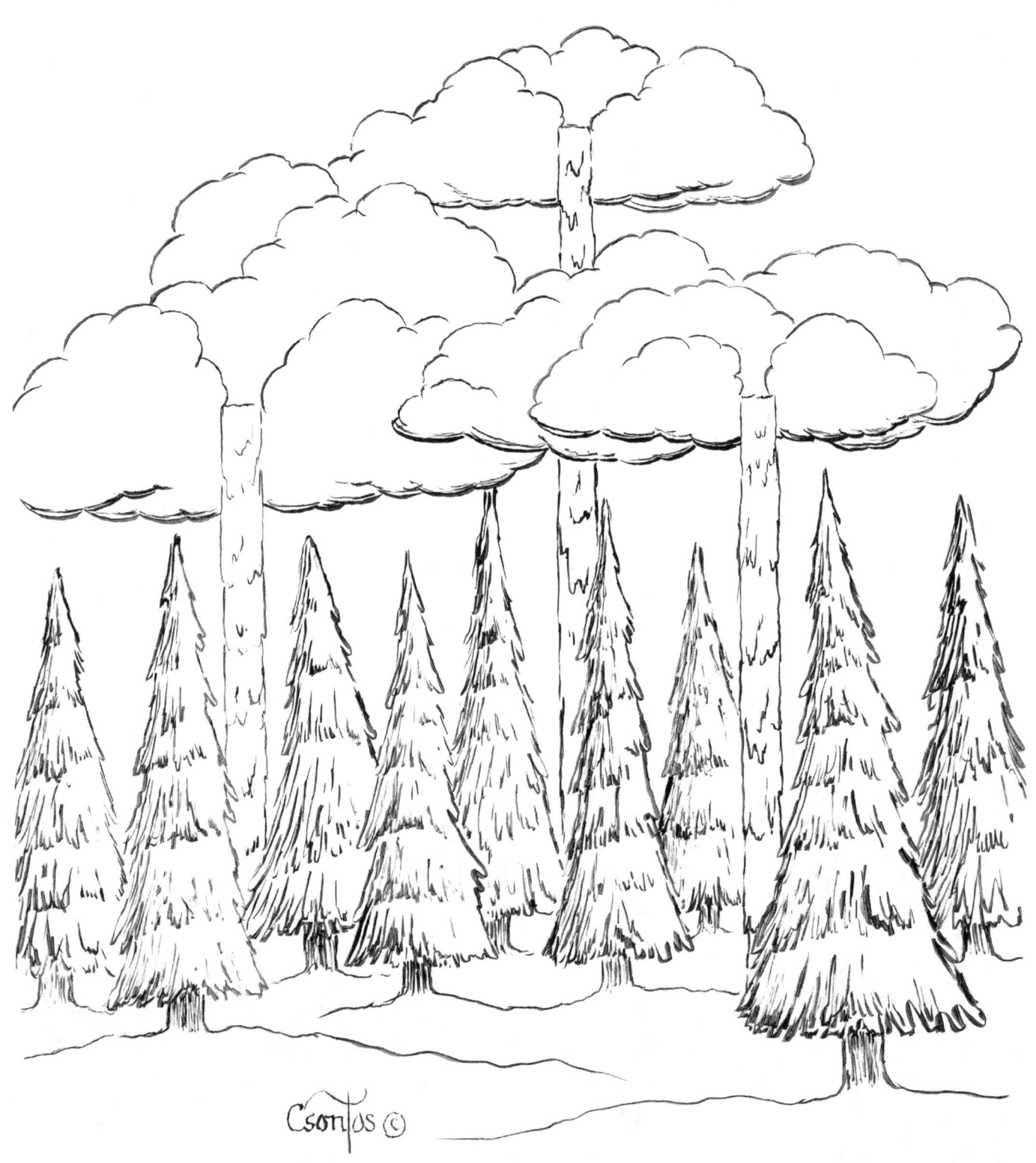

WATERING THE BIG TREES - ink - pen & brush

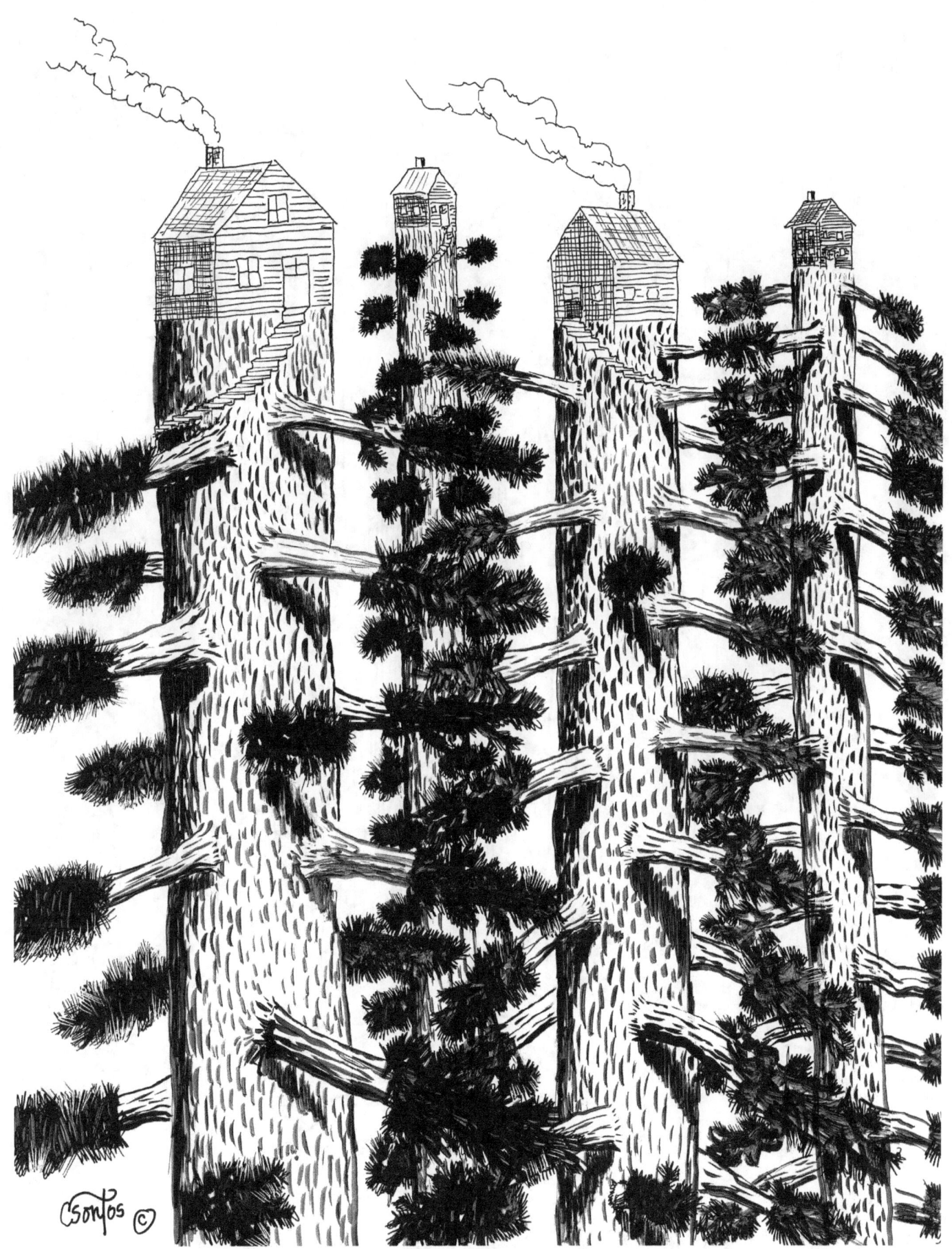

TREE HOUSES - ink - pen & brush

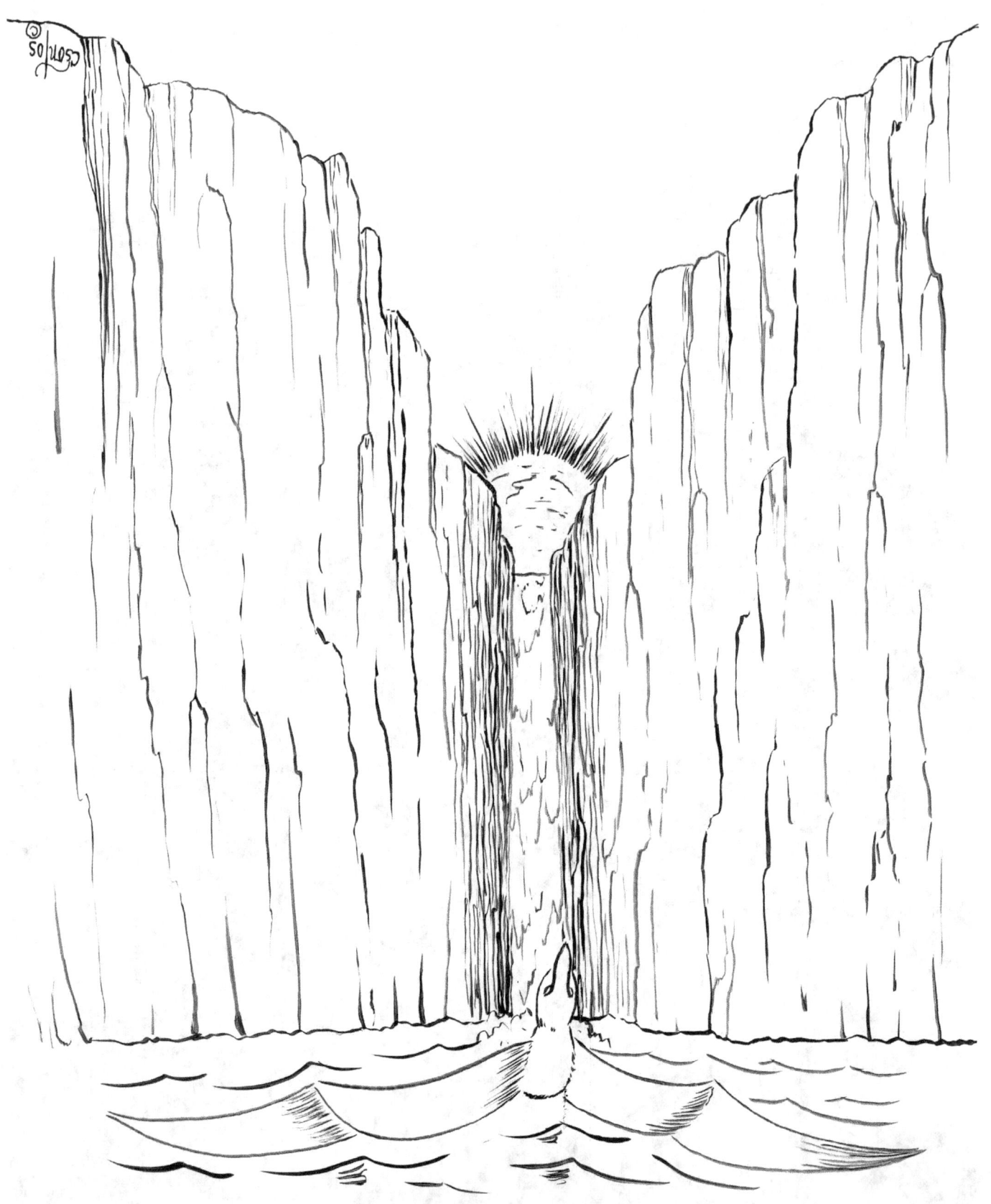

CANYON FALLS - ink - pen & brush

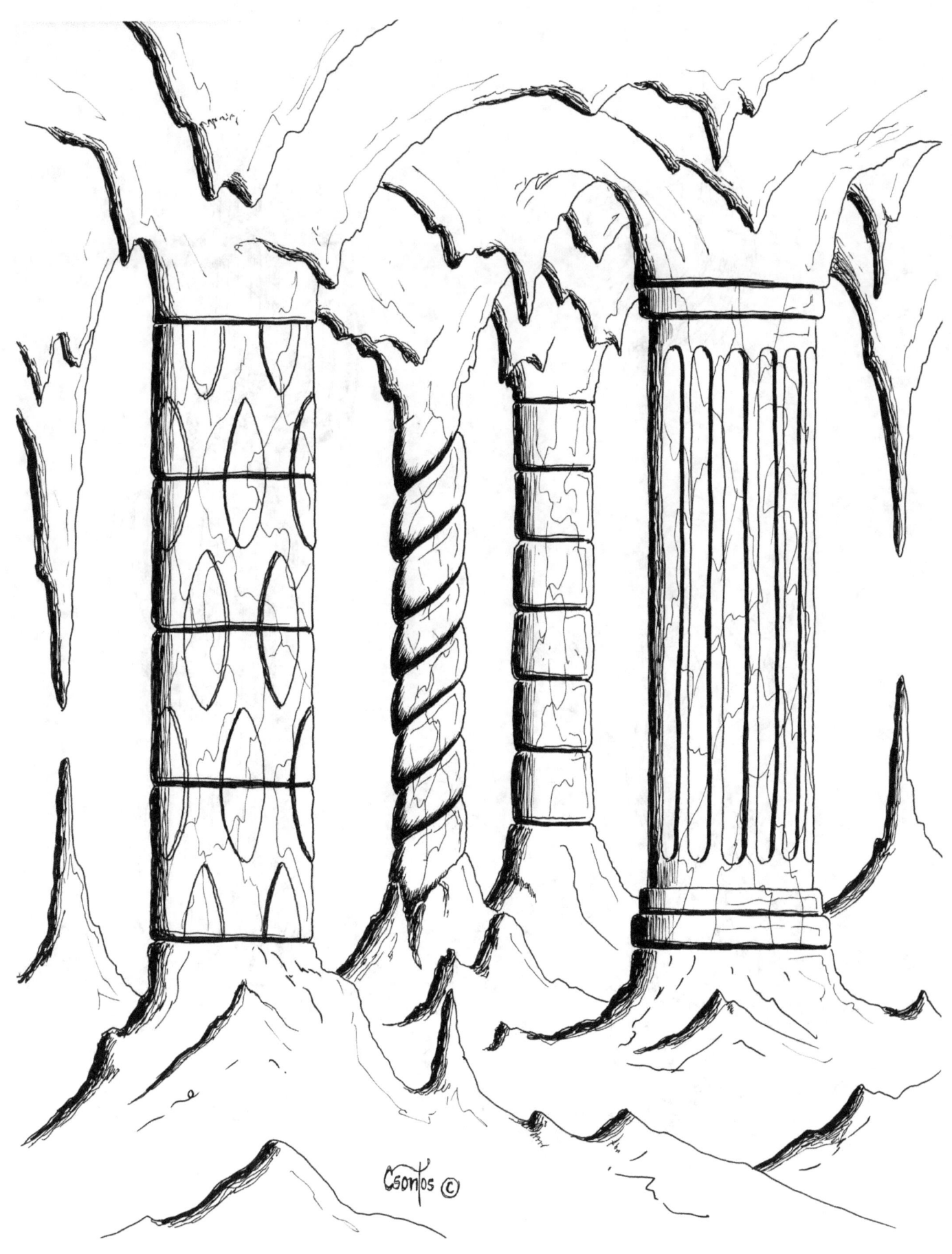

COLUMNS - ink - pen & fine tip marker

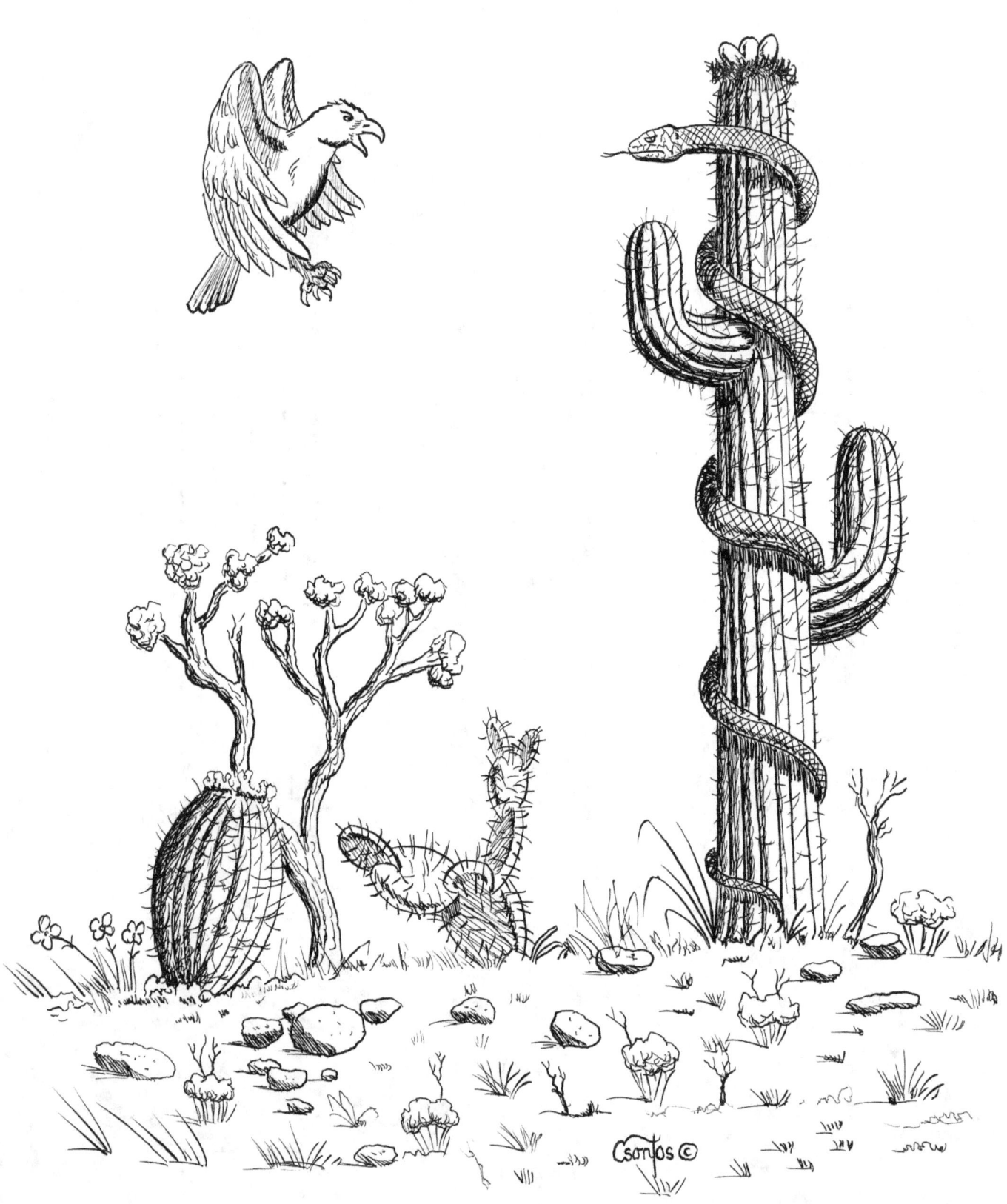

STICKY SITUATION - ink - pen

Book Illustrations

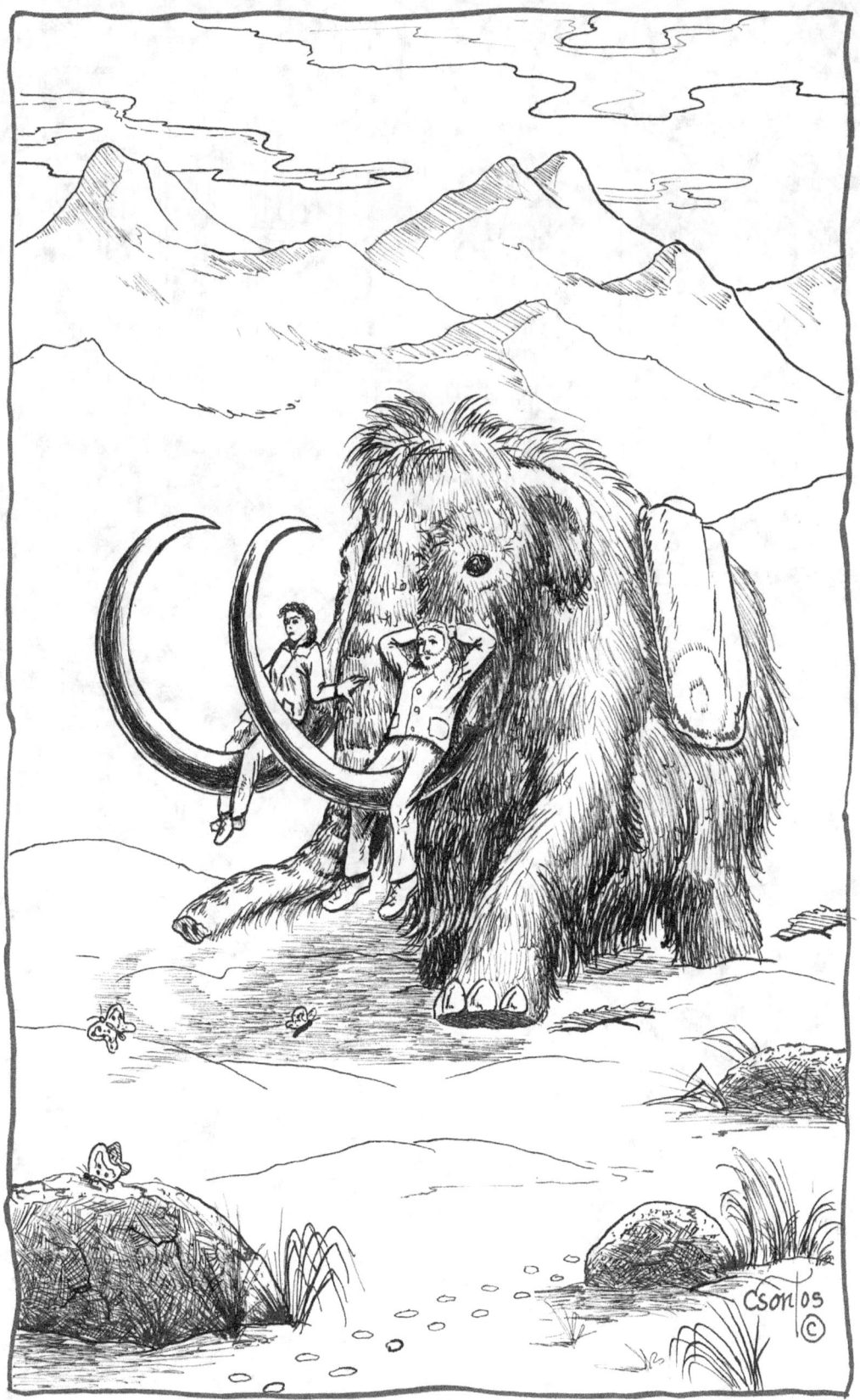

HITCHIN'' A RIDE - ink - pen

This section are some of the illustrations I did for the science fiction novel 'One Sided Doors'. I put a few others in my book 'The Art of Visualizing Black and White'. They were not created using the abstract sketching technique but I did have to visualize the scene after reading the section of text they referred to.

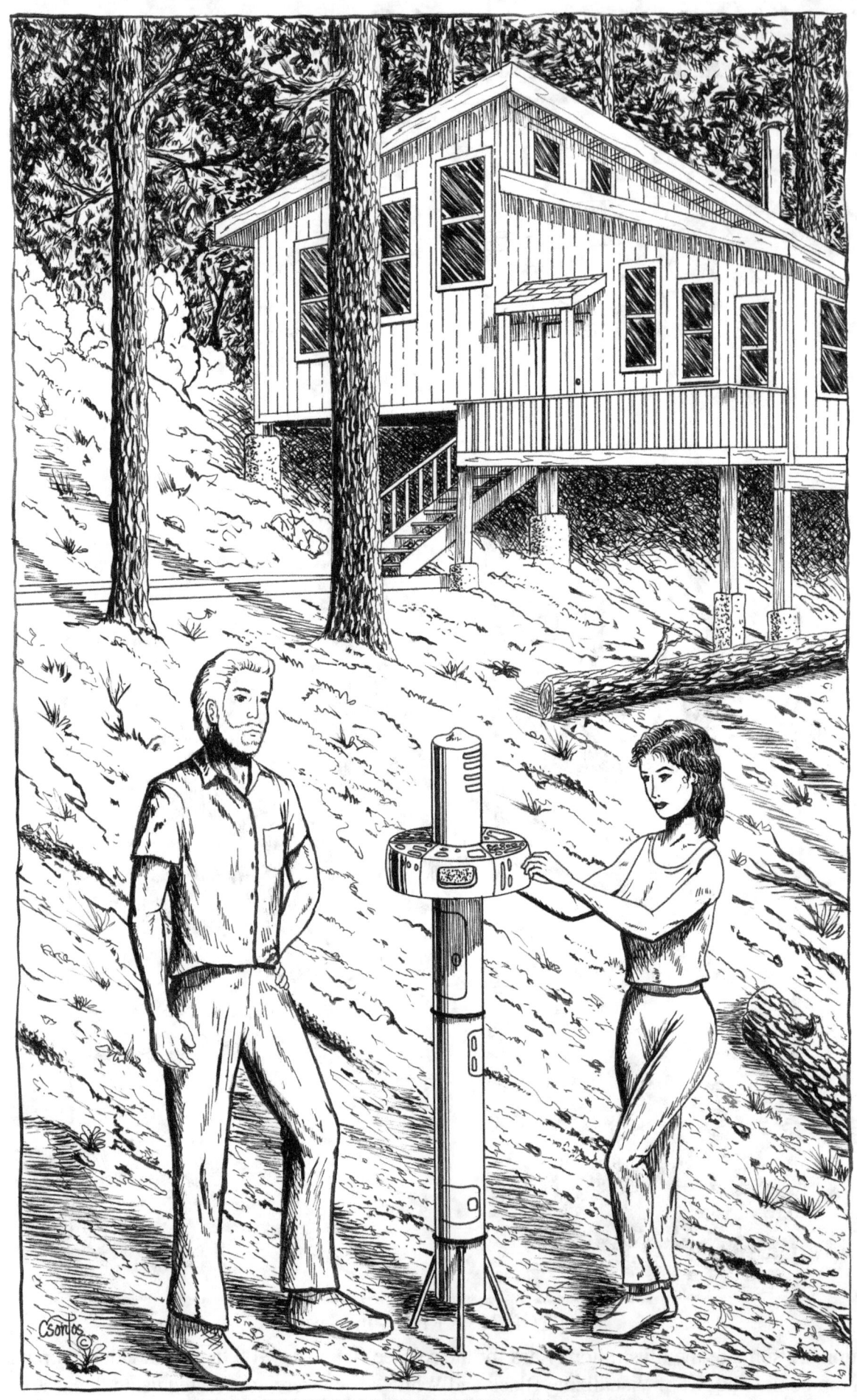

THE LADY FROM THE FUTURE - ink - pen & brush

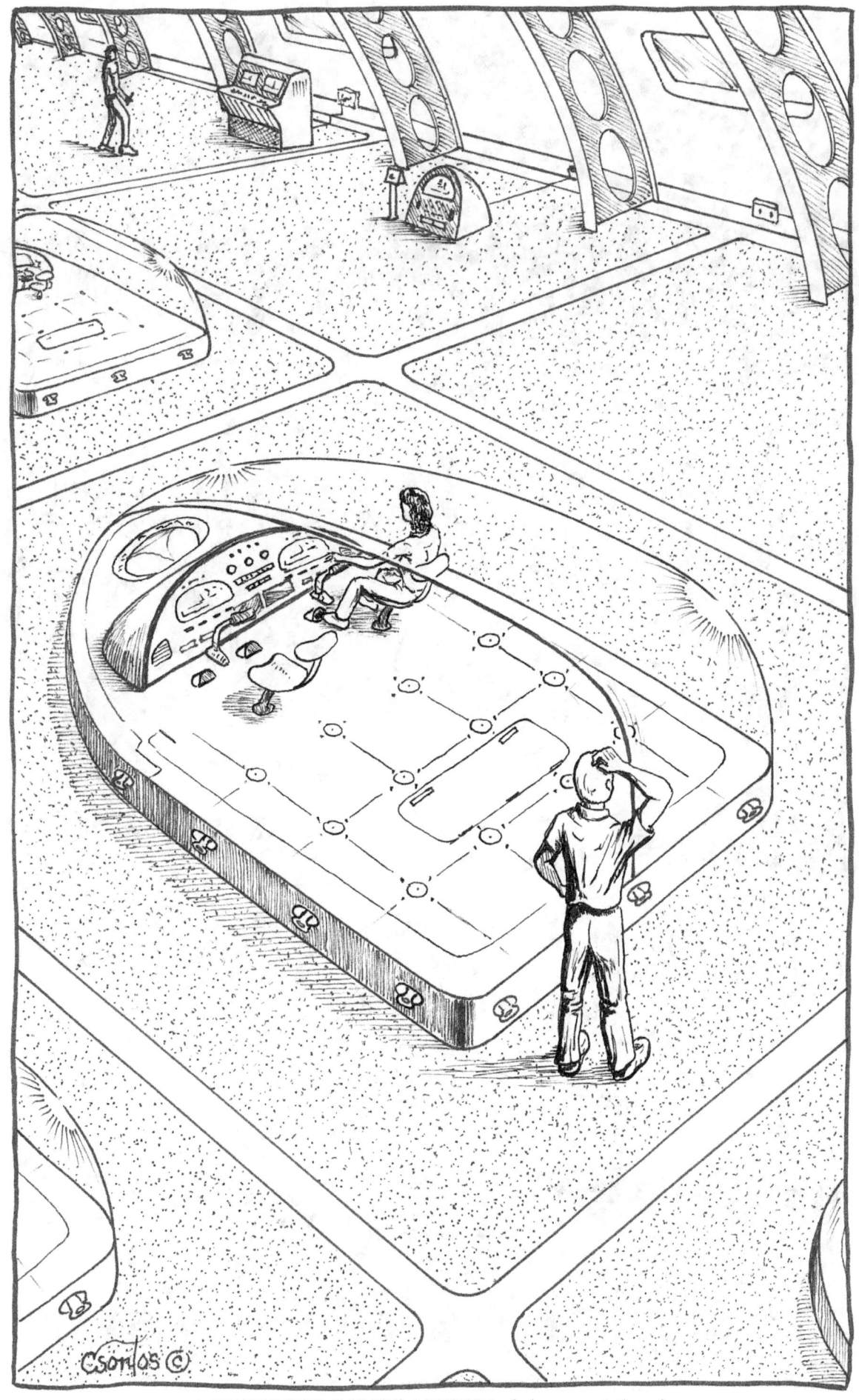

A PUZZLING CONTRAPTION - ink - pen & brush

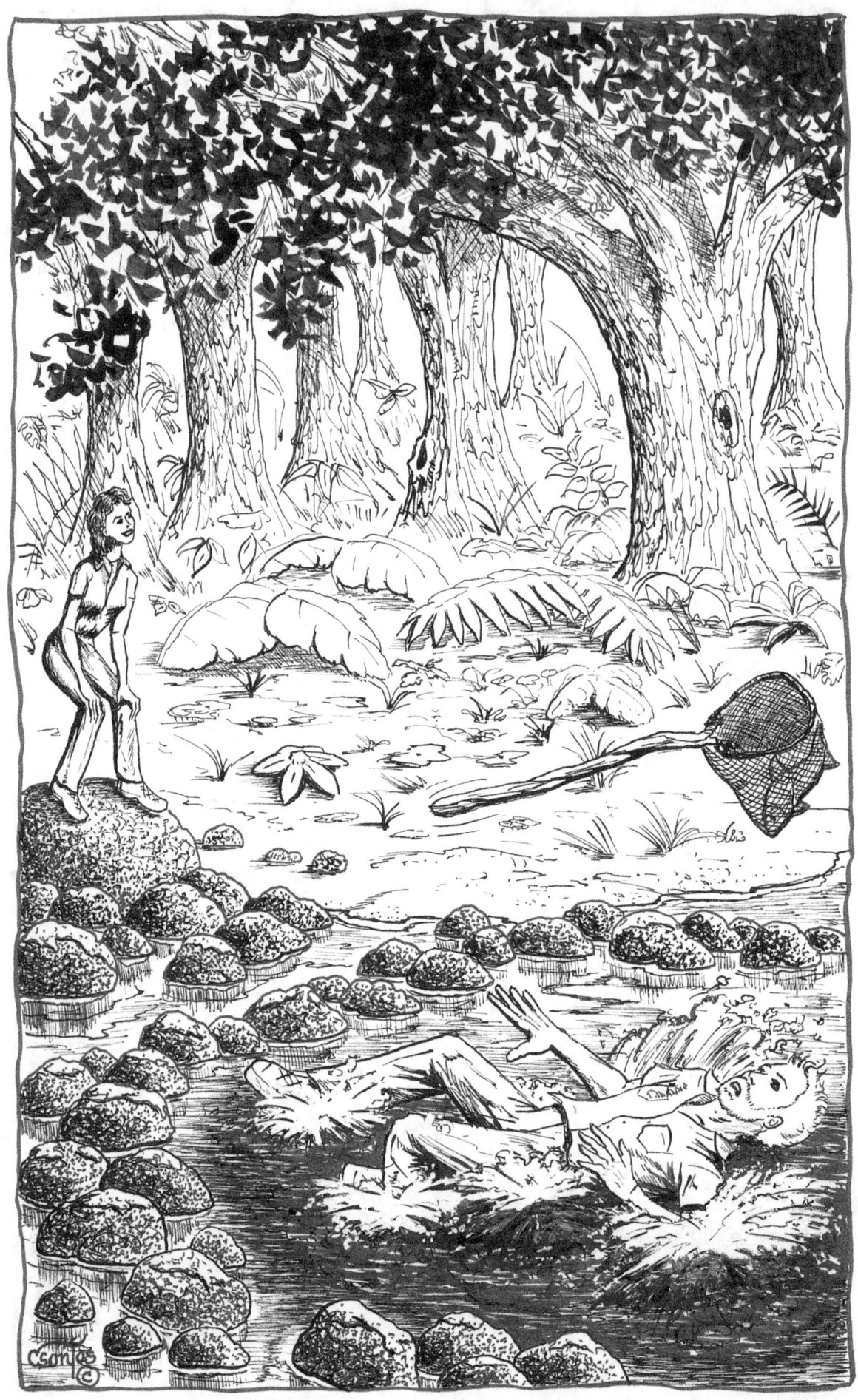

CATCHING A FISH - ink - pen & brush

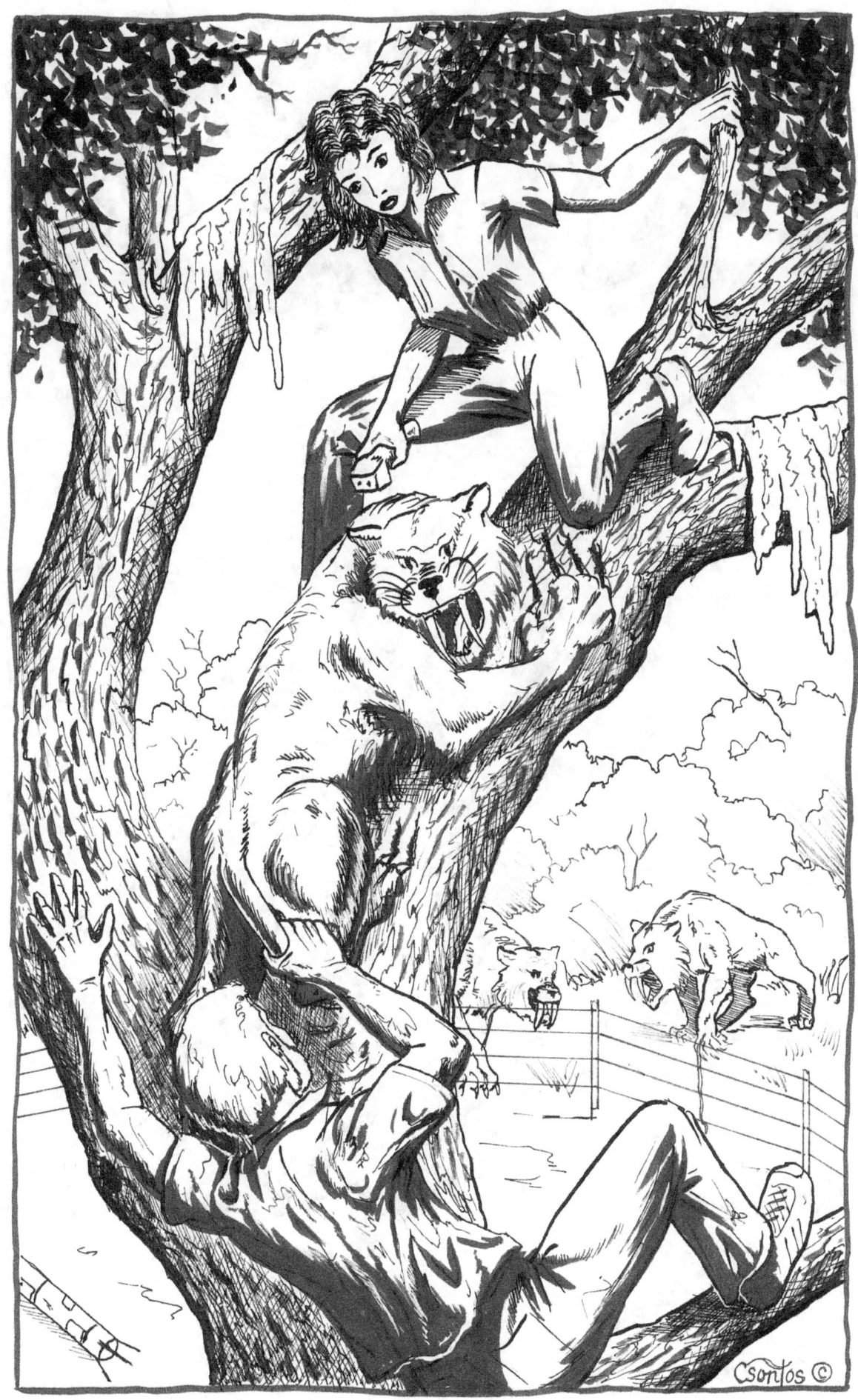

DISTRACTING THE SABER TOOTH - ink - pen & brush

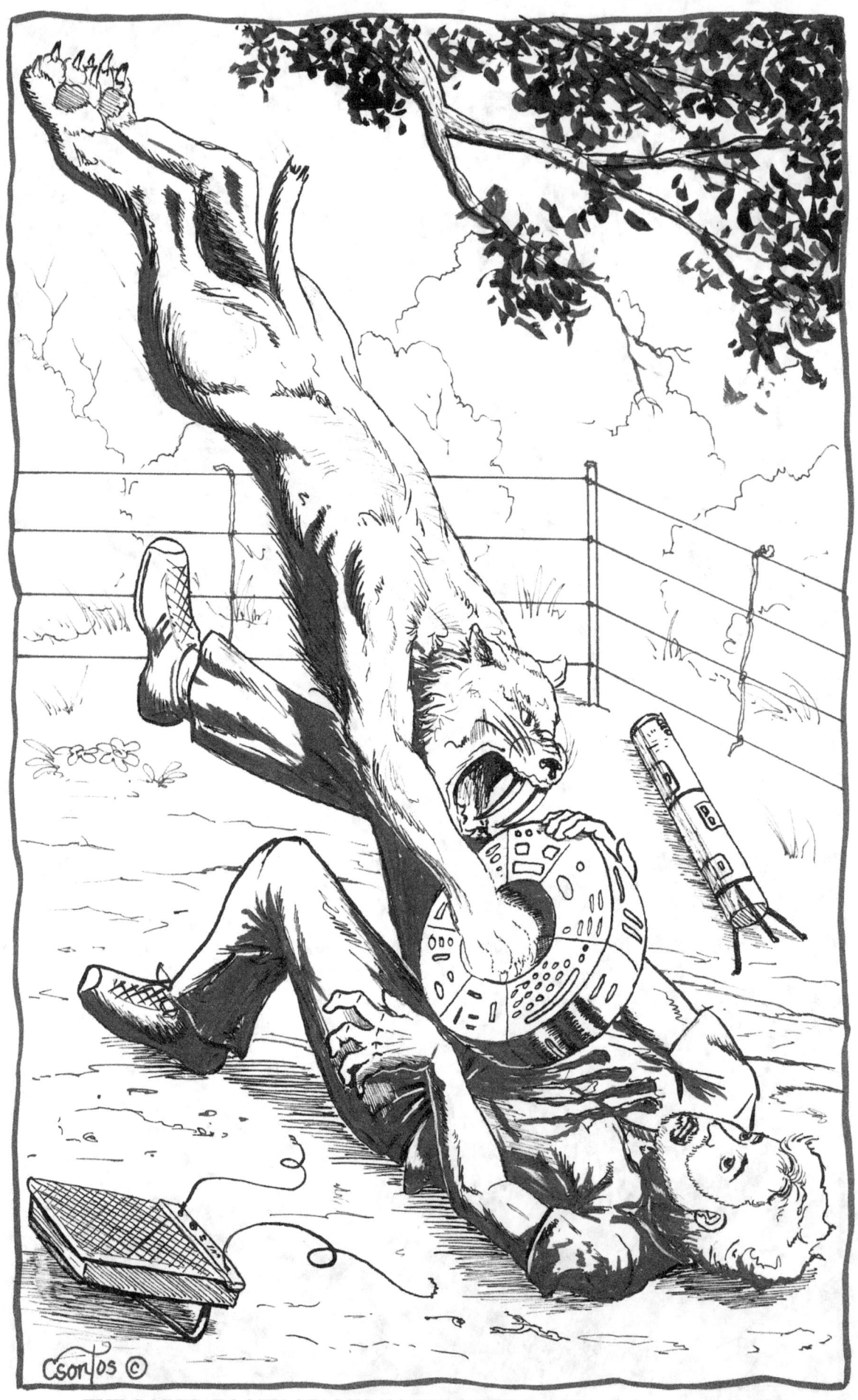

THE SABER TOOTH STARTS TO DEMATERIALIZE - ink - pen & brush

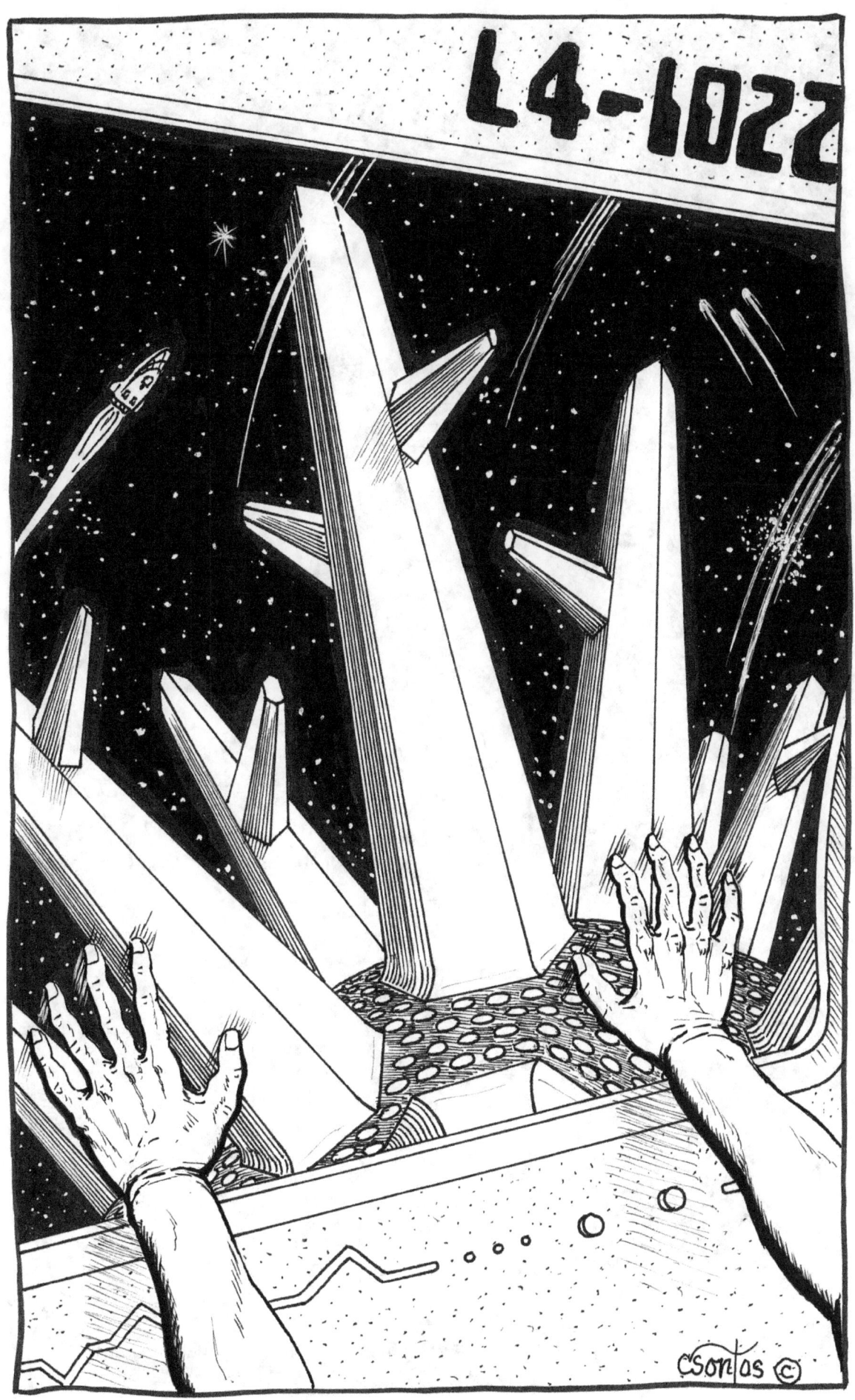

LOOKING OUT THE SPACE STATION WINDOW - ink - pen & brush

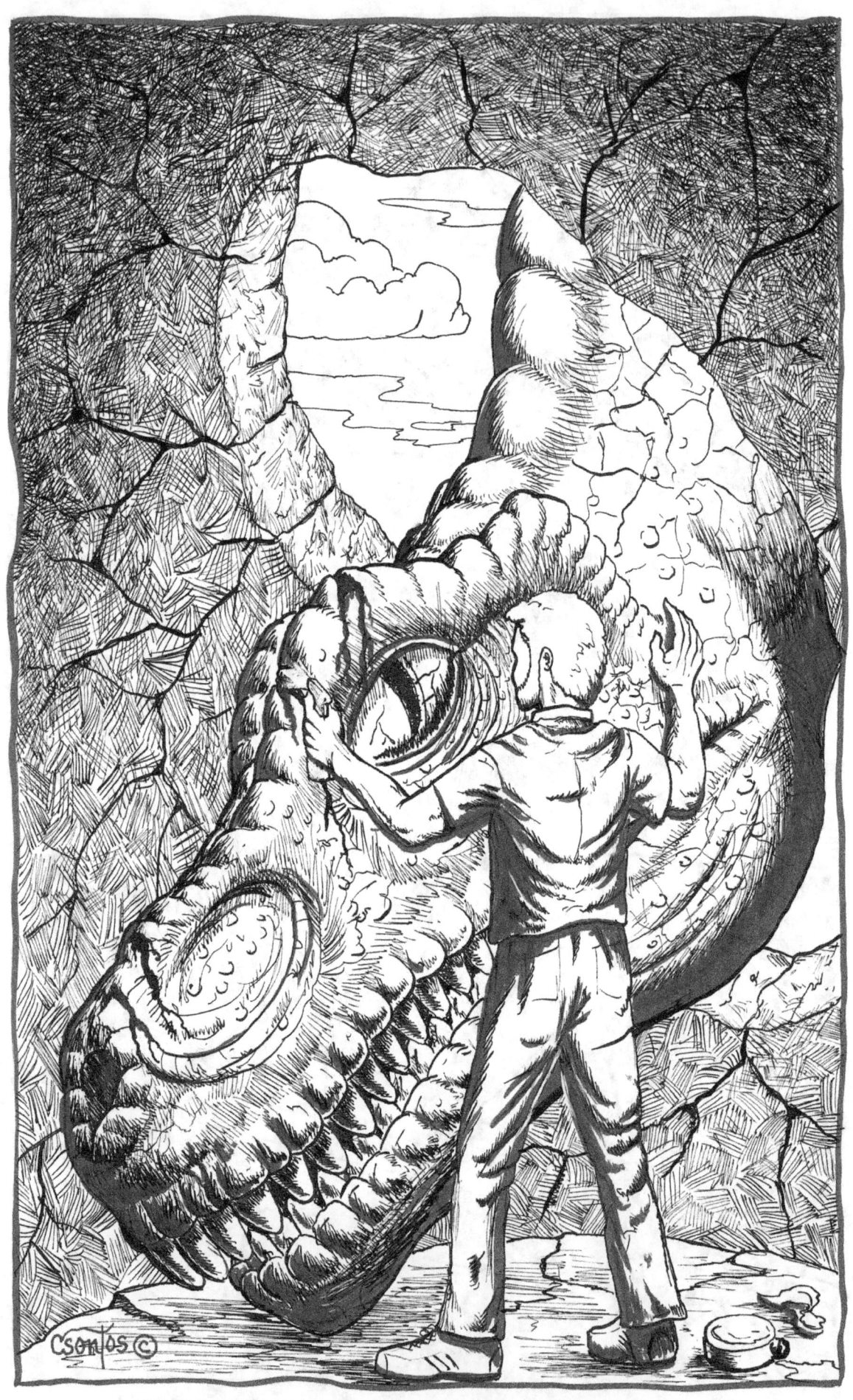

TENDING TO A CUT ON T-REX'S HEAD - ink - pen & brush

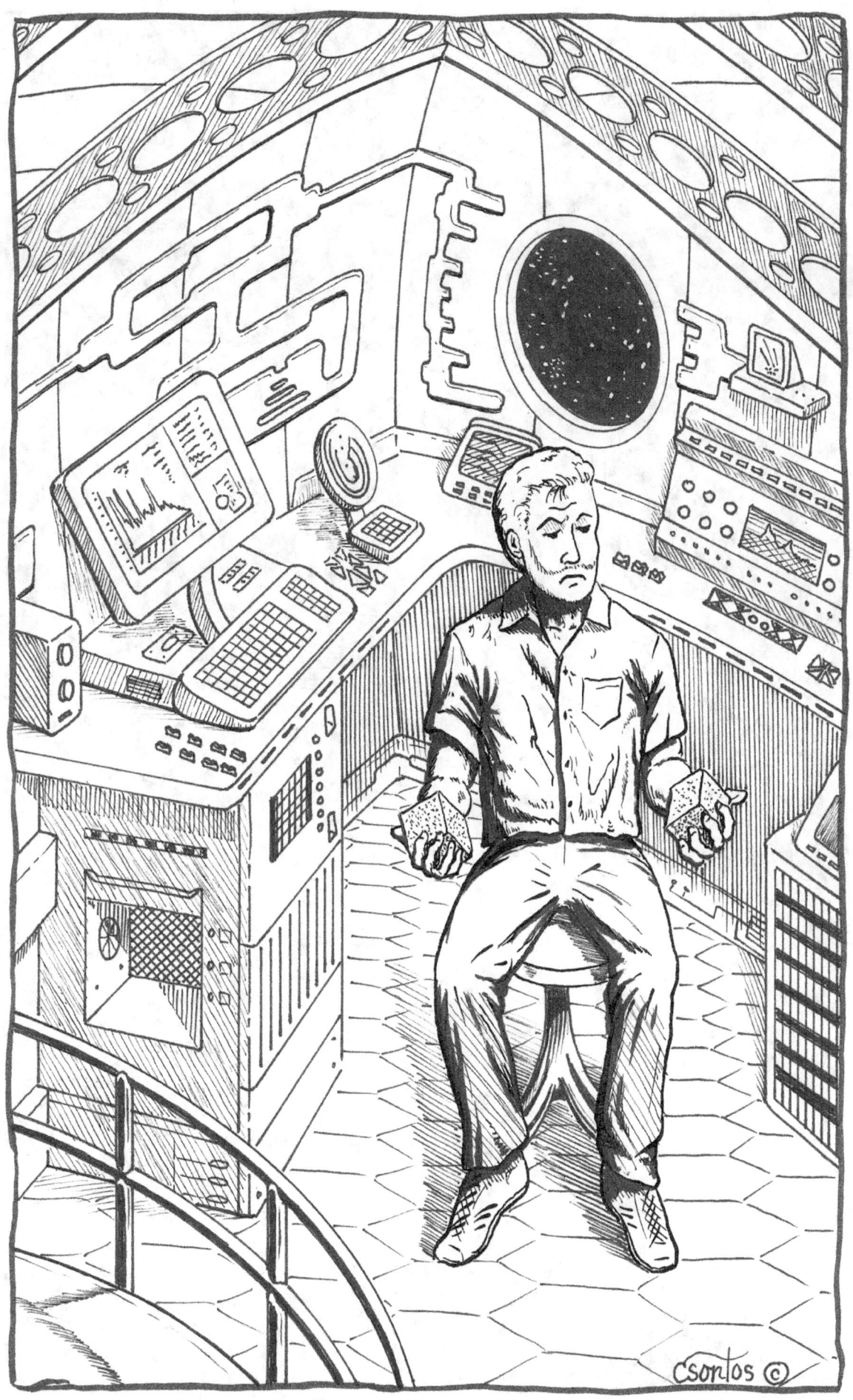

WHICH CUBE IS THE RIGHT ONE? - ink - pen & brush

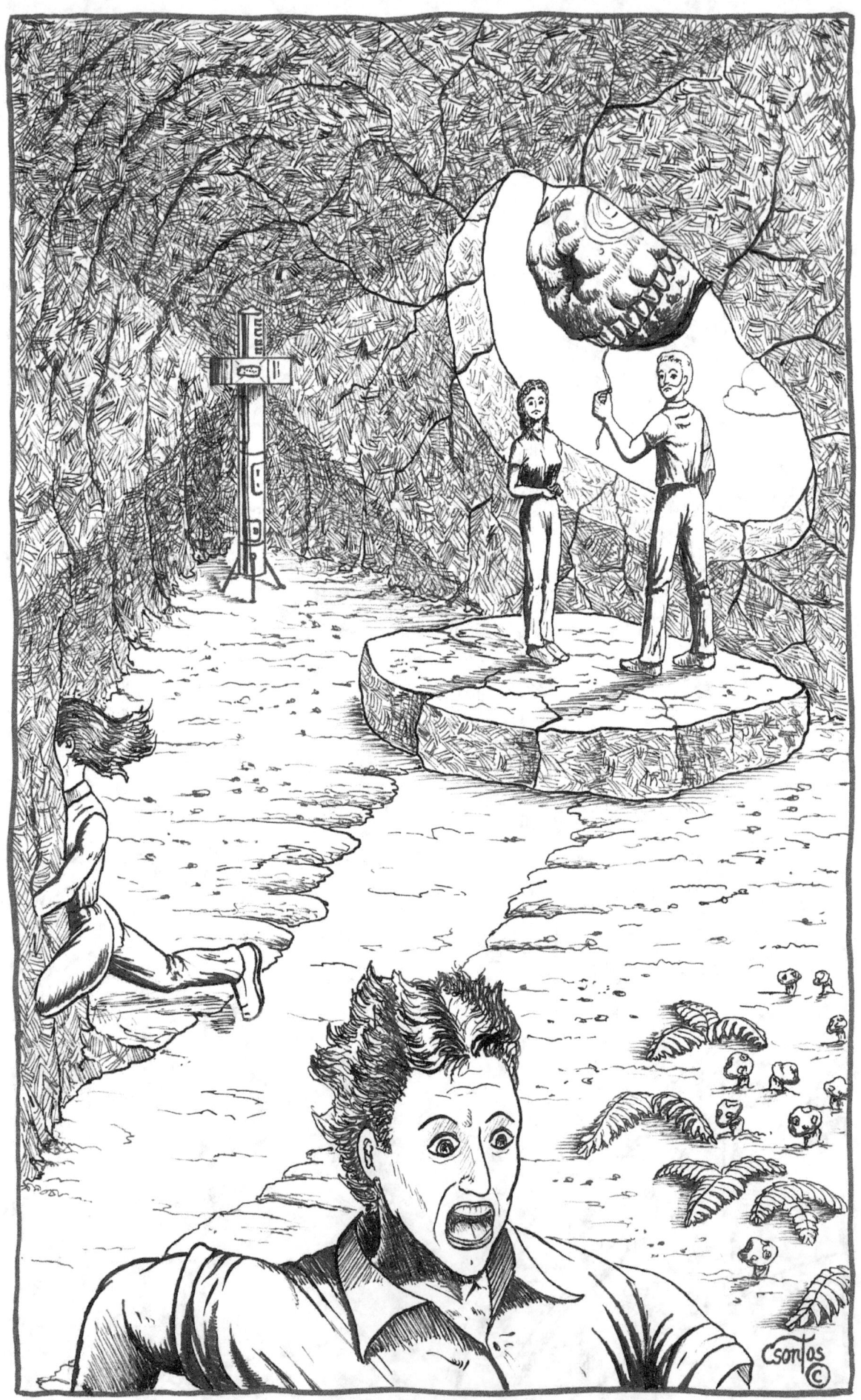

AFRAID OF A HOLOGRAM - ink - pen & brush

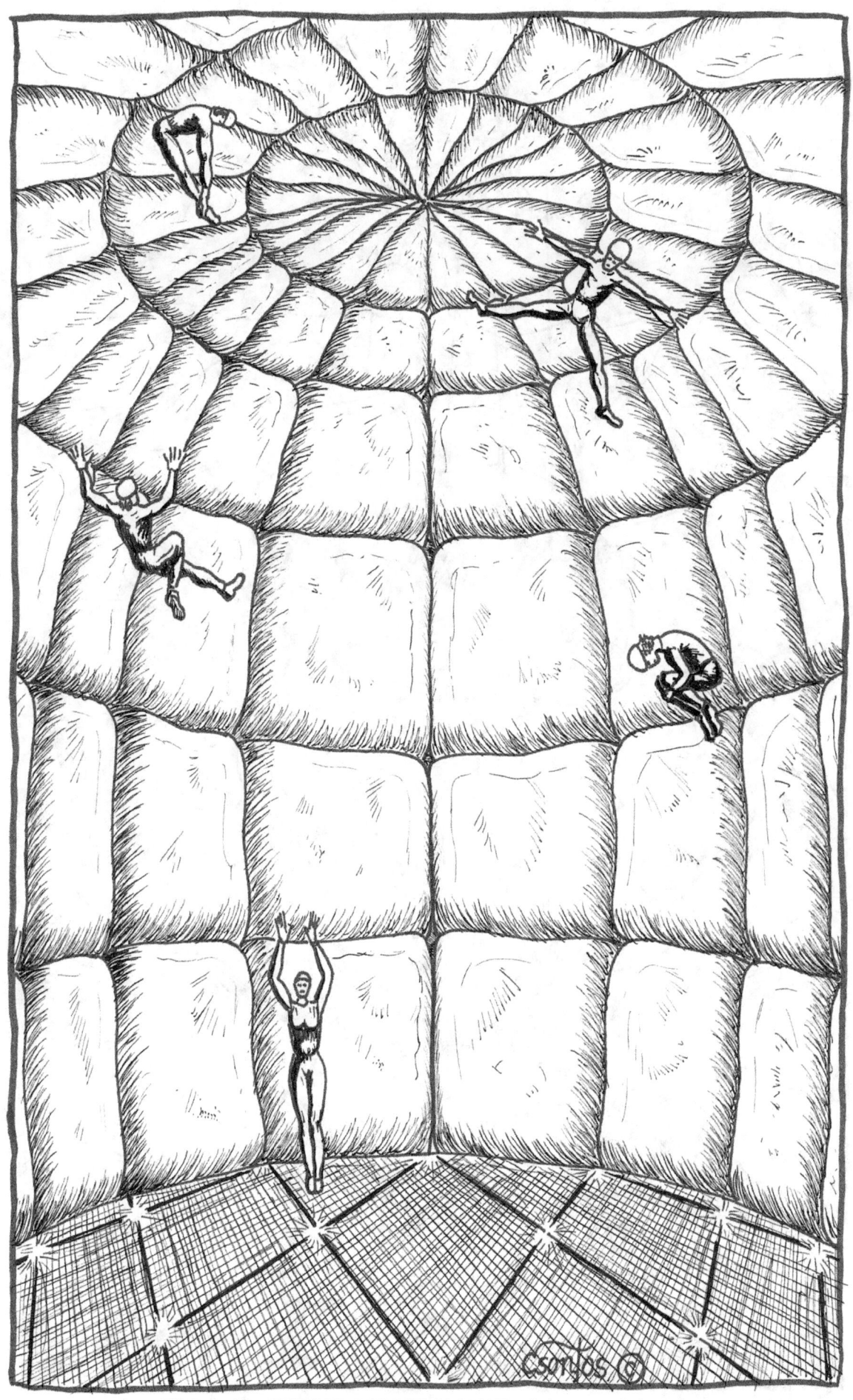

ZERO GRAVITY BOUNCE HOUSE - ink - pen & brush

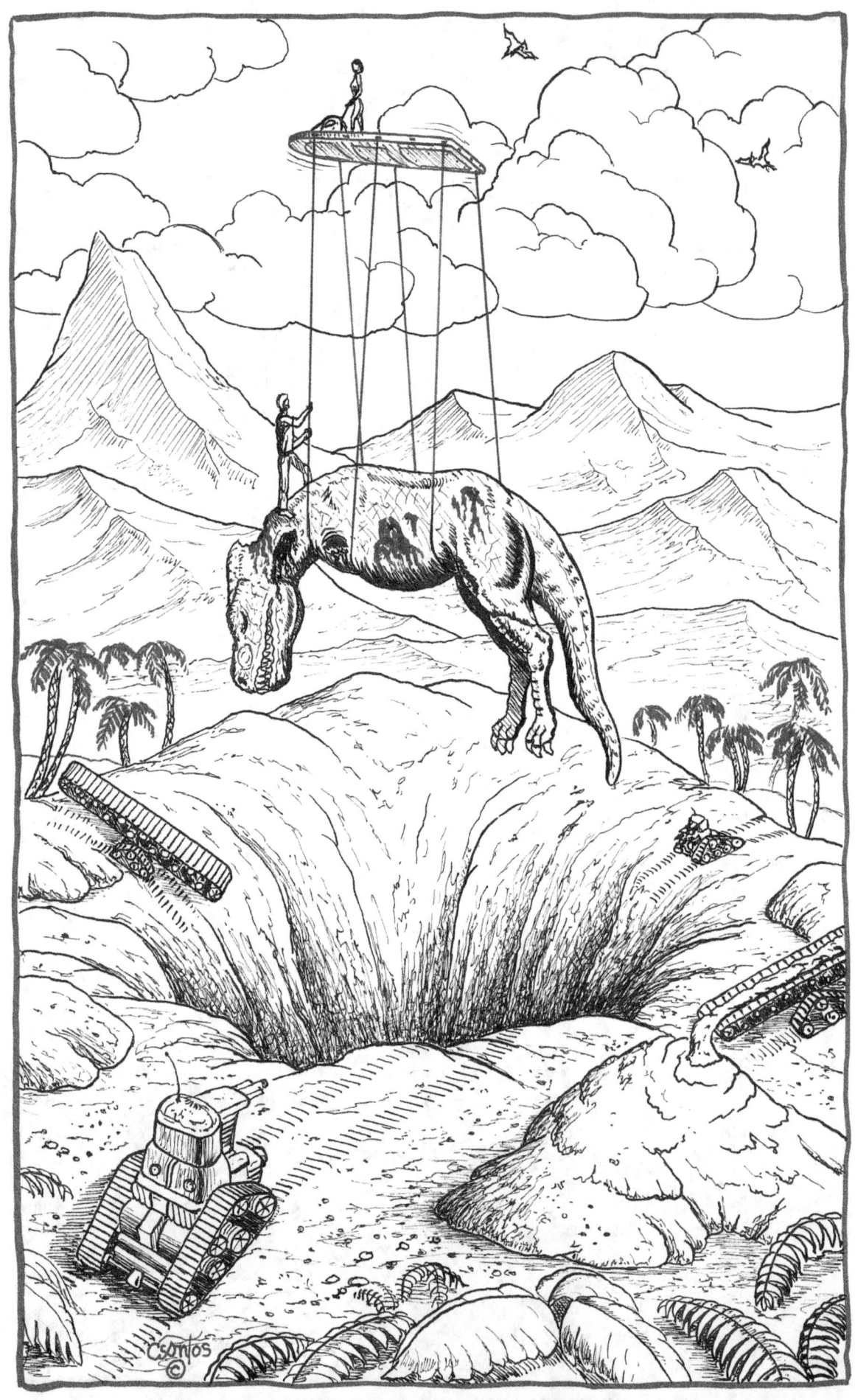

BURYING A FRIEND - ink - pen & brush

Life Drawing

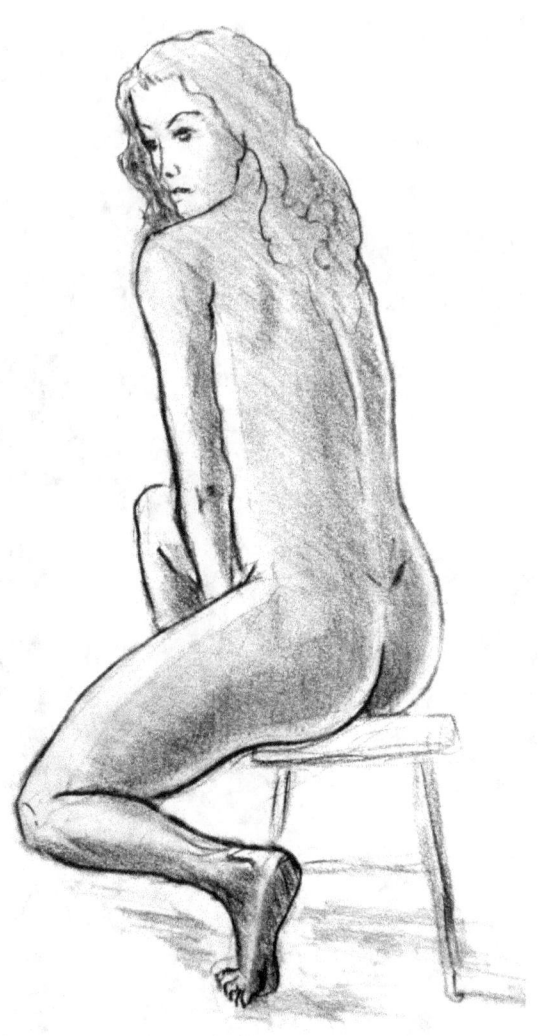

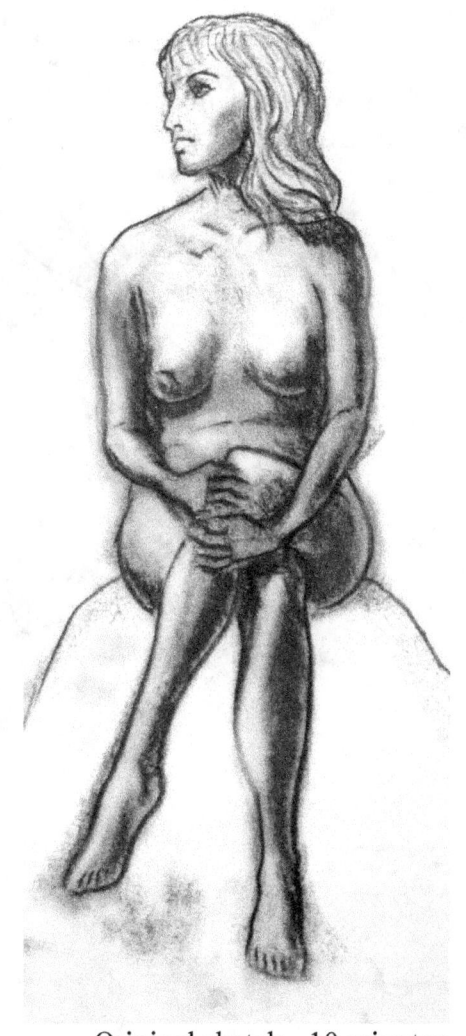

Original sketch - 5 minutes
Rework - 5 minutes
6" wide x 12" high

Original sketch - 10 minutes
Rework - 5 minutes
5" wide x 13" high

These life drawing images are not really results of visualizing but I wanted to include them in this volume. I felt the models had a visual thought of their pose before they conveyed it physically. And the way I draw from life is this: I try to take a mental snapshot of what I'm looking at and then I see it developing on the paper almost like a photograph materializing in a solution. I could then actually redraw (almost trace) the scene from memory. That approach may be considered visualizing. Unfortunately my mental camera is a little out of focus so I prefer a quick sketching approach of the main bone intersections to get a more definite resemblance. Also most of the best poses were ones which were sketched in a gesture mode in about two to three minutes and then reworked from memory. The third line, which is the shadow line, was the hardest to memorize. The gesture poses were the most unique and the model could usually hold them long enough to where the artists or myself could get the basics down. I tried to remember to make little notes about what was going on in my head at the time of the sketches such as focusing on the shadow side or the highlight side or just basically anatomy. I also wrote down the time each drawing took for the original sketch and the time I put in reworking the image during session breaks. Also the size of the sketch. I went quite large on some and small on others. The larger sketches were harder to keep in proper proportion. I did several as smaller versions (less than 8"x8") because I thought they would take less time. For some reason they took almost as long as the larger ones. All the life drawing images were done with charcoal pencil except one.

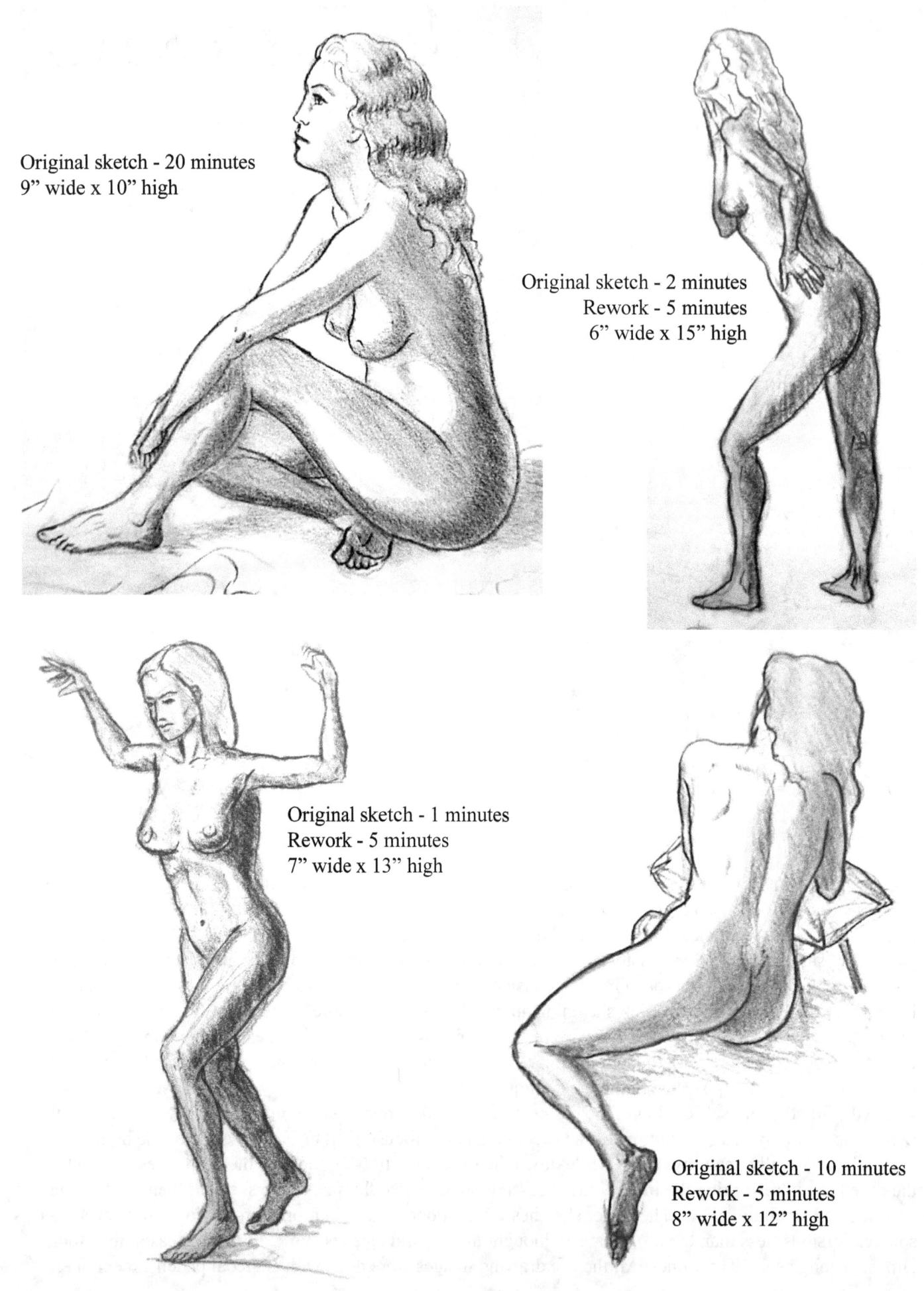

Original sketch - 20 minutes
9" wide x 10" high

Original sketch - 2 minutes
Rework - 5 minutes
6" wide x 15" high

Original sketch - 1 minutes
Rework - 5 minutes
7" wide x 13" high

Original sketch - 10 minutes
Rework - 5 minutes
8" wide x 12" high

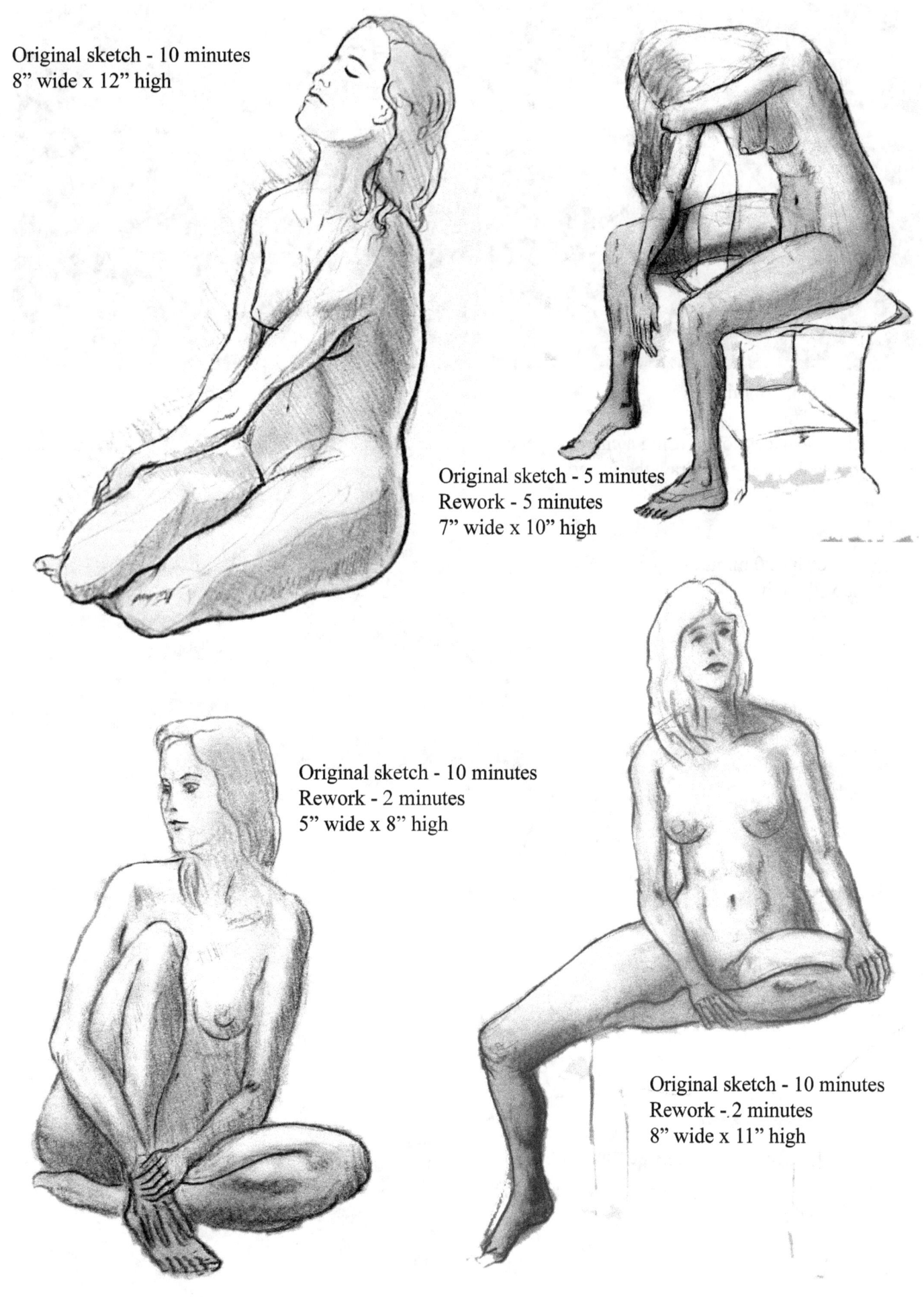

Original sketch - 10 minutes
8" wide x 12" high

Original sketch - 5 minutes
Rework - 5 minutes
7" wide x 10" high

Original sketch - 10 minutes
Rework - 2 minutes
5" wide x 8" high

Original sketch - 10 minutes
Rework - 2 minutes
8" wide x 11" high

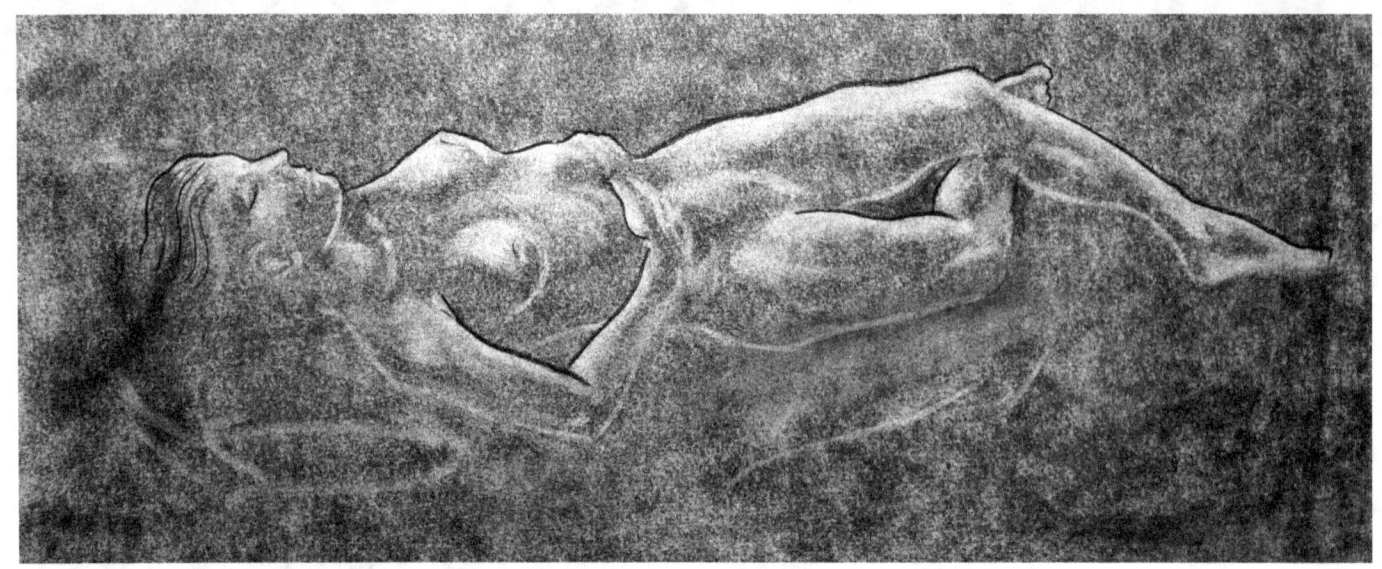

Original sketch - 20 minutes
19" wide x 7" high
This is the one exception to using a charcoal pencil. I used a charcoal stick to cover an entire sheet and then used a kneadable eraser to draw the image.

Original sketch - 20 minutes
18" wide x 7" high

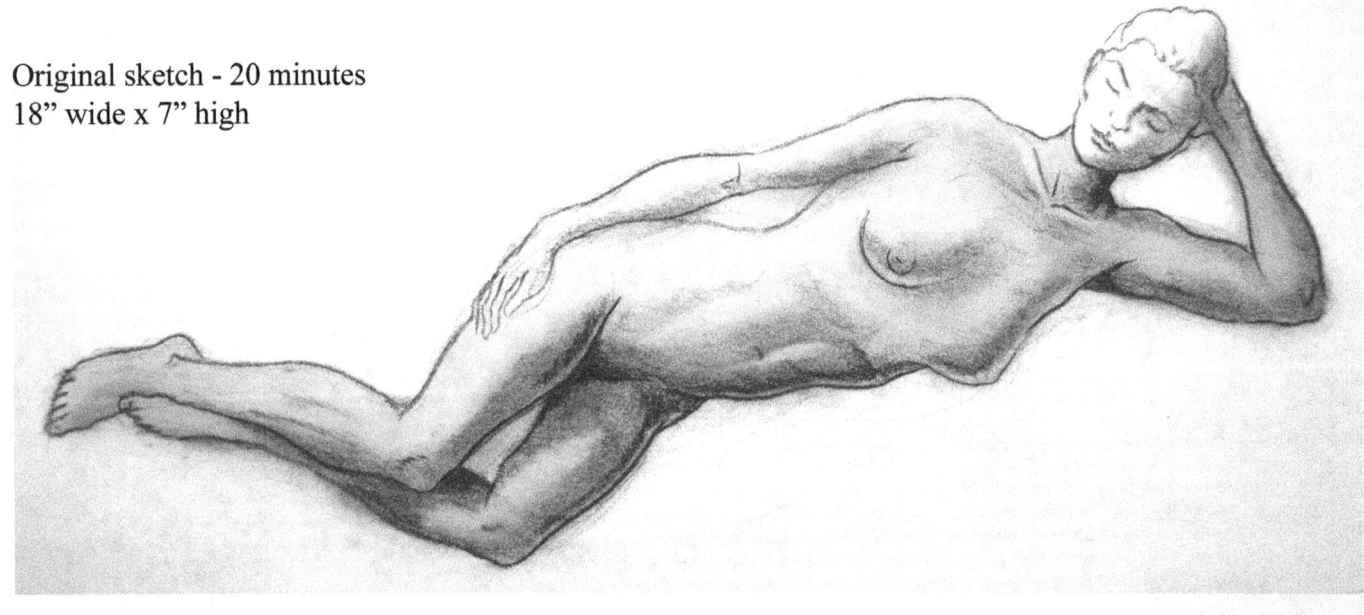

Original sketch - 20 minutes
17" wide x 7" high

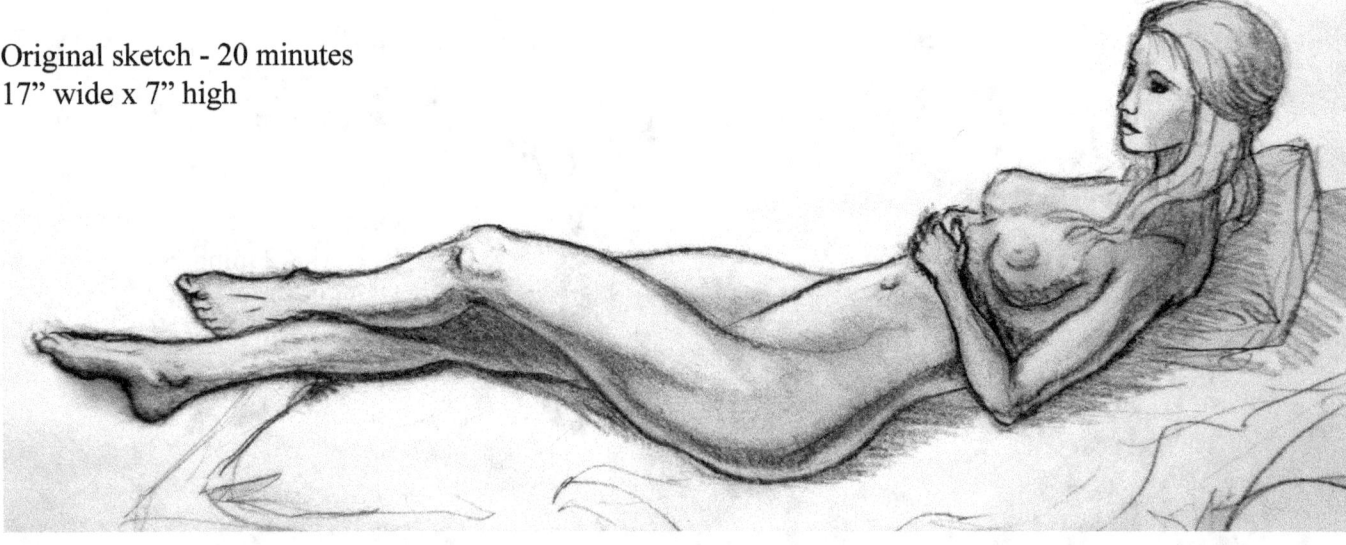

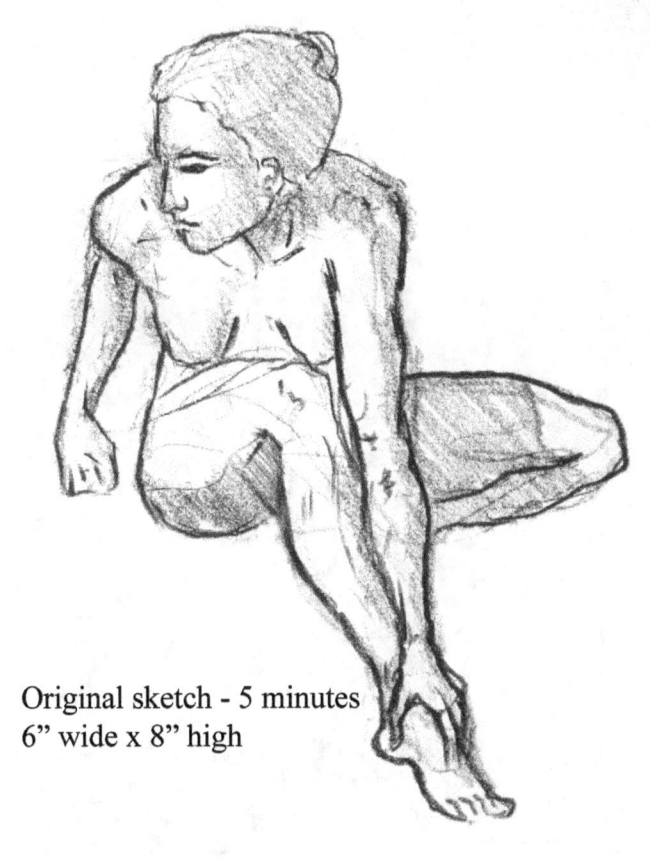

Original sketch - 5 minutes
6" wide x 8" high

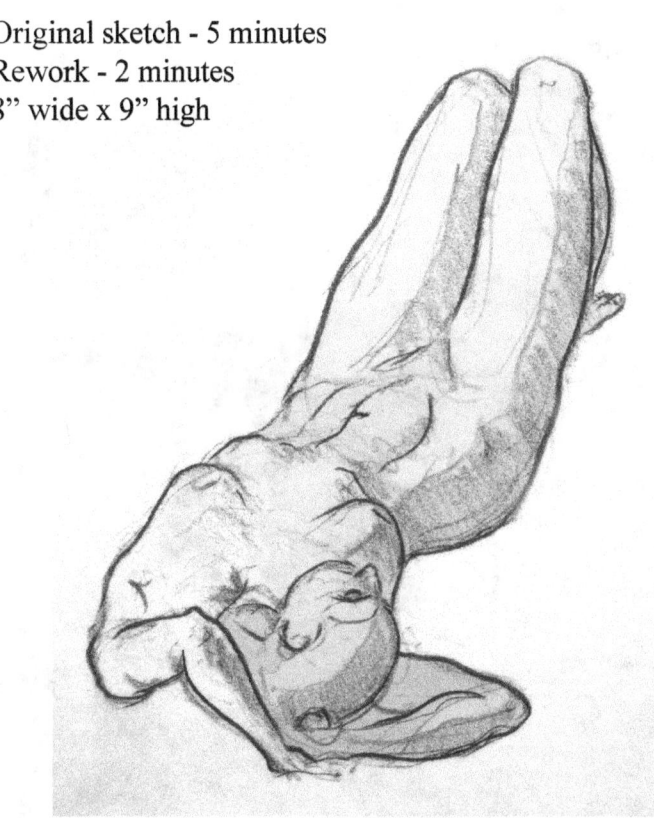

Original sketch - 5 minutes
Rework - 2 minutes
8" wide x 9" high

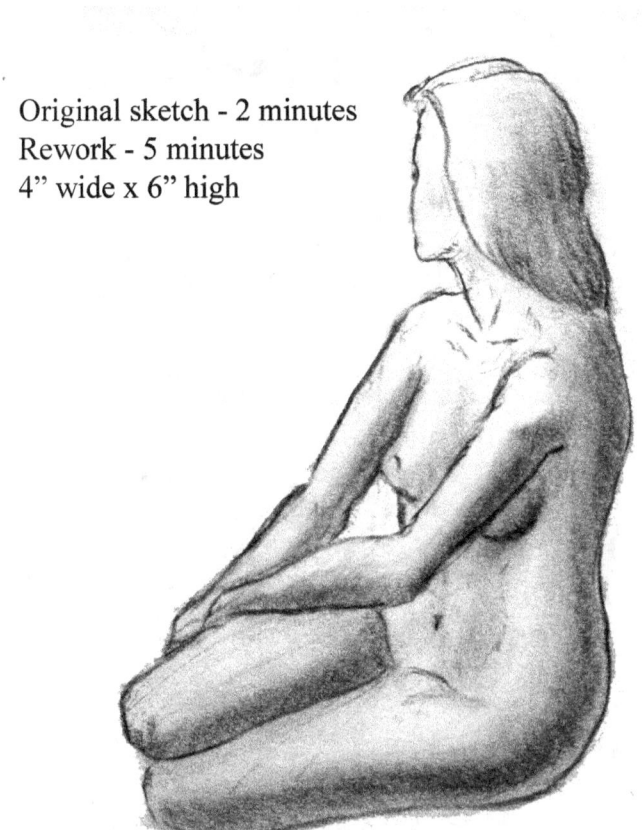

Original sketch - 2 minutes
Rework - 5 minutes
4" wide x 6" high

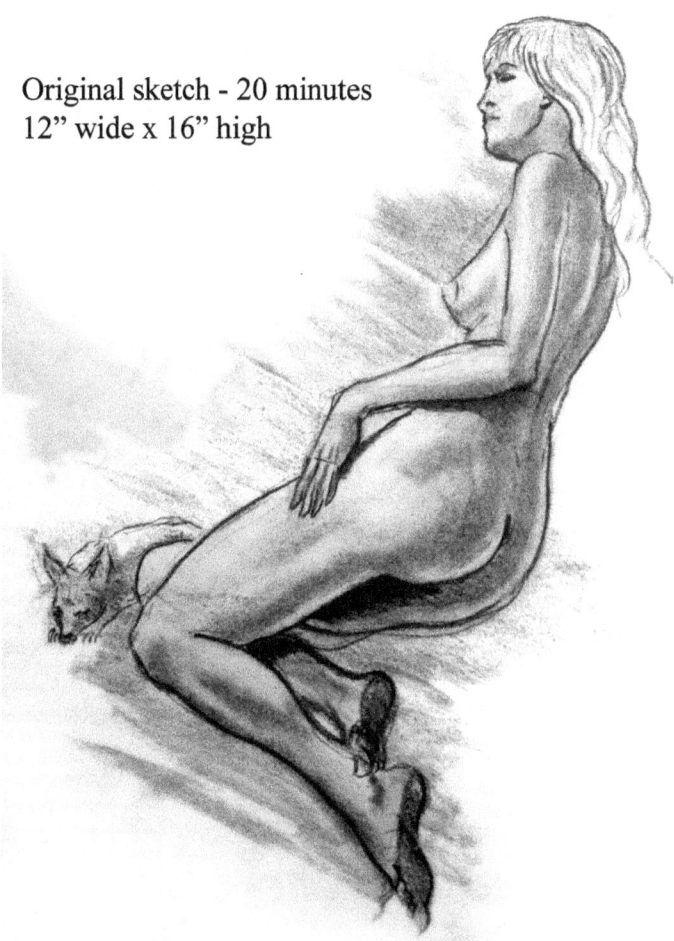

Original sketch - 20 minutes
12" wide x 16" high

Original sketch - 10 minutes
Rework - 3 minutes
10" wide x 10" high

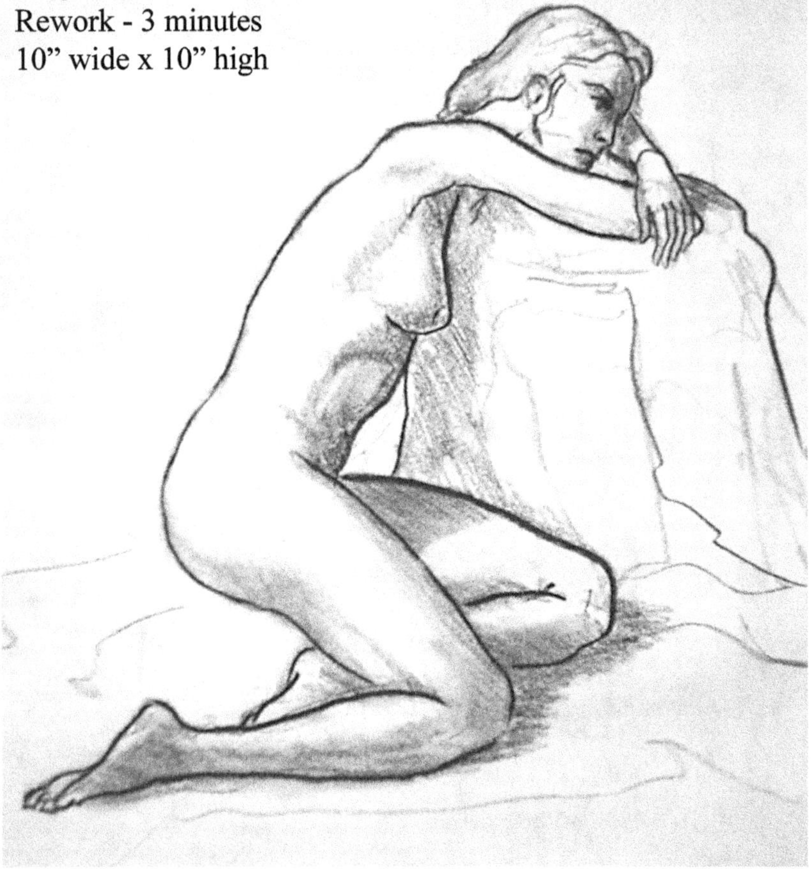

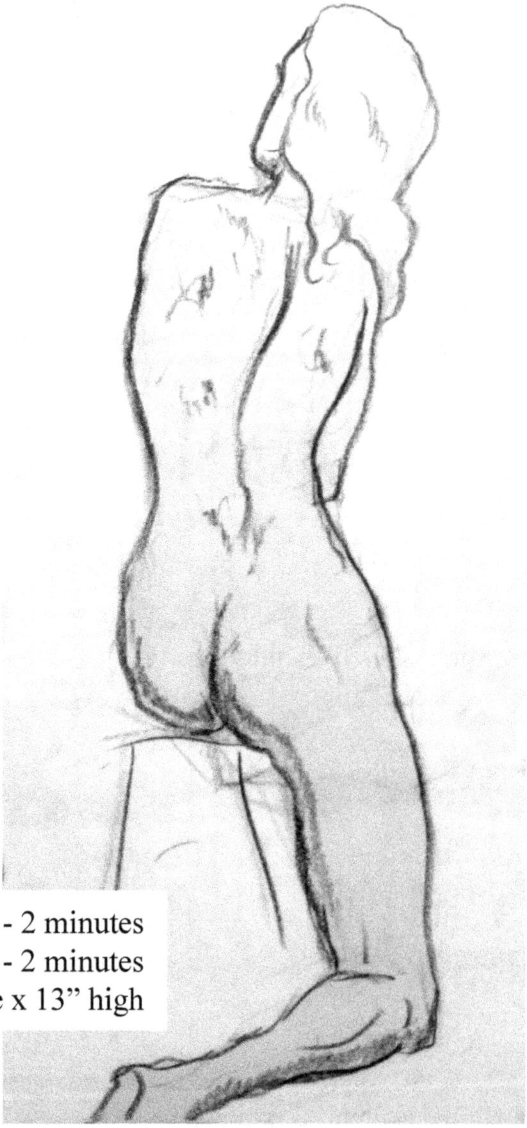

Original sketch - 2 minutes
Rework - 2 minutes
5" wide x 13" high

Original sketch - 20 minutes
13" wide x 10" high

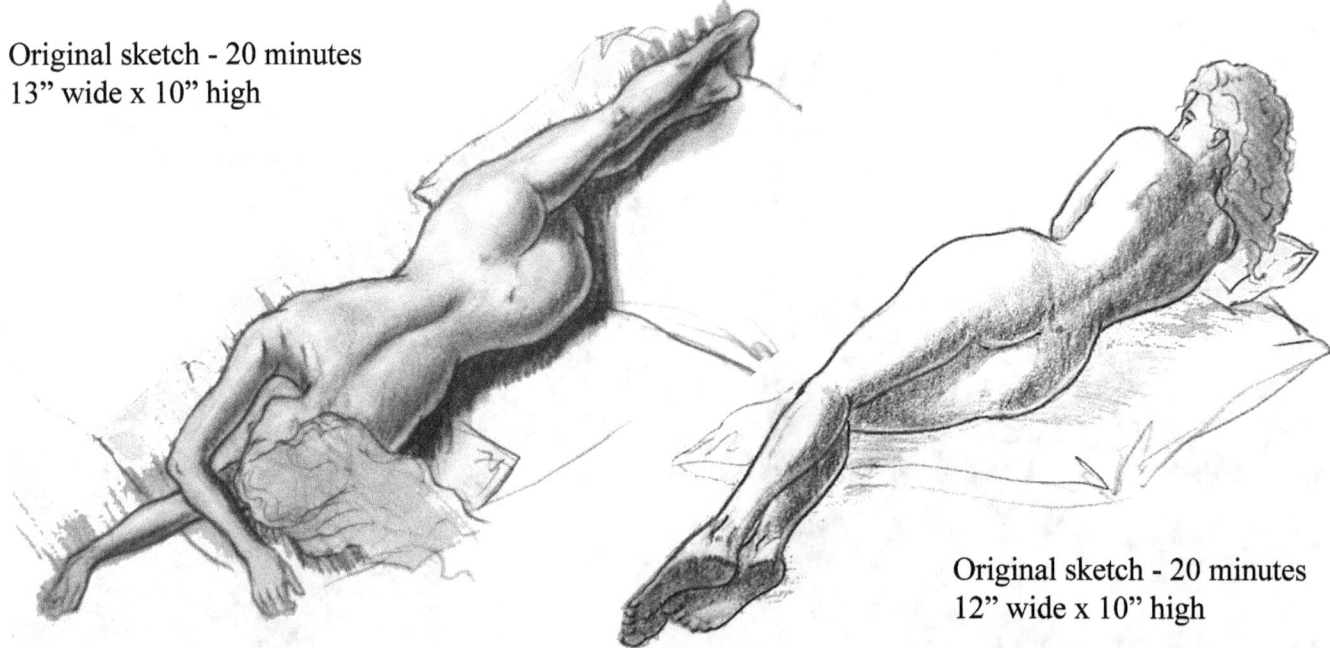

Original sketch - 20 minutes
12" wide x 10" high

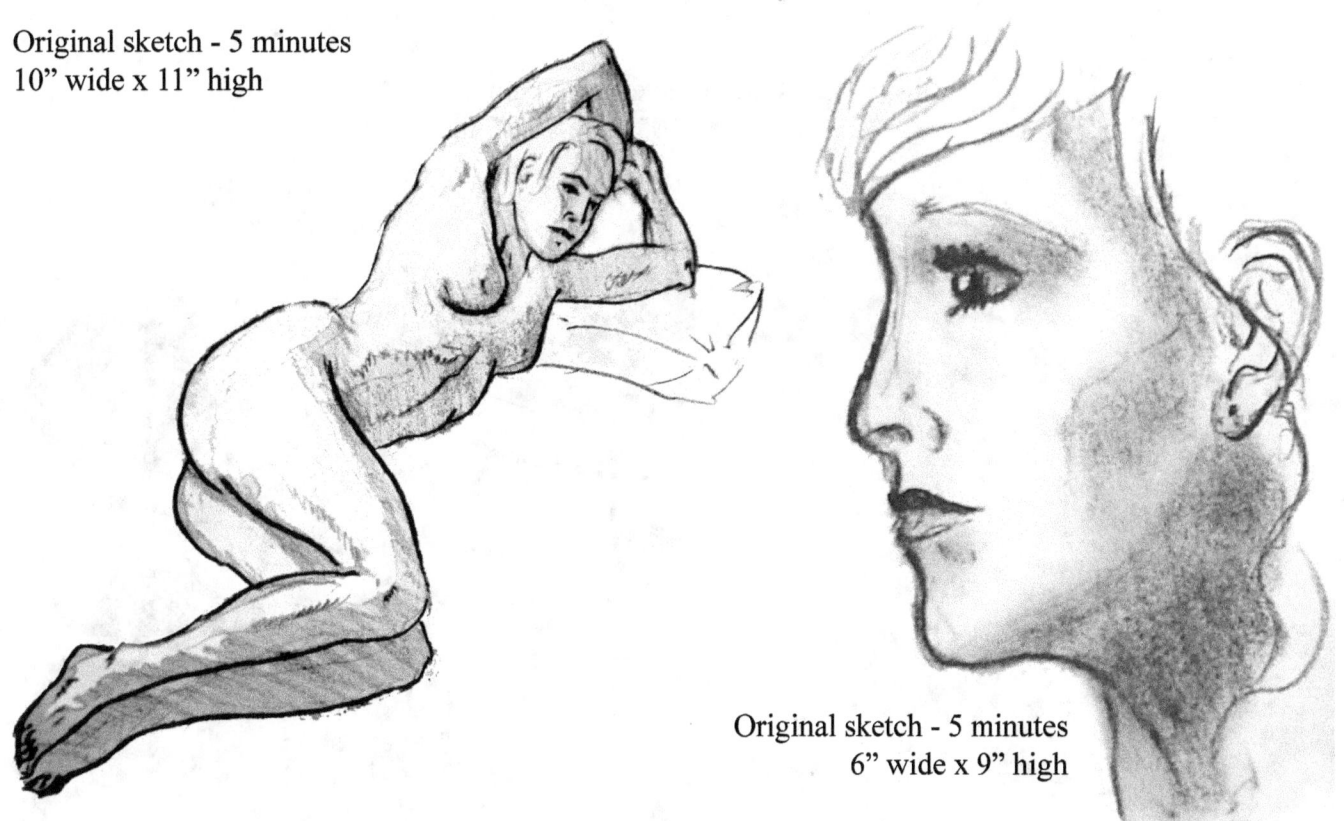

Original sketch - 5 minutes
10" wide x 11" high

Original sketch - 5 minutes
6" wide x 9" high

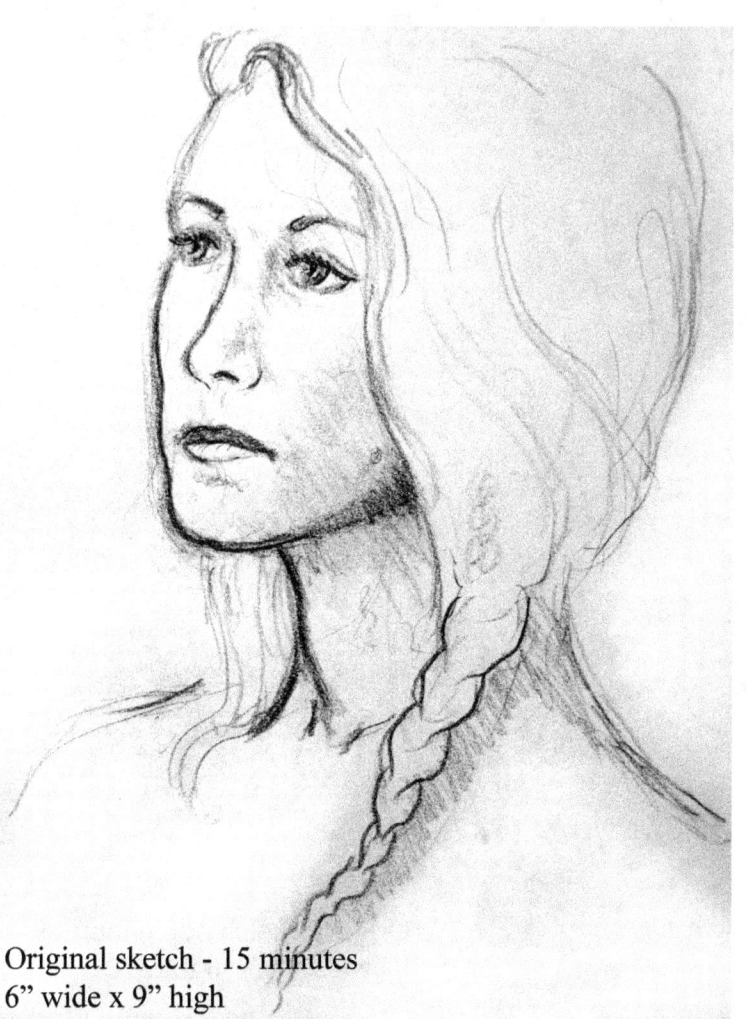

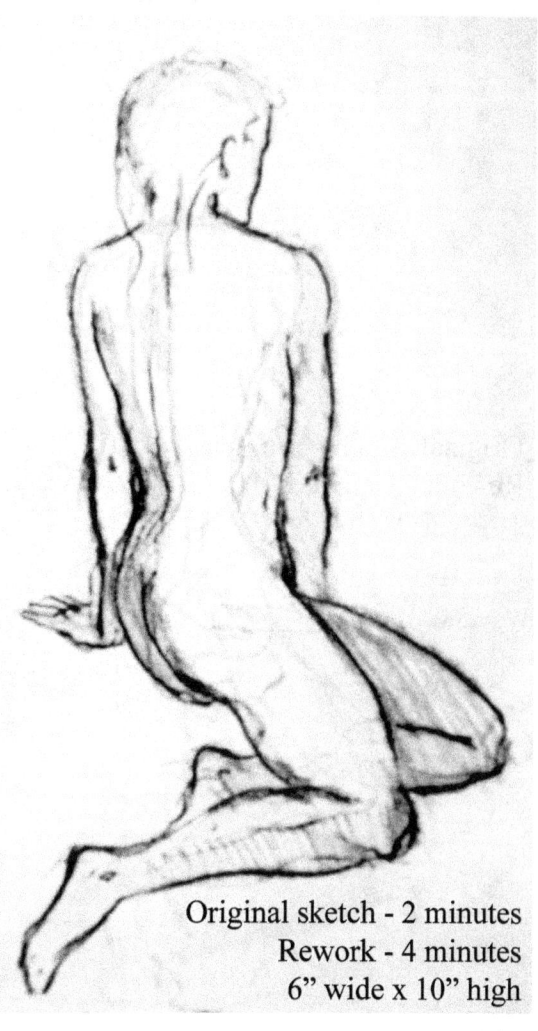

Original sketch - 15 minutes
6" wide x 9" high

Original sketch - 2 minutes
Rework - 4 minutes
6" wide x 10" high

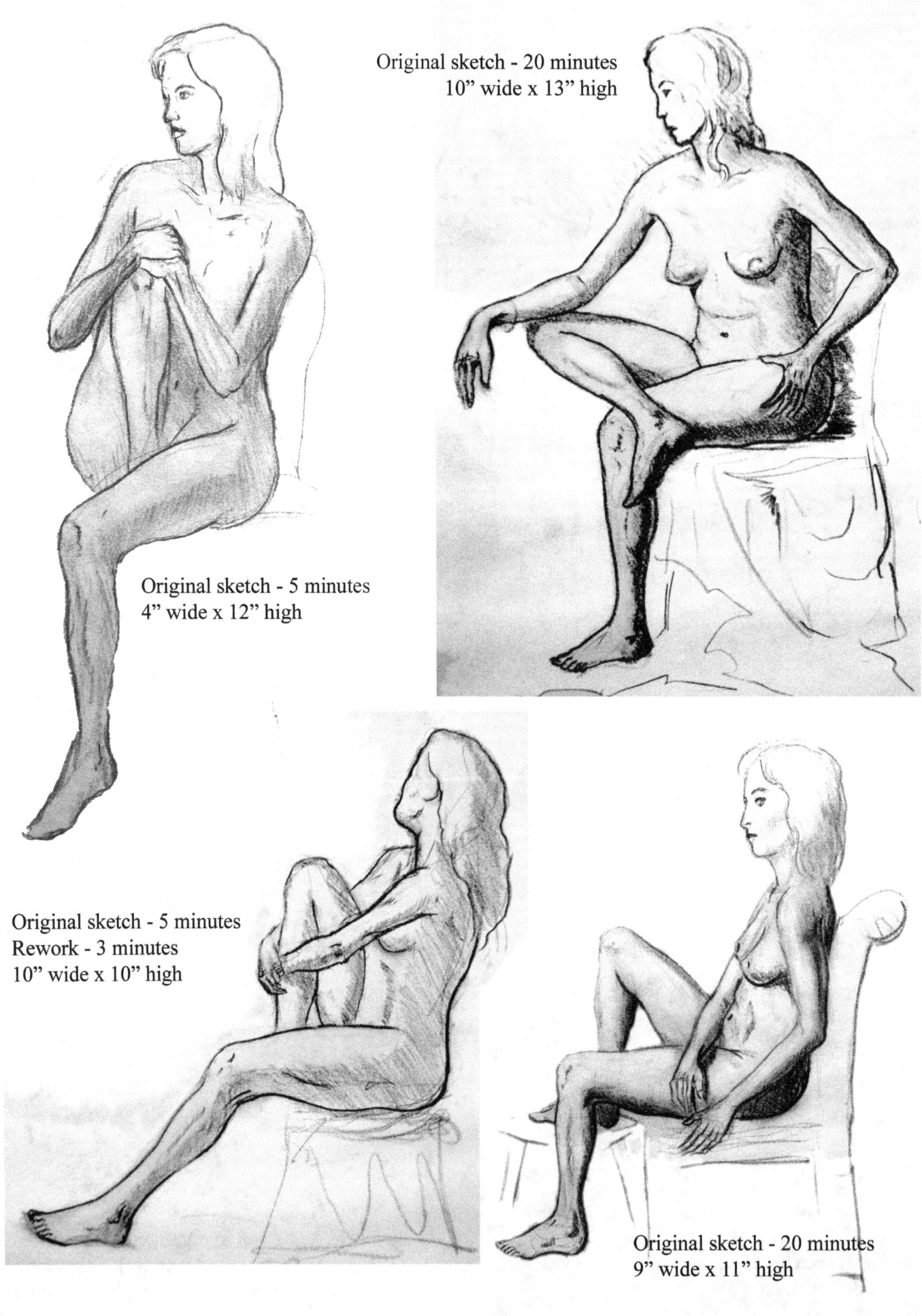

Original sketch - 20 minutes
10" wide x 13" high

Original sketch - 5 minutes
4" wide x 12" high

Original sketch - 5 minutes
Rework - 3 minutes
10" wide x 10" high

Original sketch - 20 minutes
9" wide x 11" high

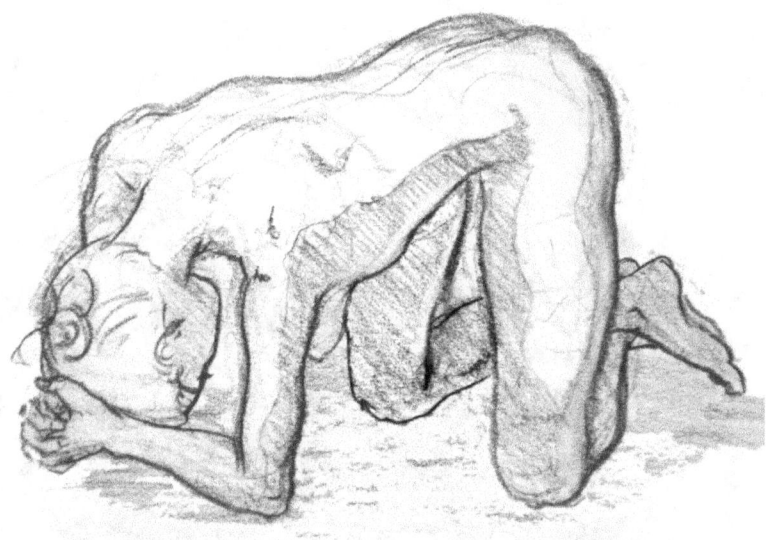

Original sketch - 5 minutes
Rework - 2 minutes
9" wide x 7" high

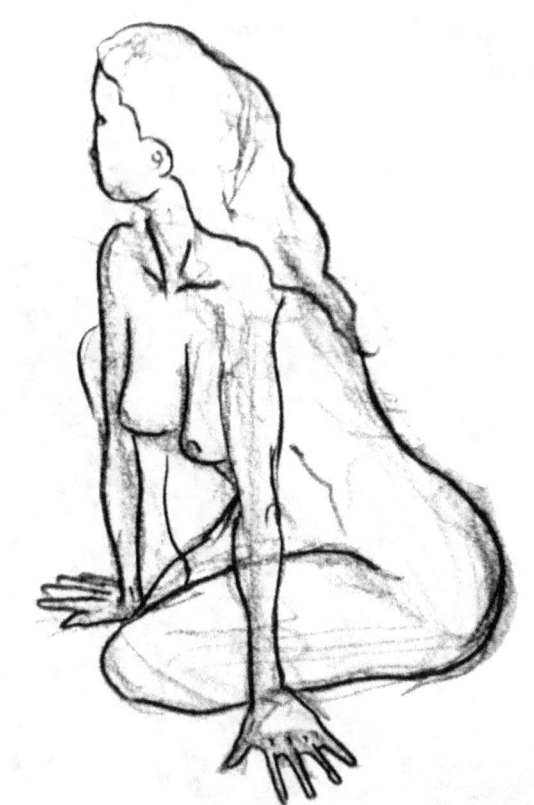

Original sketch - 3 minutes
9" wide x 14" high

Original sketch - 2 minutes
Rework - 3 minutes
5" wide x 8" high

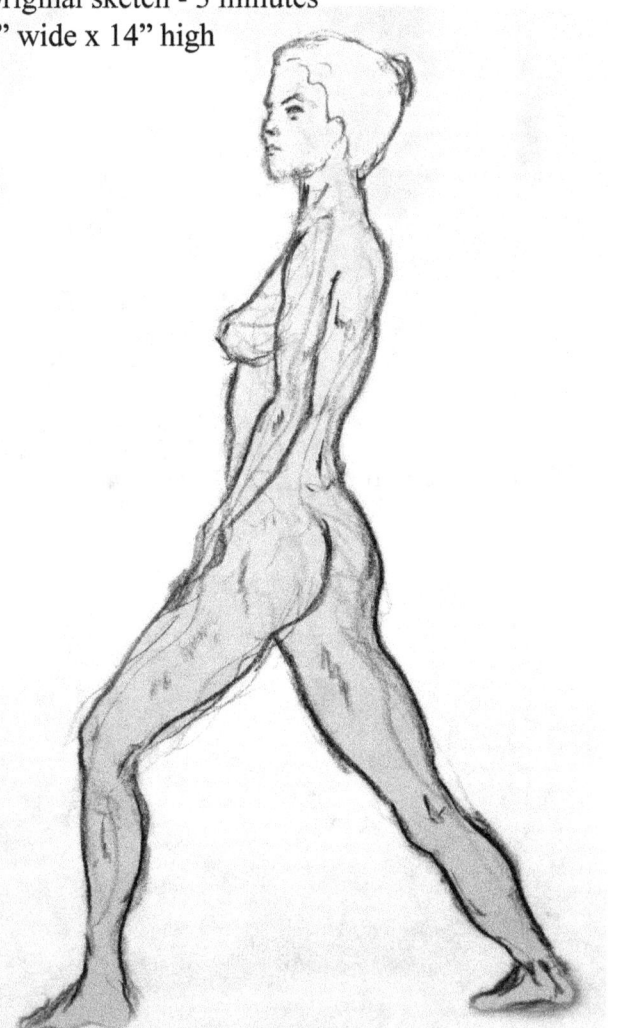

Original sketch - 1 minutes
Rework - 5 minutes
7" wide x 9" high

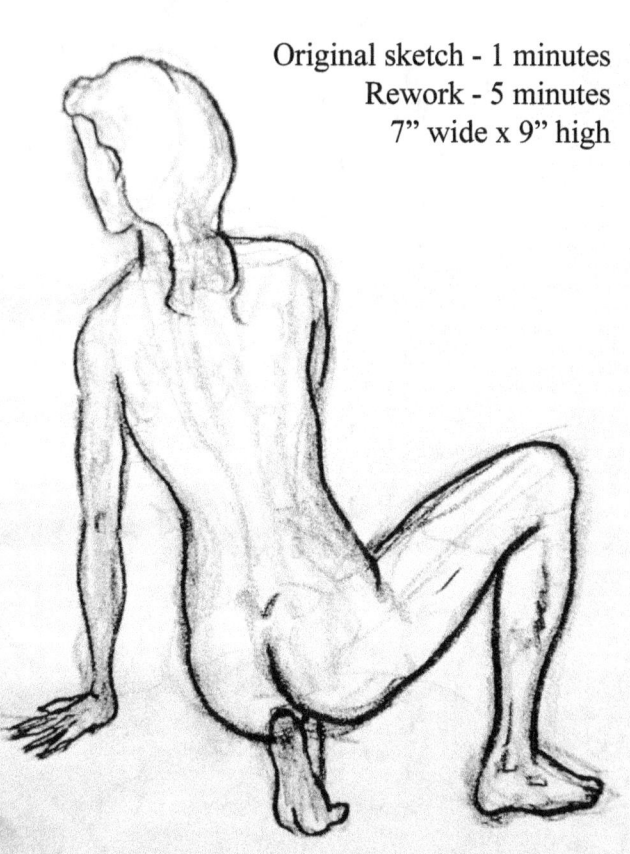

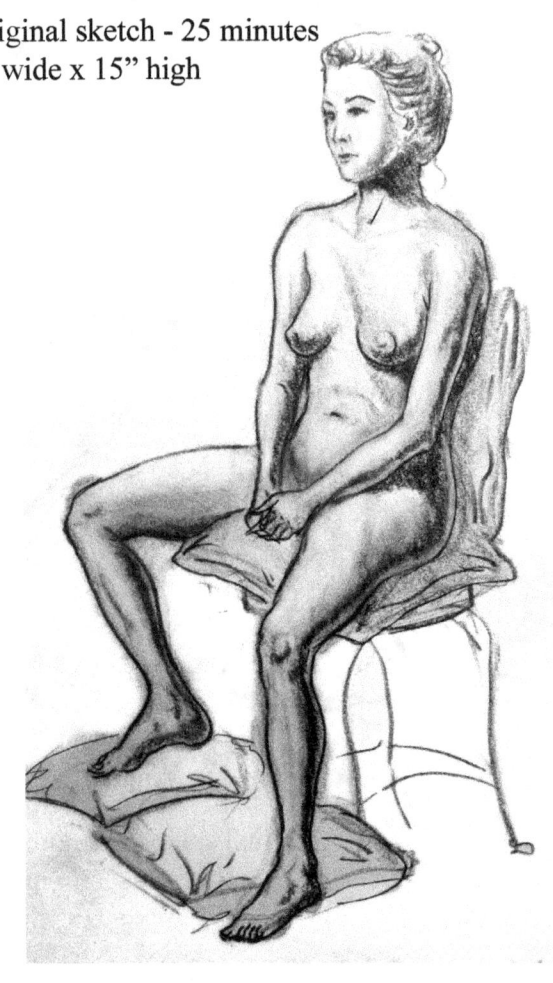

Original sketch - 25 minutes
9" wide x 15" high

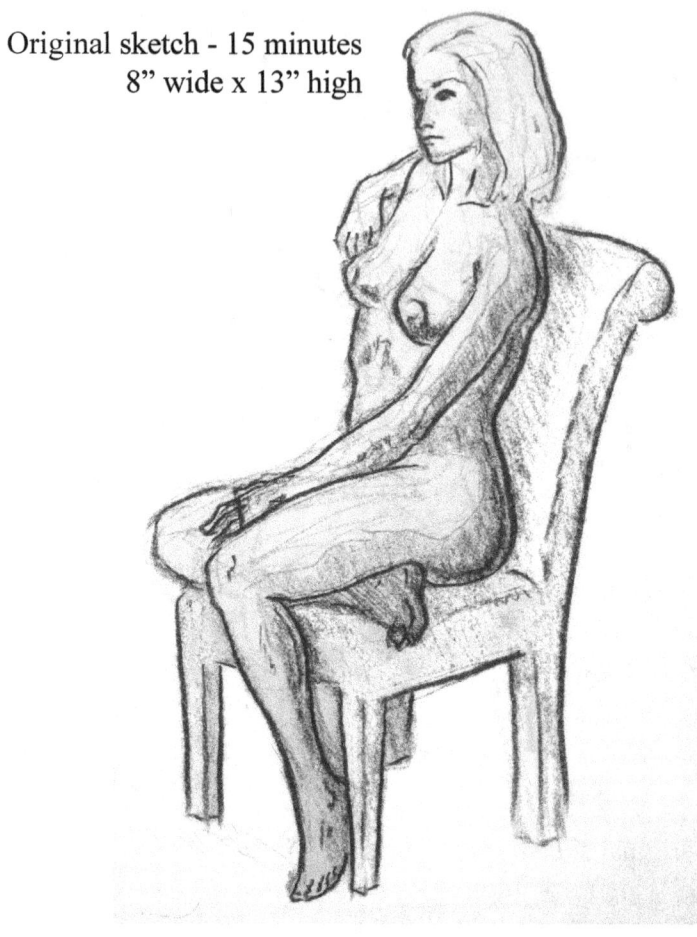

Original sketch - 15 minutes
8" wide x 13" high

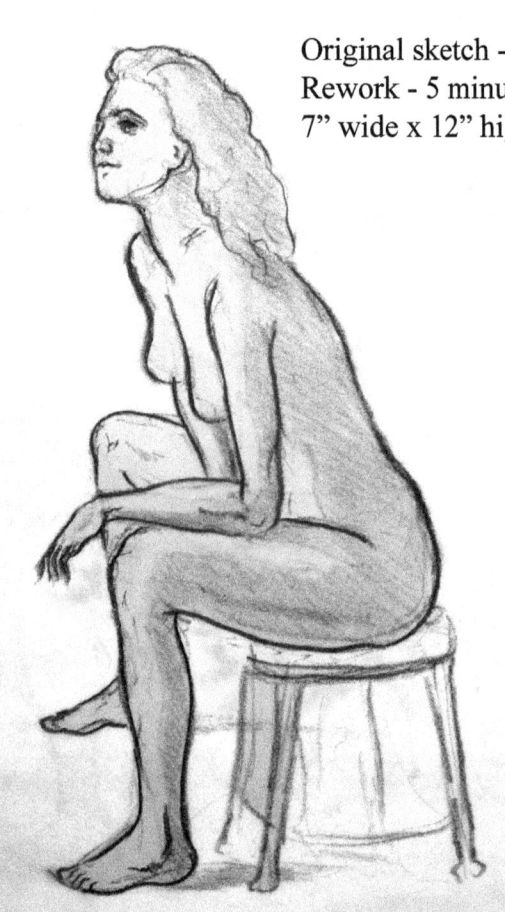

Original sketch - 5 minutes
Rework - 5 minutes
7" wide x 12" high

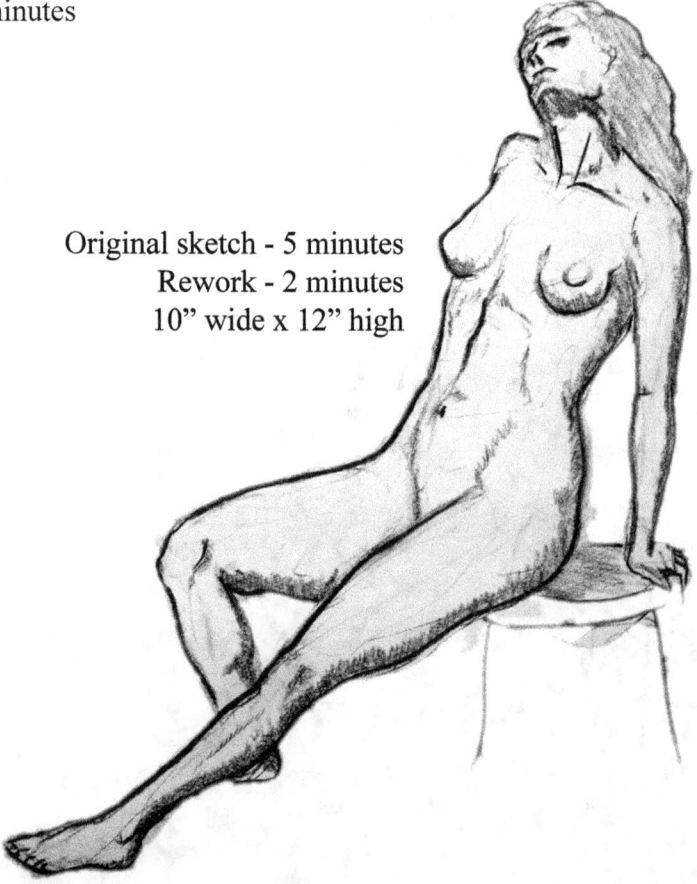

Original sketch - 5 minutes
Rework - 2 minutes
10" wide x 12" high

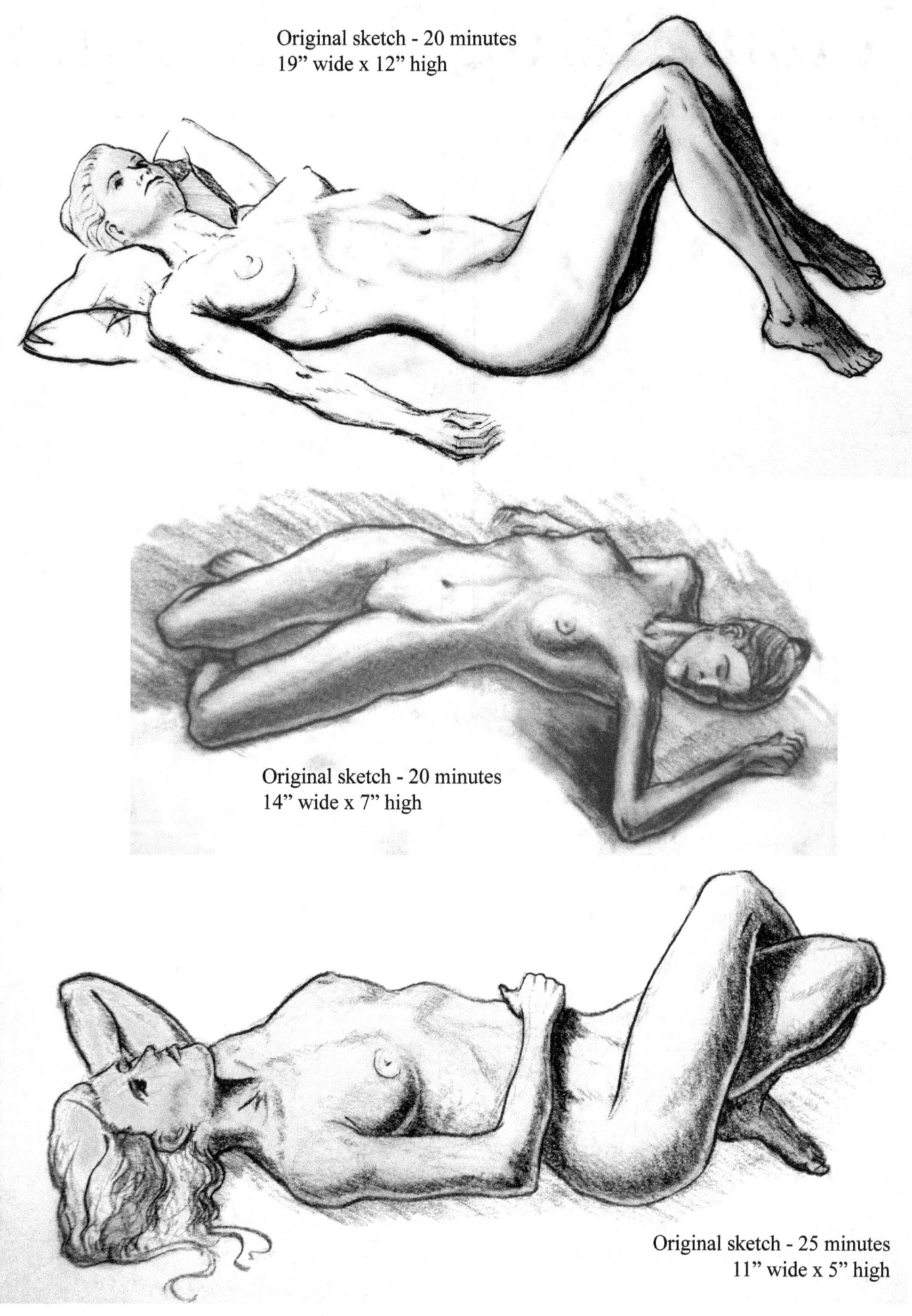

Original sketch - 20 minutes
19" wide x 12" high

Original sketch - 20 minutes
14" wide x 7" high

Original sketch - 25 minutes
11" wide x 5" high

Visualizing Technique

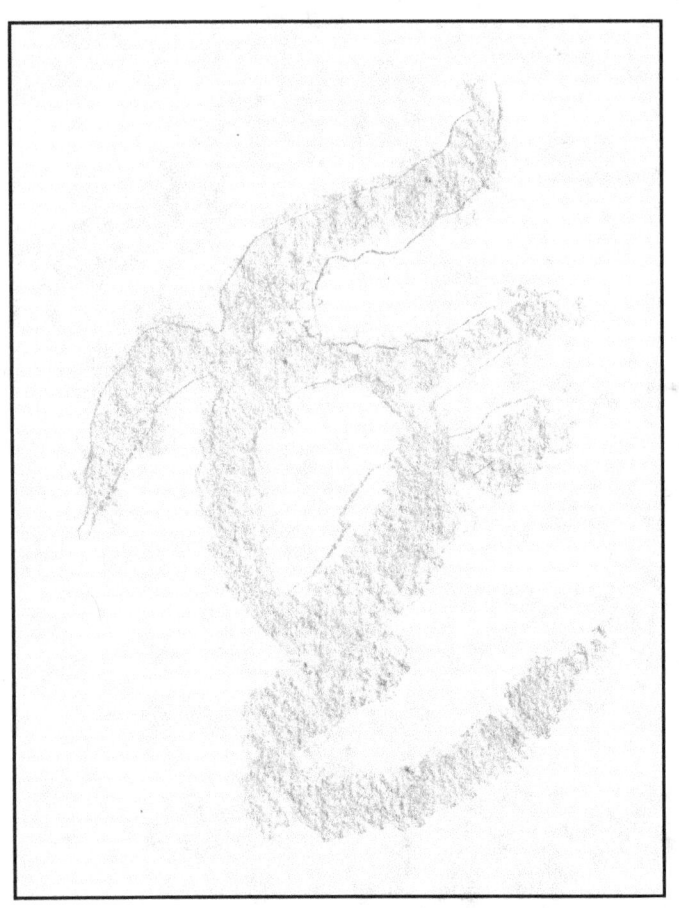

Initial sketch done with a 6B pencil held at a low angle.

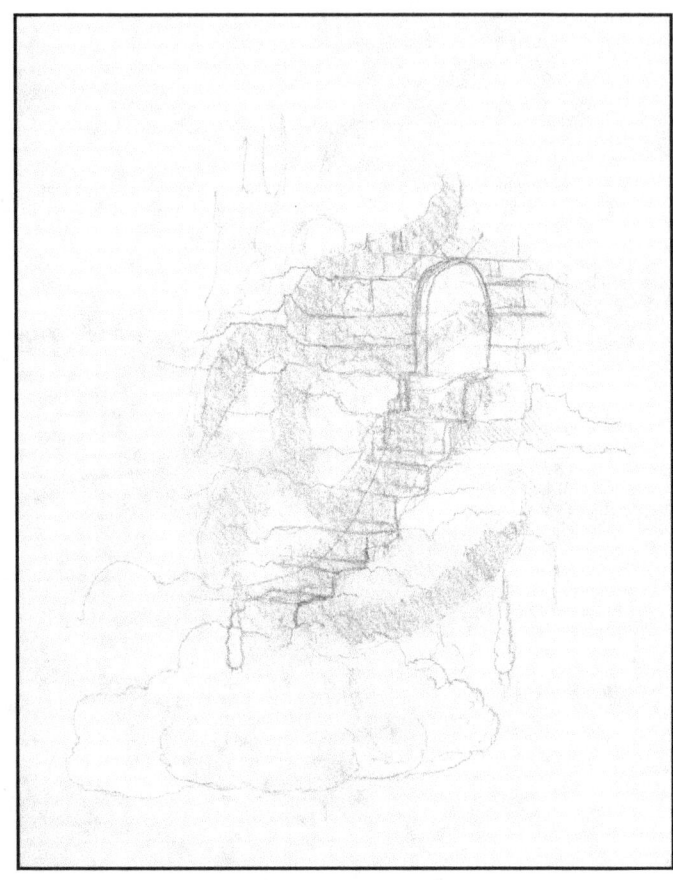

Second stage with a regular HB pencil.

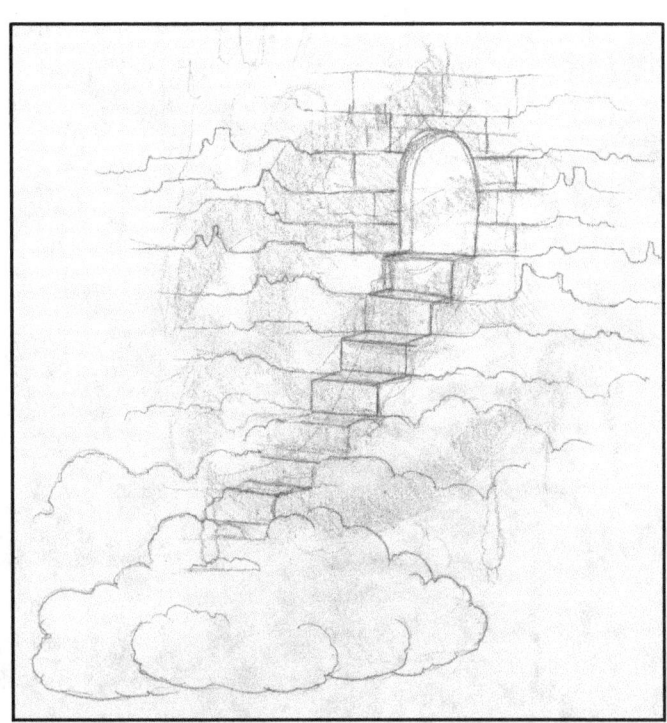

Third stage where I've refined the idea. This is usually where I make changes if necessary.

The initial sketch as you can see, was done with a 6B pencil held at a low angle. Nothing immediately came into view even after rotating the paper. This was probably due to the fact that I knew this image was going to be the step by step technique tutorial for this book so a bit of artistic blockage came into play. So I next switched to a HB pencil and used it as you would a regular pencil. After about a minute imagery came into view. It was a surrealistic depiction but I decided to go with it because the step by step techniques I've shown in my other books were more of a representational nature. I am only trying to show that imagery can be found in any abstract shape. If I wanted to show a representational image (such as a critter) then I would of continued sketching abstractly or just started over on another piece of paper. I did see a set of eyes and a nose starting

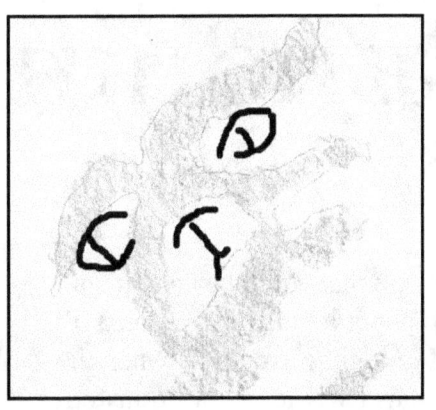

to emerge in the initial sketch but for some reason I did not go with it. When I decided to finish this image I attached a better grade of paper over the copy paper with the abstract sketch. I did this because I saw toning in the image and wanted to use pencil and not pens or Photoshop. I supposed I could of refined the idea better to get a more thought provoking reaction, even out of myself, but for some reason I did not. However I do see aspects in it that may be used in an oil painting.

Rough idea of the eyes and nose I saw originally.

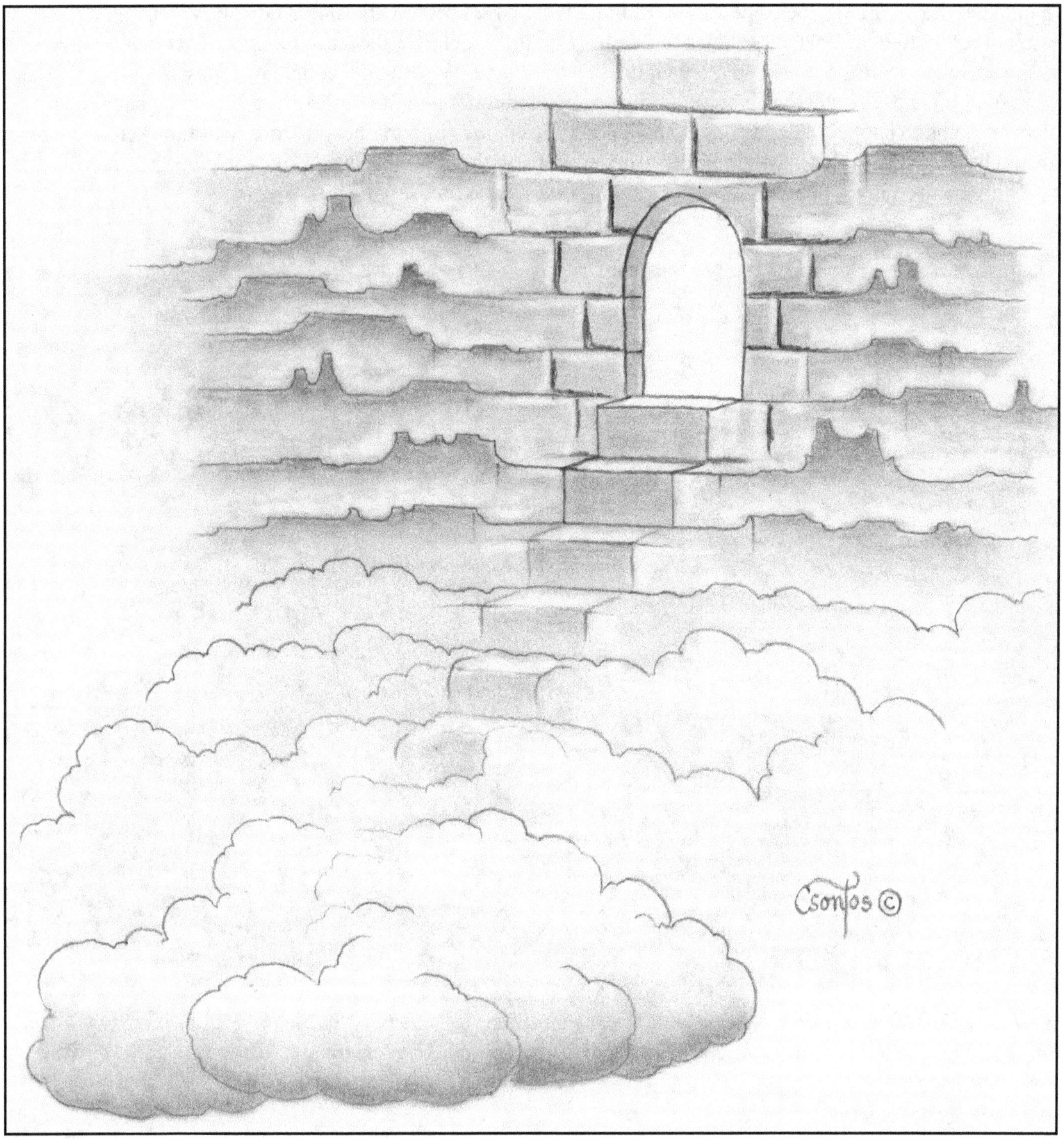

STAIRWAY TO MONUMENT VALLEY - The finished piece done on a better grade of paper.

Addendum

As I mentioned on the previous page, I though I saw some aspects of the image that could be used in an oil painting. It must have stuck in my head because as I started to sketch on paper an idea for my next oil painting the result below is what came out. However it was not as easy as I thought it would be when the idea originally came into being. After I thought I had the imagery completed as I would like it I transferred the idea to the painting panel. Then after studying it for a bit I redrew the ship again and again and again. I do not really like to constantly sketch and redraw on the panel itself because it tends to get messy with graphite. I also redrew the archway, the Goddess's head, and the serpent a couple of times as well. I also went over the entire water area a second time because I did not like the initial effect. This is what almost always seems to happen if an idea or even a partial idea comes into my head before I start to sketch abstractly. However I think the redundant work was worth the effort because I like the piece and it will probably be used in a calendar. The color version is viewable on the website.

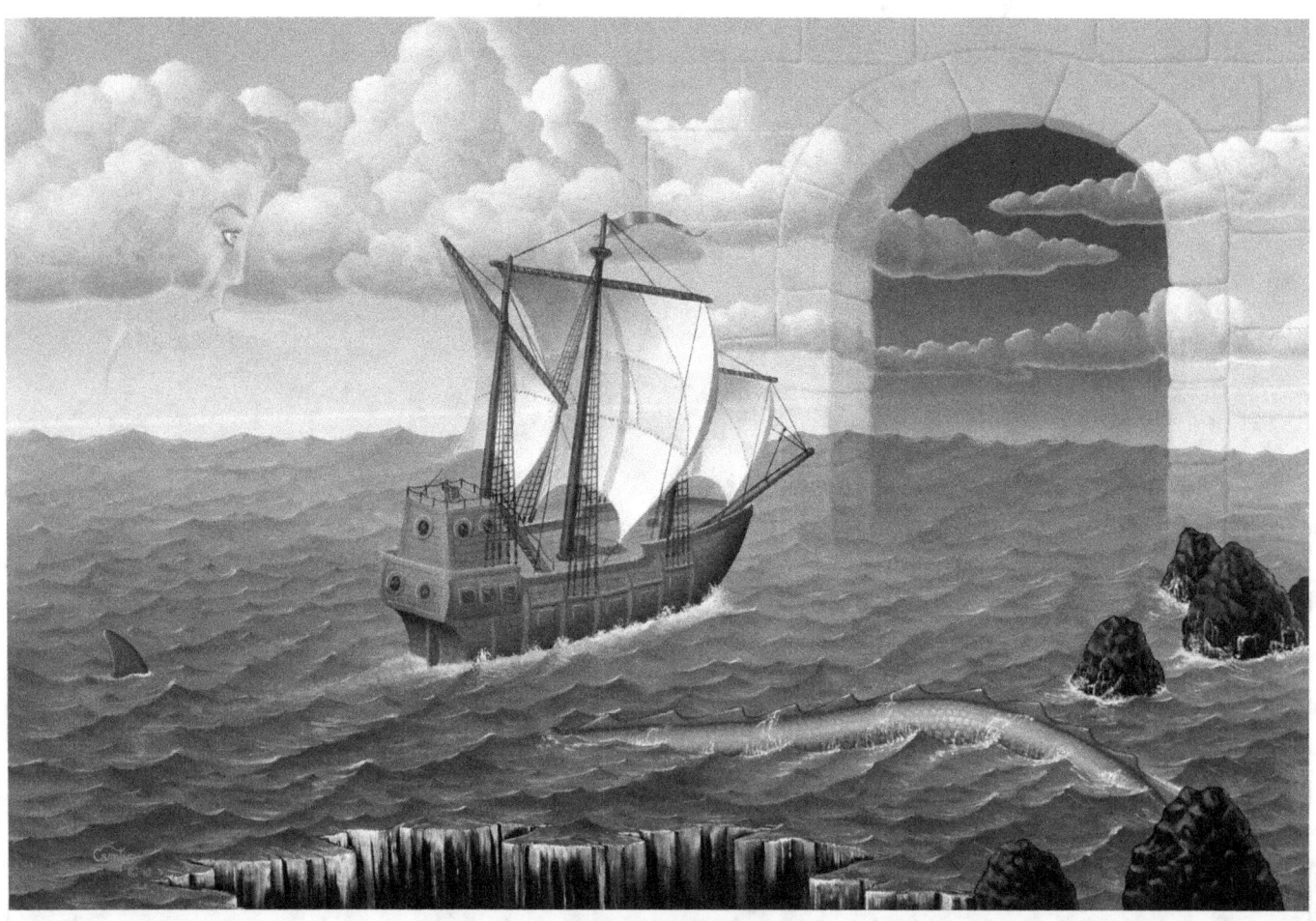

SAILING INTO THE NIGHT - the full title is 'The Goddess of Wind Persuading the Patchwork Ship to Sail Into the Night and Away From the Perils at the Edge of the Sea'. The original is oil.
24" x 36"